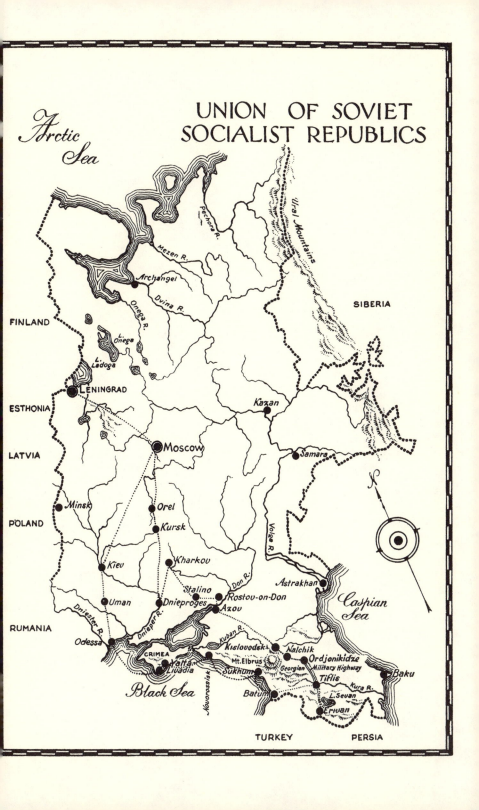

SOVIET JOURNEY

SOVIET JOURNEY

LOUIS FISCHER

GREENWOOD PRESS, PUBLISHERS
WESTPORT, CONNECTICUT

Library of Congress Cataloging in Publication Data

Fischer, Louis, 1896-1970.
    Soviet journey.

    Reprint of the 1935 ed.
    1. Russia--Social conditions--1917-   2. Russia--
Description and travel--1917-   I. Title.
DK267.F53 1972   914.7   72-136529
ISBN 0-8371-5450-2

Originally published in 1935 by Harrison Smith and Robert Haas,
New York

Reprinted by Greenwood Press,
a division of Williamhouse-Regency Inc.

First Greenwood Reprinting 1973
Second Greenwood Reprinting 1974

Library of Congress Catalog Card Number 72-136529

ISBN 0-8371-5450-2

Printed in the United States of America

INTRODUCTION

A mountain of articles and news dispatches and a whole library of books have been written about the Soviet Union. I have sinned myself. Yet most of the writing, including a large part of my own, has been inadequate. For I regularly meet foreign visitors in Russia who have read a great deal about it and are yet surprised at every turn by things they had not expected to encounter; often they also miss things they had expected to encounter.

The fault is not altogether ours. It is extremely difficult to give the outsider a picture of a foreign country, and especially of so quickly changing a foreign country as Soviet Russia. This book is my attempt to do so. I want to try to make the reader see, hear, feel and smell Russia. I want him to travel with me on trains and boats, go with me into homes and factories, probe with me the private thoughts and private life of various kinds of Soviet citizens. I would like to make Russia concrete and real to the person who has never seen it or whose knowledge is incomplete. I will stress the permanent fundamentals which enable one to watch future developments.

I will discuss problems, but I will do so less from the abstract point of view and more from the standpoint of the human being who struggles with those problems. People— men, women and children, Russians, Tartars, Armenians, Jews and a dozen other races, commissars, peasants, beggars, homeless waifs, writers, leaders, etc.— will walk the pages of the volume.

Everything I write I know because I have seen and heard it myself.

Louis Fischer

CONTENTS

Contents

ILLUSTRATIONS

Photographs by Julien Bryan

SOVIET JOURNEY

Chapter I

OLD AND NEW, OLD AND YOUNG

Leningrad.

Leningrad is obviously a big city. The telephone wires are underground and the absence of poles gives the wide avenues an air of majestic spaciousness—and emptiness. Though the population has grown since the revolution, the streets seem desolate. But then Baedeker remarks that before the war, too, St. Petersburg looked deserted. There is less automobile traffic than in Moscow. The trolley alarm signals are not a third as long or raucous. The tarred, hexagonal wood blocks of the street pavements hush all sounds. Leningrad has culture and dignity. It is quiet. It lacks the staccato tempo of the usual Soviet city.

I walk down the Nevski, the chief promenade of the former capital. Its new name: "Prospect of the 25th of October" (the fateful day in 1917 when Lenin engineered his coup d'état) remains on the street plates only, for the hearts of the people find no valid reason for the rechristening. The clothing emporium of So-and-Sosky and Co. is now the Leningrad Coöperative Supply Association; it displays pictures of Stalin and Kirov and Bolshevik slogans to disguise its lack of goods. On the Kazan Cathedral, which retires from the street front in a gigantic brown stone crescent, floats the red flag, and a huge sickle and hammer has taken the place of the cross in the center of the halo on the triangular frieze. The old Slavonic Bible inscription on the cornice has given way to "The Soviet Academy of Science: Museum for the Study of Religion";

inside is an anti-religious museum. An old woman makes the sign of the cross on her breast as she goes by.

At the bottom of the Nevski, in the square of the railway station, rises an equestrian statue. The granite pedestal is like a huge block from an Egyptian pyramid. The horse resembles a rhinoceros heavy and long of body, and short of leg. The legs are wide apart in order the better to support a ponderous master. Alexander III, father of the last Czar, sits there, a flat Tartar disk cap on his big round head. No neck. Upright and rigid, his expanded chest recalls the gorilla's. His legs are short and fat. The whole looks like an unconscious caricature of Czarism. Its squatness, immobility and heaviness express the brute strength, inflexibility and stupidity of the autocracy which erected it. The Bolsheviks preserved this monument as they did those of Peter the Great, Catherine the Great and Nicholas I which stand in Leningrad. But they apparently could not resist the temptation of pointing an unnecessary moral. So into the granite base, in big block letters, the word "SCARE-CROW" has been cut, and under it this verse by Demjan Bedni, Communism's popular bard:

My son and father were executed by the nation,
But I, condemned to posthumous ingloriousness,
Stand here a pig-iron scarecrow for a country
Which has forever discarded the yoke of autocracy.

The dead stones spell out the epitaph of Russia's past. Much more so the living people. With the dashing troika and its liveried driver, the men and women who sat in it have also disappeared. A new type of person dominates the streets of Leningrad—and the life of the Soviet Union: the workingman and the peasant. They have came into the center of town from their factory faubourgs and villages. They fill the former aristocratic quarters and the old haunts of the nobility. They are short and heavy-set; fine facial features are rare. But vigor and health spurt from every pore. Most of them are young. (Where are the old?) This is a strong unspoiled generation. None other could have borne the trials and sacrifices of two difficult decades and remain capable of the enthusiasm and energy required to rebuild a backward country. Suffering and insufficient food may have reduced their stature but not their fecundity, nor their vitality, nor their capacity for exhilaration and enjoyment.

A platoon of Red Army soldiers passes. A fellow five-feet six in height stands out among them, and a six-footer towers like a giant. They do not dress or march as well as American or British or German soldiers, and their knee-high leather boots knocking at the sharp cobbles of the side streets lend them an air of clumsiness. But they sing. The Red Army is a singing army. One man, usually a high tenor, renders a couplet, and the rest join the refrain in deep full-throated bass. They sing lustily and briskly. Self-made music makes marching more rhythmic than the best band. The populace looks thrilled, and the onlooker is caught by the spirit.

Peter built Petersburg on the marshes of the mainland, but the Russian rich erected their summer homes on the islands in the Neva. Today the rich are gone. They are either dead or working for the Bolsheviks or serving tea in glasses in Paris and Prague cafés. Their villas see strange sights. They have been converted into rest homes and sanatoria for the workingmen of Leningrad. Every villa and suburban cottage of Leningrad is devoted to that purpose, and every factory hand in Leningrad receives at least a fortnight's vacation by the river. I visited several of the rest houses. One had belonged to the owner of the Triangle Rubber Factory; its crystal chandeliers, marble staircases, marble halls and big windows giving a full view of the Neva reflect his wealth and moderately good taste. The structure is densely populated. I talked to the directrix and the doctor on duty. The vacationist pays nothing. The National Social-Insurance Fund provides the quarters, the food and the service. This is a house for men only. One hundred metal workers were now living in it. Women find accommodations in other buildings nearby. The day begins with gymnastics, and is featured by excursions into surrounding districts, lectures on political subjects, games, dancing, concerts, and four meals. The inhabitants are not sick. They merely need relaxation, good air, a holiday spirit, and better nourishment than they usually have at home. They were getting them all.

Through the window one could see girls in shorts and brassieres rowing in speedy shells and sculling boats. Girls in the same uniform, and men with shorts or without bathed from the low river bank. Everybody was taking full advantage of Northern Russia's brief summer. The sleeping quarters, therefore, were quite deserted. Although the beds stood rather closely together in the big, lofty, oak paneled chambers, cleanliness ruled throughout. I found only one man indoors. He was preparing for an afternoon nap. He was sixty-three, worked in a Leningrad factory as a mechanic, received a monthly old-age pension of 180 rubles from the state but continued to hold his job because it afforded him additional income. Altogether he had 350 rubles a month. "Do they compel you to take morning exercises?" I asked. "No," he grinned with a toothless mouth. "I am too decrepit for that—unfortunately."

The open air beckoned but I remained to see the dining hall. I took today's typewritten menu from the bulletin board, and got yesterday's from the chief's files. I reproduce today's.

BREAKFAST. Coffee with bread and butter, and cheese, each person consuming 10 grams of coffee, ⅛ of a liter of milk, 30 grams of butter, 25 grams of sugar, 50 grams of cheese, and 650 grams of bread—for the whole day.

LUNCH. Milk soup with home-made noodles, and meat pie, each person consuming ⅛ of a liter of milk, ³⁄₁₀ of an egg, 140 grams of flour, 16 grams of butter, a trace of yeast, 4 grams of sugar, 80 grams of meat, and 20 grams of onion.

DINNER. First dish: pea soup each portion of which contains 60 grams of peas, 80 grams of meat, 20 grams of carrots, and 20 grams of onion. Second dish: fried fish and kasha containing 140 grams of fish, 7 grams of butter, 4 grams of tomatoes, 10 grams of flour, and 50 grams of kasha. Dessert: an apple tart consisting of 70 grams of flour, 5 grams of sugar, 10 grams of butter, 30 grams of apple jam, and some milk.

SUPPER. Macaroni with scallions containing, per person, 80 grams of macaroni, 10 grams of butter, and 20 grams of scallions. For dessert a jello consisting of 30 grams of huckleberries, 20 grams of sugar, and 20 grams of potato flour. Before going to bed, the vacationist may have a cup of milk with a few slices of bread.

The doctor would under no condition allow me to enter the kitchen without donning a freshly-laundered white apron much too small for me. Those worn by the cooks and scullery maids were noticeably dirtier than mine, but the prominently displayed laws of cleanliness were observed at least in the letter. All hair was to be covered, finger nails manicured regularly, aprons changed regularly, and street clothes left in lockers outside. The list of commandments ended with an injunction to wash hands after visits to the lavatory.

I took one last glance at the rich, wood-paneled dining room and its long and broad oaken table where the rubber manufacturer might have seated sixty or seventy wealthy or betitled guests, and then entered the balmy sunshine. I stopped to interview two workingmen-vacationists; in a moment a crowd had gathered around me. "Do you mind the big common quarters?" I asked.

"No," came one answer, "our own sleeping accommodations are sometimes worse than these."

"Do you mind being on vacation without your wives?" Laughter. "Oh," said a worker, "we can manage without them for two weeks." "Before the revolution," said another, "most of our wives lived in the villages and we stayed without them for months."

"How many of you are members of the Communist party?"

Six raised their hands. I counted heads. Thirty-three men and women. But most of them were "udarniks" or enthusiasts of labor, people who had undertaken to increase their individual output. "Why then," I demanded, "are you not Communists?"

A man of forty or thereabouts, dressed in a sleeveless shirt, trousers and sandals, offered to reply. "You see," he began, "we have just become literate. To be an active Communist one must understand theory, and something of Marx. You must be able to teach others. You must submit to a severe discipline which demands time. We are Communists. We think and live like Communists, but we don't join the party."

"What do you earn?" I pointed my finger. "250 rubles." "400 rubles." "190 rubles." There was obviously a wide range of wages.

"Are you better off than you were before the revolution?" I now inquired.

"The food is worse." The speaker was a man of seventy. His remark raised a storm. The young and the middle-aged proceeded to attack him. "Would you have gotten a pension before the revolution?" a workingman cried. Our septuagenarian admitted that he was the recipient of a 160 ruble monthly pension, yet he stood his ground. He kept smiling and repeated: "The food is worse."

"Did women receive three months pregnancy leave from the Czar?" a girl asked him. "Was it prohibited to discharge a woman during pregnancy?" another woman urged. "Why, we couldn't have come within a mile of this mansion before 1917," a worker affirmed, and others nodded assent. "Did you have free medical aid before?" Yet when the argument was finished no one had denied the old fellow's assertion.

Then the inevitable happened. I have been at an interview with Joseph Stalin; I have interviewed peasants in Bokhara. The procedure is always the same: after you have extracted your information from them, they reverse the tables, and put their own questions to you. "How are the workers faring in Germany?" "In America?" "Is Fascism growing in the United States?" "Have you unemployed insurance?" "Does the unemployed worker receive support from the state?" "Ah," declares a gnarled man whose beard is streaked with gray, "you must make a revolution."

"America is not ready for revolution," I plead. Laughter. "No, indeed," says a brawny muscular Russian, his spherical head shaved clean to make it look like a billiard ball. "No. With ten million unemployed, most of them permanently, and with farmers plowing under cotton or being paid not to grow food while others starve, you are not ready for a change." His audience smiled appreciatively. "That's just what our bourgeoisie thought in 1917," a listener exclaimed. I beat a hasty retreat. Their minds were made up.

A boy had dismounted from his bicycle by the side of my automobile. "Where did you get this bicycle?" I said in a deep threatening voice putting my open hand on his head. He raised his face to me and winked. He had understood the tone. "My father bought it."

"Who is your father?"

"A worker in the Putilov factory," he said proudly.

"Is it a Soviet product?"

"Yes, of course, don't you see the mark?"

"How old are you?"

"Eleven."

"Do you read books?"

"Yes."

"Like to go to school?"

"Yes."

"Do you have a good time in life?"

"Yes. Very much. Anything else you want to know?" and lifting one leg behind him, he was off.

A young woman passes wheeling her bicycle. She wears a pair of white, rubber-heeled and soled shoes, a tight skirt reaching about two inches below her bare knees, and a tight, sky-blue jersey sweater which makes her pronounced round breasts even more prominent. I asked her where she got her bicycle. She got it from her trade union as a reward for good work at her lathe. She is on vacation here.

The streets of the island are full of people obviously relaxed and bent on merry-making. They are enjoying the last warm hour of the summer's day. Every house is marked "Rest Home" of such-or-such a trade union. One big mansion, formerly the property of a railway constructor, has been set aside as a club. Here there are small and large music rooms, a café, library, war preparedness room, chess and checker room, reading room, etc., etc. In the court is an open-air cinema for some 500 spectators. I visit the café. It is packed. The prices are moderate. The place is clean. The food seems to be excellent. The massive buffets are the ex-owner's. The beautiful ebony, mahogany and young oak tables too. One is surprised not that there is a scratch here and there on the precious wood but that these treasures are intact at all after seventeen years of public use. As I look around, café patrons invite me with their eyes. They love to talk. A woman is sitting at a table with her husband and boy. They have come out from town to visit her. The family is treating itself to ice-cream. When it is machine-churned ice-cream, the Russians always advertise the fact with the sign: "Machine Ice Cream" in loud letters. Anything mechanized is supposed to be better.

The war preparedness room of the clubhouse contains posters telling the civil population, in simple pictures, what to do in case of a poison gas attack from the air. Another diagram sketches the growth of foreign military forces. A big chart shows the detailed cross-section of an army rifle. Below the picture is a list of the names of the rifle's parts. By touching the end of a wire to a rifle part and the other end to its name one lights a bright electric bulb. If the bulb fails to light the guess has been wrong and one must search for the correct designation. To judge from the crowd, this rifle is a great attraction.

Such subtle influencing of the Russian mind is ubiquitous. The staircases and halls of the clubhouse are decorated with colored discs, blocks, and modernistic statistical figure-charts graphically comparing the old and the new, and vividly proclaiming Soviet progress. To understand them it is not necessary to know a word of Russian. They are equally intelligible to the illiterate mujhik and the foreigner. One example: a drawing of a blast furnace. Beside it, four blue inclined buckets from which molten pig-iron flows in a tongue of red flame. On a line with them stands a capitalist. This represents Russia's iron production in 1913. Each bucket equals 1,000,000 tons. Below, the situation in 1923 is indicated with one half of one red bucket. But by 1928, there were four red buckets, by 1932 five and a half, and by 1934 ten.

A former millionaire came to see me in my hotel room this evening. We have mutual friends in Moscow. He is sixty-seven years old. Between 1915 and 1917 he earned 2,000,000 gold rubles collecting timber from the peasants and selling it to the Czarist government for war purposes. When the Bolsheviks took over, they put him to work at a similar task and paid him 2 pounds of bread a day. We spoke for more than an hour. He was not bitter. "The Czarist régime was pretty bad," he declared once, "and I don't wonder that the common people wanted to get rid of it." But the Bolsheviks "must learn how to trade. They are the worse merchants in the world." For years he had thought the Soviets would fall. But in 1932 he burned 400,000 Czarist rubles, the equivalent of $200,000 in gold. With their smoke went his hopes of a restoration. He realized that a new world was in the making all around him. He regretted not to be part of it. In Leningrad they knew him too well to give him a job, and in Moscow, where he could find work he would have to live with his children who, though they might politely welcome him, would nevertheless be displeased. They sent him money occasionally.

My millionaire occupies one room in the house he formerly owned. There had been a quarrel yesterday. A workingman beat his wife. The neighbors interfered. "She is my wife and I do with her as I please." Others disputed his rights over her. "A wife is no longer private property." The neighbors decided to try him before the comradely court of the house which had no authority to punish but could pronounce social censure. And then they retired. "He is a counter-revolutionary," was one person's parting gift. Wife-beating is not just wrong in the Soviet Union. It is anti-Bolshevik. And it is everybody's business.

Leningrad is having its northern white nights, and daylight continues for twenty-four hours. It is difficult to go to bed. The streets are alive with pedestrians long after midnight, and I hear their tramp beneath my window. I have been reading an article in today's "Pravda" entitled "Socialism and Equality." Anything which is printed in the "Pravda" is the accepted view of the ruling Communist party. "Socialism," the article begins, "in no sense tends to ignore or suppress all the varied individual talents, urges, tastes and requirements of human beings." No regimentation. "On the contrary, socialism presents an unprecedented possibility for the development of such capacities, abilities and talents." The capitalists, on the other hand, talked much about equality but actually maintained a system of economic exploitation which produced tremendous inequalities in wealth, social position and political influence.

"Equality in general," A. Leontiev, the author of the "Pravda" article continues, "is an empty abstraction." There are natural differences which cannot be wiped out. "A man is not the equal of a woman, but to erase that inequality would mean to destroy mankind. In other words, the question is not one of eliminating the natural distinguishing characteristics of individuals but of the destruction of the social functions of inequality." Socialism, accordingly, strives to make it impossible for one class of people to become superior by taking advantage of another, less-favorably situated class. "By equality," Stalin declared in January, 1934, "Marxism understands not the leveling of personal needs but the elimination of classes."

"It is obvious," Leontiev proceeds, "that there is no equality and can be no equality between a conscientious workingman and a loafer, between an 'udarnik' or labor enthusiast and a lazy man, between a devoted toiler and one who lies on his side. . . . You cannot use the same yardstick to measure different people; one is stronger, the other is weaker." Even in the perfect future society of Communism, Leontiev believes, there will be no equality. For the principle of the Communist millennium-to-come is: "From each according to his abilities; to each according to his requirements." But abilities vary. Moreover, where one person will require a violin the other will want a permanent wave. . . .

And so to bed.

Chapter II

ARISTOCRATS AT WORK

In the summer of 1932, I needed a vacation. That meant that I needed to get away from newspapers, books, my typewriter and inquiring tourists. I wanted, moreover, to study the life of Soviet Russia's "aristocrats." So I had myself invited to the Putilov factory in Leningrad, one of the largest and oldest in the country. For a week I lived on the territory of the plant in a room that trembled all day and all night from the blows of a 2-ton hammer in the blacksmith shop nearby. I saw men at work, at play, at meals, and in their homes. I went swimming with them. I went to their classrooms. I attended their political meetings. I visited the factory's school for the training of young mechanics, its hospitals, rest homes, farms, club house, yacht club, and Communist party offices. For the Soviet factory is not simply a place where a man works seven hours a day only to rush home and forget all about it. It is the center of his life.

I gathered many impressions and made many friends. About two years later, I thought I might go back to Putilov's to see how things had changed. This was one of the reasons for my trip to Leningrad. The moment I arrived at the Astoria Hotel, therefore, I telephoned Paul Otz, the director of the big plant. He sent his car for me immediately. I talked with the chauffeur.

"I used to work in the tractor foundry," he said. "But my lungs are bad and they gave me this job."

"Then you must be pleased," I commented. "This is much better."

"No," he replied. "There I was producing something. Now I am merely serving somebody."

The factory covers an area of 7 square miles, a little city in itself. Inside the gate, the chauffeur pointed out how much cleaner the plant has become in the last two years. And indeed, many roads have been asphalted and some open spaces are either being turned into lawns or paved so that less black dust flies about. Young trees line the pathways. The chauffeur was proud of this achievement. Director Otz mentioned it to me. Numerous workers called my attention to it. "We are making our factory beautiful," they said.

Some parts of Putilov's have been standing for over a century. Others, the tractor and turbine shops, for instance, are as modern as any industrial unit in Western countries. Its sewage system dates back to 1805. From time to time it was probably repaired and reconstructed, but the age-long open wood troughs through which the waste flowed down to the sea remained. Now they are being removed and replaced by concrete pipes about a yard in diameter. The smell which accompanies the work of exhuming the troughs is not exactly of the pleasantest. Putilov's is also installing a new water main which will, for the first time, give the factory a steady supply of fresh water from the Neva.

I was particularly interested in seeing the turbine plant which was just being finished in the summer of 1932. Immediately opposite the entrance, I stumbled over what the Russians call "a medical point" or a first-aid center. The factory had four such "points" as well as its own hospital.

At each "point" a physician is permanently on duty. I talk to the physician. He came to work today at 8 a.m. and will stay until 8 p.m. Then he will be relieved by his colleague. He works thirty hours in six days. He earns 260 rubles a month here, but fills another position for several hours on alternate days. He does this to raise his standard of living, and the government permits it because the establishment of "medical points" in all the thousands of Soviet factories and the introduction of medical service into tens of thousands of distant villages has produced a very perceptible shortage of physicians. This "point" serves 8,000 Putilov workers. Its personnel consists, apart from physicians, of six nurses and three maids. They handle approximately 100 cases a day, most of them cuts, bruises, and simple surgical cases. There is no charge. A serious case receives preliminary treatment at the "point" and can be transferred to the central hospital by ambulance in six minutes. I inspected the closets and drawers. The "point" had plenty of bandage, plaster, sterilized cotton, instruments and anesthetics, but an insufficient supply of pyramidon and luminal.

Inside the turbine shop, I looked for the propaganda. Slogan signs are always an important feature of a Soviet plant. Close by the entrance stands the Red-and-Black board. Red for distinction; black for bad work. "Do you mean to say this is the way to work for Socialism?" reads the inscription at the top of the black half, and there follows a list of workers' names and a description of their criminal misdeeds: arriving late, leaving the lathe unswept at the end of the shift, loafing on the job, etc., etc. A name remains on this social pillory until its owner's record has improved.

Work in an organized manner.
Work in a cultural manner.
Work full seven hours.

I found this admonition in the turbine foundry, on the walls of buildings, and on red streamers drawn across shops. "Work full seven hours." There is no evidence that a Soviet workingman, even though he be an "udarnik" or labor enthusiast, overworks himself. He has the leisurely way of the Slav. The Soviets are endeavoring to inculcate habits of industry and a love of work. They have succeeded only in part. At times, to be sure, when an important production or construction task must be finished by a certain date, the authorities manage to inject the sporting spirit and stimulate all persons concerned to strain hard towards the demarcated goal. Often a sweeping élan of work is called forth which produces truly astounding increases of output. Then there is public praise for those who contributed towards the victory. But usually, even though almost all factories pay on a piece-work basis, the employee keeps a considerable volume of energy in reserve. Knowledge of this fact has induced many Soviet factory directors to arrange end-of-the-month "storms." Whenever a plant falls behind the plan of production handed to it from above, a fourth-week spurt is organized in order to carry the factory over the top. The workers are then urged to "take the plan by storm," and, not infrequently, they join in the game and open up the sluices of their reserve energy. But the government, to which all the factories—and all the mines, railroads, oil fields, and land—of the Soviet Union belong, strongly disapproves of these storming tactics. It prefers to see an even curve of production. There has been some improvement. But the individual output of a Soviet workingman is relatively still quite low. In 1932, Putilov's employed 34,000 men and women. Today it produces just as much with only 28,000. I am sure, however, that a more rational use of equipment, further mechanization of "dirty work," and also additional speeding-up by the workers themselves would enable the factory to reduce its staff much more.

This matter of speeding-up is complicated. It cannot be solved only by propagandistic appeals to "work full seven hours." Here is the situation: a worker makes twenty bolts an hour and is paid 5 kopeks per bolt. This is the norm. He accordingly earns 1 ruble an hour. By and by he becomes more proficient and begins to turn out twenty-three bolts an hour, and later twenty-six. His wages rise correspondingly. Now the management argues: "This is just what we have been trying to achieve. We are raising the standard of production. Part of this rise is due to our improved managerial efficiency. Moreover, the worker is not yet exerting himself to the full. We will therefore lift the norm. Henceforth he must do twenty-five bolts an hour; and we will pay 4 kopeks for each bolt."

What is the result? The worker must cut twenty-five bolts an hour to earn the same ruble. He resents this measure. He decides that by raising output he merely raises the norm and is thus working against himself. Nevertheless, he cannot persist in this attitude too long, for if he produces another bolt per hour he earns an extra 4 kopeks. And since he wants those 4 kopeks, he speeds up.

A Soviet factory hand's chief incentive is his desire to earn more. More often than not, he does earn more if he works more and better. But there is another incentive, the social incentive. For it cannot be doubted that a Russian worker who is politically ripe regards himself as part-

owner of his factory and behaves accordingly. In the restaurant of the turbine shop, I engaged a man in conversation. He was a typical Slav with flaxen hair and blue eyes.
His face was intelligent, his head long and tipped with a
blond beard. He had perfect ivory teeth. In reply to my
question he stated that their food was satisfactory now,
but admitted that it had been bad. Apropos of food, he
told me a story. "Recently," he recounted, "a girl in our
department was running her lathe badly and spoiling it.
We complained to the department chief, but he was lenient
with her. So we men went to the head office and had her
discharged. Why? Because that lathe was bought with the
food we had not eaten last year and two years ago, and
we didn't want her to ruin it." The department chief who
stood by my side confirmed the tale.

The logic of this story is simple enough: the workingman believes he owns his factory because he knows he has
paid for it, often by pulling in his belt or by accepting
a smaller salary. And he hopes that his property will soon
be giving him a bigger dividend than it does now. He trusts
that the near future will be more pleasant than the present.
He remembers that the present compares favorably with
the recent past.

The turbine shop counts many expensive foreign machines. Almost all of them have an inscription like this
painted on them: "Comrade, your lathe costs 17,500 gold
rubles. Take care of it." I asked several men whether such
an appeal meant anything to them. They answered in the
affirmative. One worker said: "In order to buy this machine, the Soviet government had to export butter, eggs,
etc., which we would otherwise have consumed ourselves.
If I destroy my lathe we will have to sell more butter and
eggs abroad to buy another."

I approach many machinists and shout questions into their ears so that they may hear me above the roar of the shop. A young fellow, about twenty-eight, has been at the plant for five years. He started as an unskilled hand for 60 rubles a month. He took technical courses. Now he gets 250 rubles. He has stopped studying because of crowded living conditions. A second workingman, aged twenty-six, was engaged on rough "dirty" work as late as 1932. Now he operates a complicated lathe. Earns 175 rubles. Of course, he does not operate his lathe with unimpeachable efficiency. It will not live as long as it would under the hand of a mechanic with ten years' experience. But what can the management do? The manager of the tractor foundry tells me he employs 1,300 people. He could use 400 more but cannot find them. And Director Otz informed me later that he is forced to send agents to railway stations to waylay incoming peasants and entice them with all sorts of promises to take jobs in the factory. He also recruits men in neighboring agricultural collectives. All persons in authority at Putilov's believe that it will be years before they have a sufficient supply of skilled and installed labor.

While I spoke with the manager of the turbine shop, a bell rang loud and long, and there was a rush to the exit. The bell announced the lunch hour, and nobody lost a second. Before I could walk upstairs, the restaurant was crowded. Each section of the plant has its restaurant. Each worker gets two meals a day in such a restaurant. In the morning, one can have tea, brown kasha or buckwheat gruel, sausage sandwiches and rye bread for between 60 and 70 kopeks. Lunch at the turbine shop consisted of: macaroni soup, 30 kopeks; a 125 gram meat cutlet with cabbage, 74 kopeks, or pork with kasha, 1 ruble and 30 kopeks, and unlimited quantities of tea at 6 kopeks a glass. 200 grams of bread were served free with each meal. In addition, anybody could buy himself up to five sandwiches to eat on the spot or take home. A ham sandwich with 25 grams of ham costs 53 kopeks; a cheese sandwich with 20 grams of cheese, 35 kopeks.

I spent two hours in three Putilov restaurants. In one, spoons were the only eating utensils. In another, spoons and forks were available. The third supplied knives, forks and spoons. I noticed quite a number of plates containing left-overs. All people answered "Yes" when I asked them whether they were getting enough to eat. But all people likewise declared that prices were excessive. Every worker can have two satisfying meals a day at Putilov's. He needs only one supplementary supper at home. This makes his wife's life much easier. Those two meals, however, cost him 2 rubles and that puts a rather big hole into his budget.

The average wage at Putilov's is 185 rubles a month. Rent averages 8 per cent of income throughout the Soviet Union. At the Putilov coöperative store, a man's ready-made suit sells for 60 to 80 rubles, silk for 10 to 18 rubles a meter, and a pair of shoes 15 to 33 rubles. Clothing prices, therefore, are reasonable. But food costs are still much too high.

A concert took place in one of the restaurants during the second half of the lunch hour. Two men played accordions and three women accompanied them by whistling through combs against which they held pieces of paper, while the workers, their stomachs full, sang Russian folk and revolutionary songs. This music interval, a working-man explained to me, "puts us in good humor for the rest of the day." Putilov's has just organized its own music school where employees are taught to play instruments, to write and read music, and to sing.

Outside, in the spaces between shops, some workers played volley ball and "gorodki," a simple Russian game distantly related to ten-pins; others watched or lay around and smoked. A number ran to the library. Every Soviet factory has a library for its personnel. I made a visit to the "book base." This base supplies reading matter to the forty-one branch libraries of the Putilov factory which are located in the very shops where the men work. The base possesses 93,000 volumes—30,000 of them political, 30,000 on technical subjects, and 33,000 fiction, plus 20,000 volumes for engineers on complicated scientific topics. At the moment, 11,500 books were out, but the chief librarian explained that the figure was low because many were on vacation. Besides, people read less in summer time. Thus, the librarian of the electric bulb shop in the Moscow Electrozavod once opened her records to show me that only 1,171 workers had borrowed books in July, but 1,875 in September.

I asked the Putilov librarian about the literary taste of the Putilov staff. The older workers, she said, usually asked for the pre-revolutionary classics, but the younger ones read avidly of both the old and the new. There was a great demand for Tolstoi, especially for his "Resurrection," "Anna Karenina" and "War and Peace." Gogol was popular and so also Turgeniev and Russia's greatest poet, Pushkin, but Dostoyevsky had fewer readers.

Of foreign authors, Jack London was the great favorite. His works were sometimes literally "read to pulp." I heard the same report in other cities. A Moscow magazine recently picked twelve workingmen at random and asked them questions about a number of prominent foreigners. Five had never heard of Prof. Albert Einstein. One woman wrote that he was a great musician. Two knew nothing of Charles Lindbergh. One thought he was a writer; the same woman called him "a comic artist." But all had read Jack London, and all went to the trouble of expressing their love for him. The Putilov librarian explained, in answer to my query, that the Russians relished tales of adventure and stories of man's struggle with nature. The Arctic was near to them. "Besides," she added, "London was a socialist." (Lenin himself used to enjoy Jack London —the tales that are full of true pathos—but he laughed at some of his "false, middle-class sentimentalism.") There is also a considerable call for Dreiser, Zola, Upton Sinclair (Sinclair Lewis is not so well known) and H. G. Wells. Russians used to have a weakness for O. Henry, but now he finds few readers. John Dos Passos is becoming quite popular.

Maxim Gorki is the most favored Soviet author at Putilov's. Then follow Sholokhov ("And Quiet Flows the Don"), Panferov ("Bruski"), Serafimovitch ("Iron Stream"), Alexei Tolstoi, Novikov-Priboi, and the poets. The workers often complained that the style of Soviet writers was poor compared to that of the classics. Nevertheless, they wanted books and more books. André Malraux, the French novelist, asked a Moscow workingman why he read. "In order to learn how to live," he replied.

Many rank and file workingmen take out books on technical subjects too. There is a great thirst for scientific knowledge in the factories because new foreign machines and new production methods are being introduced which the workers want to understand. Moreover, the management encourage the men to make their own suggestions for improving production. In every Soviet plant, one finds bulletin boards to which employees have pinned notes scribbled sometimes with pencil on scraps of paper hastily torn from a copybook. These notes are rationalization proposals. It may have occurred to a lathe turner or a furnace tender that his task could be simplified; it may have occurred to him that a slight change in his machine would eliminate waste and economize time. He shares his thought with his fellows and with the engineers. If necessary, a draftsman puts the man's ideas in to a blueprint. A workingman with special inventive abilities is likely to be sent to a school for inventors. In the Putilov blacksmith shop, a prominently displayed typewritten announcement recorded a number of rationalization schemes which had been adopted. Comrade Ivanov, whose suggestion saved 3,500 rubles, had received a 1,000 ruble premium. And so on down the list of eleven names.

After two hours with Director Otz in which we discussed the entire gamut of problems facing a Soviet factory chief, I repaired to the workingmen's living quarters. Bad housing is one of Russia's worst curses. Before the revolution, dwelling accommodations were poor and terribly inadequate. Since the revolution, the cities have grown and standards have risen, but construction has failed to keep pace with the new demand. The situation at Putilov's, accordingly, reflects a condition which may be encountered in other centers as well. Only 4,000 of Putilov's 28,000 employees inhabit new, modern coöperative apartments. They are well-lighted, well-built, and furnished with bathtubs and similar elementary requirements which in Russia, however, are regarded as great achievements. I visited several homes. A workingman had been fortunate enough to get a three-room apartment. The rent was moderate. He might have kept it for himself and his wife and child. But no! He sub-let one room to one brother and another room to a second brother. The second brother and his wife later took in a nephew of eighteen as a boarder. I asked why they did it. "Well," came the reply, "he had to live somewhere." Now they were all crowded, but they did not seem to mind. They did not seem to understand why one and the same room could not serve as dining room and study by day and bedroom by night. . . . It is interesting to look at a Soviet apartment house in the evening. Most of the windows are lit up—because practically every room is a bedroom and living room.

I spent little time in these comfortable coöperative houses. I preferred to study conditions in the temporary barracks. These are two-story wooden buildings stuccoed inside and out for warmth. In front of one barrack stood a woman holding a child. I asked whether she would be good enough to show me her living quarters. She was very glad to do so—and she was very glad to talk about herself. She is a type-setter. Her husband is a bookkeeper at Putilov's. Her child is only two weeks old. She had returned from the clinic only eight days ago. She was now having her two months' post-clinical leave, "vacation-by-decree," the Russians call it. Her boy of seven was in a summer camp. Her sister had come up from Kiev to help while she still was weak. The baby was immaculately dressed in a part of the white layette supplied free of charge by the hospital. In its mouth was a sucker. The mother understood my glance. "Yes," she said apologetically, "the doctor prohibited it. But feeding time is nearing and I am afraid she will cry."

"Let it cry," I heartlessly advised. "But don't let it form bad habits." Mother did not seem convinced.

I inquired whether she had wanted the baby. She answered "Indeed" with spirit.

"Do you have birth control information," I asked.

"Yes," she replied. "The doctor in the clinic, however, gave me something I had not known."

I went from this meeting to the rooms of the single men which, as might have been expected, were bleaker and dirtier than those of the unmarried women. In the girls' dormitory, I simply walked down a corridor and knocked at random on a door. A gay "Come in" was heard, and I entered. Six iron beds stood end to end along the long sides of the room. Near each bed was a small table with the inevitable powder box, soap, a paper-covered book, here and there a hand mirror, a purse, etc. One girl lay on her cot covered with a pure white linen sheet which did not conceal her contours. Her naked arms were exposed. She wore a blood red headkerchief. She and the two other girls in the room had been reading. Not one of them showed the slightest embarrassment at the sudden appearance of myself and the men and women who accompanied me on my tour of inspection. There was no quick hiding of a bit of underclothing, and no hasty attempt at making-up. The Russians are simple and uninhibited.

I proceeded to interrogate one of the girls. She was an assistant locomotive driver at Putilov's. Earns 165 rubles a month. Pays 2 rubles a day for breakfast and lunch at the factory restaurant, and spends 30 rubles additional a month for food at home. Each girl prepares her food separately in the kitchen downstairs. She is never hungry. Just now, she is on a month's vacation. She had received that month's salary in advance.

"Why a month instead of the usual fortnight?" I inquire.

"Because my job is regarded as injurious to the health." She is spending the first half of her vacation at home.

"What do you do?"

"I lie on the fields getting sunburnt. And when I get bored I go into town to an amusement park." In eight days she would enter one of the rest homes on the Neva islands for a two weeks' stay. "There is always a lot of jolly company in those places. The food, too, is as good as in a fine restaurant. I had a wonderful time there last summer."

She pays 15 rubles a month for rent.

"Aren't you crowded?"

"No," she replied swinging around as if to say: "See how much room we have." Four days ago she bought a dress for 16 rubles, "half a dress, really," she added with a smile, and took it off a hanger to show. A plain cotton print of the kind one sees in all Soviet streets. Three months ago she bought an excellent cloth coat for 85 rubles. That too hung above her bed. Ordinarily, she had about 30 rubles a month left for spending on cinemas, theater—once a month—carfare, etc.

Polya had borne up very well under my machine-gun cross-examination, smiling, and even volunteering information. I was ready to go further.

"How old are you?"

"Twenty-three."

"Married?"

"No," and then, when I had paused to muster courage, she spared me some embarrassment by adding most naturally, "But I have a friend." Soon she was giving me a brief autobiography. I repeated this performance in another room and encountered the same healthy readiness to talk frankly about personal affairs. These girls in the barracks were earning just a little less than the average Putilov salary, and they were all apparently well and happy. But they all hoped that next year they would be housed in good stone dwellings.

Chapter III

"BOOKS AND THINGS"

Kornei Chukovsky did me the honor of calling to see me shortly after I returned from Putilov's. Every child in the Soviet Union knows Stalin's name. Every child in the Soviet Union knows Kornei Chukovsky. He makes them happy. Chukovsky is Russia's best authority on Nekrassov, a nineteenth century poet. He knows Shakespeare backwards and forwards. He was an esteemed literary critic before Russia became Bolshevik, and it is probably a bit irritating when people forget this branch of his activities and speak of him only as a writer of children's books. But Chukovsky cannot be irritated very long. His red, full face always beams. His bulbous nose, the target of many a caricature including some by himself, always shines. His steel gray hair smiles. As he talks he regularly passes the whole length of an expressive finger along the tip of his nose.

An entire generation of authors of children's books, not excluding Marshak and Ilin, the creator of "Russia's New Primer," has sat at Chukovsky's feet. But none excels the master. He read some of his poetry to me. One need not know a word of Russian to enjoy its rhymes and rhythm. Some of it he wrote for his little daughter. For months he sat over her sick-bed reciting to her, or composing extemporaneously to cheer her. But she died.

Chukovsky is really proud of his work for the young. Hundreds of thousands of parents learn his books by heart, together with their children. I am one of the well-rewarded hundreds of thousands. Children's literature is a tremendously rich branch of Soviet literature. A special publishing house exists for it. Maxim Gorki, the Nestor of Soviet art, pays considerable attention to it. It has been the subject of much discussion by important political leaders. At one time, in fact, Chukovsky was under a dark Bolshevik cloud. Lenin's widow herself, Nadezhda Krupskaya, attacked him because he produced non-political, individualistic tales for children instead of writing about tractors and blast furnaces. The authorities then considered Chukovsky "harmful" and his books were not printed. Mothers, fathers and children mourned and combed the antiquarian shops for old editions. Today, however, a fresh sensible wind has blown away the cloud. Chukovsky is rehabilitated and endlessly popular.

He tells, actually he acts this story: "They come in on tip-toe and whisper: 'If it weren't for the children, we would of course never, believe us never. . . . Only for the sake of the little ones. . . .'

"Abashed, I reach for my purse.

" 'Please no, no. We ourselves will pay all. And believe us, we will never tell anybody, never. We do this for the sake of the children, believe it. You are a father too. You will understand.'

"Their faces show suffering. Their eyes beg.

" 'We have our own paper,' they whisper, 'we are from Saratov. We will only make a copy, only a copy.'

"I feel myself drawn into a conspiracy."

And then the secret comes out. These visitors to Leningrad from the distant Volga want to make copies of some of Chukovsky's children's books which are sold out. He is accustomed now to such "beggars." They knock at his door almost every day. All over the country one will find manuscript copies of his works and of other books for the young. This situation is several years old and is sure to continue for a number of years.

One naturally deduces that children's books are not published in large quantities in the Soviet Union. "That's an optical illusion, an aberration, a mirage. Yes, that's the

A Soviet cartoon showing eager children waiting for a "drop" of Chukovsky's "Wash Till You Make a Hole."

word—mirage," Chukovsky exclaims. Chukovsky speaks excellent English. "In pre-revolutionary days," he continued, "if any one of my children's books, say "Moi-do-dir" ("Wash Till You Make a Hole") was published in a microscopic edition of 6,000 to 7,000, the market was saturated. The readers of those times were supplied.

"But today? The same book appears in 250,000 copies and on the third day you can't find one in the shops. And then the reader complains that 'Moi-do-dir' is not being printed at all, and he comes to me privately to make a manuscript copy."

Chukovsky is not alone. "Every Soviet child now reads children's books," he says. "All editions are quickly sold out. Gaidar's "School" sold 100,000 copies; the same writer's "Distant Lands" 135,000. Barto's "Little Brothers" 290,000, Marshak's "The Postman" 400,000, and "Moi-do-dir" 400,000. You could throw ten times as many children's books on the market and it would still remain incompletely satisfied." Recently ex-Commissar of Health Semashko complained in the Moscow "Izvestia" that there was no use publishing children's books in editions of 250,000. They disappeared in three days from the book stalls of the larger cities, and the provinces never even saw them. A 250,000 edition of Chukovsky's "Moi-do-dir," Semashko writes, was sold out in three days. Children's books, Semashko insists, must now be published in "mass edition." He demands that the Children's Book Publishing House receive more paper from the government factories. In 1935, this house will print 300 to 400 titles in 300,000,000 volumes.

Chukovsky's "Crocodile" has been published abroad in English. He has translated European children's classics into Russian. He has gone West many times and has many foreign contacts. On almost all occasions when I have seen him, he carried a 4-inch thick scrapbook into which Shaw, H. G. Wells, Sir Edward Grey, etc. have signed their autographs, where some of the world's best cartoonists have made drawings, where Mayakovsky and others wrote specially composed verse, and where Repin, Russia's great painter, made a prophetic sketch on the day the World War broke out showing a crumpled Wilhelm II being carted out in a garbage wheelbarrow, etc., etc. I am asked for my autograph.

I go for a walk along the quays of the Neva. Near the bridges, men and women lean against the iron railings watching naked men wash themselves with soap and swim. But no women bathe naked. Throughout the Soviet Union, in fact, there is very little nude bathing by women and, on regular bathing beaches, very little by men. At the beaches, a woman proceeds in this manner: she pulls off her dress and slip and is discovered wearing a one-piece suit or brassieres and a pair of shorts. Having bathed and dried herself, she throws her dress and slip over her head, skilfully lowering these while removing her wet bathing clothes; the whole performance is soon completed without even a square inch of "indecent" exposure.

The quays, boulevards and amusement parks are filled throughout the evening. Couples walk with arms around one another's waists or holding hands and coyly smiling into one another's eyes. Red love. Handsome sunburnt sailors greet girls they don't know. The girls return the greeting and pass on. Or they stop and set up an acquaintance. Much laughter but not even a suspicion of rowdyism. Occasionally, a young fellow plays his own accordion: his comrades sing. A crowd listens; sometimes it joins in the fun.

I reach a mosque. A mosque in Red Leningrad. It was of course built before the revolution by local Moslems, and a beautiful structure it is with fortress walls and cylindrical minarets of pale blue tiles recalling those I once saw in Samarkand. Behind the fine grill-closed gate, in a distant dark corner of the entrance porch, a woman was making her bed on the flagstones. No question could persuade her to utter a single syllable. She was obviously a peasant. Her coat of brown homespun falling like a skirt from the tight waistbelt revealed that unmistakably. Her pillow would be the sack she had carried on her back from the village. She was spreading a blanket of the same brown homespun on the stone and preparing to lay her baby on it. She did not beg.

The sight depressed me. . . . I am not quite certain of the best way to return to my hotel. I ask a young man. He directs me, and we begin a conversation. He had seen me standing for a long time at the mosque gate. "You did not like the fact that that woman must sleep out of doors with her child?" he said.

"No," I confirmed. "Must it be?"

"In one of our weeklies recently," he replied, "I saw a photograph of American workingmen sleeping in parks and in hallways."

That was no answer, of course. But his remark brought back vividly a scene in New York. It was a cool May evening, the last I spent in the United States. As I left the subway station at 1.30 a.m., I passed rows of men sleeping in its underground corridors. A newspaper served as bedding and another as blanket. Within a block of this spot stood half-empty hotels, rich dwellings incompletely occupied and other premises where the unemployed might have been accommodated. In Leningrad there simply are not enough rooms for transients.

And so to a comfortable bed.

Chapter IV

PALACES, PROPAGANDA, AND PRIVILEGE

I found this passage in Lenin this morning: "The old (capitalist) society was based on this principle—either you rob somebody else or that somebody else will rob you; either you work for another man or he works for you; either you are a slave-owner or a slave. . . ."

The two waiters at the breakfast table are Tartars, the first exhibits of the Soviet crazy-quilt of national minorities. I ask one whether he attends services at the mosque. He says: "I used to before the revolution, but now I have no time, and even when I have time I can do other things."

I shall see palaces today. I have seen royal residences in England, France, and Germany. In Leningrad, however, the manner of showing is more interesting than the matter shown. The homes of the Czars are utilized as object lessons in anti-monarchist propaganda. Soon Czarism will be only a faint memory or a historic conception to most Soviet citizens. Russia lives so quickly that the past becomes dim in very few years. Russia has lived a century since 1917. But the Bolsheviks wish to retain certain relics of by-gone days for purposes of comparison with the different today.

For this reason, the palaces and a considerable number of churches and monasteries in Russia are being carefully preserved as museums. No hand does violence to the old material treasures. Yet the black-and-white canvas pictures of Lenin and Stalin perched on the façade of the Catherine Palace in Detskoe Selo must make the Czars turn in their graves. And a Bolshevik slogan by Lenin displayed in Nicholas the Second's private study probably has the same rotatary effect. In fact, the Czars must be spinning in their graves if they are at all sensitive to the violence which the Soviets have done to the spirit of the palaces while meticulously retaining their forms. The chief purpose of the guides is to provoke contempt and hatred for Russia's former autocrats.

The main entrance to Catherine's palace. A large delegation of workingmen is filing in. When I reach the heavy door, a white bearded giant in simple livery opens it. He says "Yes" proudly when I ask him whether he also served the Czars. He is part of the museum. He admitted monarchs. He is a bit contemptuous of the "rabble" he now admits into the hallowed precincts.

Far off on the banks of the Gulf of Finland, at Peterhof, stands another palace. Peter the Great built it. I join a group of Russians. In a forechamber we are furnished with carpet slippers to wear over our street shoes which might scratch the valuable parquet floors of the royal apartments. Close behind, a party of English-speaking visitors. I listen with both ears. The foreigners are being shown a palace; the Soviet citizens are subjected to propaganda.

To the foreigners: This is such-and-such reception hall, its furnishings brought from France or China. These paintings were hung in the reign of So-and-So. Here Czar X received a diamond present from the ruler of Y. The talks to the Soviet citizens, on the other hand, are an analysis of Russia's early history and a lesson in dialectic materialism. On the basis of an authentic chart showing the number of mercantile ships which entered the ports of Arch-

angel and St. Petersburg in the early years of the eighteenth
century we learn why Peter needed a "window into Europe" as he called his burg. To protect the "window"
he built the Kronstadt fortress on an island in the gulf.
A rude hut at Peterhof became Peter's brief stop-off during stormy voyages from the town to the citadel. But he
wished to impress foreign vessels which entered the Petersburg harbor. He wanted to proclaim to Europe that Russia
was a great Power. The modest hut was therefore converted into the expensive palace. An original document
displayed in one of its rooms gives an itemized account
of the price of construction. The guide draws our attention
to the absence of a labor cost item. Why? The answer
comes quickly from several young folks in this group:
The palace was erected by serfs. More original data elaborates the treatment accorded to these slaves, how they
were beaten, how they died in draining the swamps. Side
by side with this picture, we receive another: the pompous
but dirty splendor of this Czarist period and its uncultured, serf-owning courtiers. A letter preserved for pos-
terity establishes the budget of the court. Expenditures rose
year by year. The number of courtiers, as quoted from
the diary of a British ambassador of the 19th century, increased steadily. This is accompanied by a graph showing
the mounting taxes collected from the peasantry.

The guide then pries under the thin veneer of regal
brilliance to uncover the selfishness, backwardness and
superstition of the Czarist regime. Foreign painters are
ordered to paint *in absentia* idealized portraits of Czarinas
and Czars which would impress Europe and gratify the
royal lords. A table is spread after the manner of Catherine
the Great's state banquets. Simultaneously, we are reminded of the starvation fare in the mujhik's hut. The life

The magnificent ball-room in Catherine the Great's palace
near Leningrad

of leisure in the palace is graphically depicted by wax figures of costumed dukes and counts playing cards. Contemporaneous color sketches show the dress and coiffure modes of the period. Again an ambassador's diary reveals the secret that the immense superstructure of the ladies' false curled hair hid a wealth of parasites. The excursionists laugh appreciatively.

Public education lags. Peasant revolts multiply. A trading class is born. Europe wants Russian grain. The Czars, therefore, turn their attention towards the conquest of Southern Russia. Catherine travels to the Ukraine and Crimea. We follow her on the trip. St. Petersburg reaches out to the Black Sea, and the idea of acquiring Constantinople seizes the imagination of Russia's upper hundreds. Turkish influences consequently appear at court. Next we see how Russia's expansion into Siberia evokes an accentuated interest in China and Mongolia. A number of palace-rooms furnished at this period have purely Chinese internal decorations.

The group is especially grateful for the visit to the private church which forms part of the palace. The close connection between church and court is emphasized. Quotations from Czarist decrees enunciate the doctrine of the divine right of Czars who, according to one imperial ukaze, "are beyond criticism and opposition on earth." "In the end, however, they were not,"—the guide concludes. The Russians applaud.

When one goes from the stuffy atmosphere of the palace into the sunny reality of the parks crowded with Soviet citizens one sees what an unbridgeable chasm separates this "pre-historic" phase of Russia's past from the boiling torrential proletarian present. There is not only no return; there is no continuity between the two political systems.

At 10 p.m., as the northern sun began to set, my stroll brought me to the Neva River. The "Amur," a gray, graceful Soviet cruiser rode at anchor, and the sailors, some in brief loin strips, a few naked, swam and dived and frisked in the dark swift stream while several hundred citizens looked on. From this spot one can see many of the famous landmarks of old St. Petersburg. Just behind me rose the golden dome of St. Isaac's Cathedral, Russia's holiest, now an anti-religious museum, and in the foreground stood a beautiful statue of Peter the Great, its pedestal a tremendous rough-hewn rock. The horse prances on its hind legs, one of its hoofs on a huge python that writhes in its death pangs. Thus Peter dealt with his enemies, with Sweden, his worst foreign foe, and with the boyars at home. Soviet boys played under the belly of the beast and fitted their lithe bodies into the curves of the snake.

The platform where stands the Leningrad-Moscow train is alive with friends and relatives seeing passengers off. Since Russians don't trust themselves to be on time, they arrive at the station very early. Bouquets are handed through windows, the last calls are quickly exchanged, handkerchiefs prepared for waving and crying, and then, on the scheduled minute, without a signal, the train moves silently out of the yard for its twelve-hour, overnight run to the capital.

The train is a symbol of inequality. The "International" car, with wide, comfortable, two-berth compartments furnished with plenty of baggage space, clothing hooks, a table and table lamp, represents first class. But even here there are two first classes: some coupés have splendid little washrooms with running water attached to them, while the occupants of others use the lavatories at either end of the car. In the "International," a polite porter is always on duty, and the traveler may get biscuits and hot tea in glasses from the samovar which sings in the corner. A rung lower is second class, "soft," as Russians call it. Some of the compartments have two-berths, others four. Beds are made up here too, but they are not as convenient. Occupants can obtain food and drink only in the diner or from a waiter who irregularly moves through the length of the train. The porters are not as accommodating and not nearly as ready to keep their cars clean. Though much depends on the industry of the porter *and* on the cultural level of the passengers, a traveler will often resort to the common washrooms only in the hour of dire necessity. At the bottom of the scale comes "hard." There are no compartments. The passengers sleep on three tiers of wooden shelves. Of late, the railroads have been supplying bedding for these cars too. Frequently, the people bring their own pillows, blankets, kettles in which to make their own tea with boiled water furnished free at stations, food, etc. etc. Few "hard" passengers undress for the night. They merely remove some of their upper clothing and shoes, with corresponding effects on the atmosphere. But another kind of atmosphere prevails in "hard," the atmosphere of one big family which exchanges food and autobiographies. Foreigners with tough skins and dulled olfactory sense occasionally prefer "hard" for the opportunity it offers of making intimate contacts with Russians.

When the "hard" and "soft" passengers walk through the "International" they admire it. When the "soft" passenger passes the "hard" car he is glad he has graduated from it. At the same time, he hopes to be promoted some day to the "International." In Moscow recently my maid, who had decided to spend her fortnight's vacation in Leningrad, talked to me about the trip. I advised her to spend the extra rubles and get a mattress and pillow. She did not understand. She was sure that she would have to sit up all night. When I explained the accommodations which "hard" offered, she smiled happily. She had done all her traveling earlier in the revolution by "Maxim Gorki," in a converted freight car, that is.

Why should the engineer travel "International" and the street cleaner, or my maid, "hard"? The real reason is that the engineer is richer. The Bolsheviks recognize—they would be denying a self-evident fact if they did not—that an engineer's services are worth more than a street cleaner's. The state accordingly pays him more. This divergence of income implies varying living standards. For if the government allowed only "soft" travel and reduced the price of a "soft" ticket so that the street cleaner, and my maid, could buy one, the engineer, with a much higher salary, would be unable to spend his money, and he might just as well not earn it. (Ticket is used here, of course, as a collective term denoting all possible commodities: apartment, clothes, food, etc.) Since the Soviets reject leveling of income as destructive of personal initiative, they must tolerate a wide gamut of living levels.

Foreign radicals who abhor the sharp inequalities of capitalism, and foreign capitalists who enjoy these inequalities with gusto are alike surprised to find inequality in the Soviet Union too. But the same thing may be different. Fire is sometimes a necessity of life and sometimes an agent of death. One phenomenon may be the effect of two causes. It is not, or it should not be, the disparity between the workingman's living and the lawyer's or doctor's living which disturbs the radical in a bourgeois country. It is the difference in the social status of the workingman and capitalist. It is the discrepancy between the man who sells his labor and the man who buys it. Inequality in a capitalist country is the first step towards accumulation, and accumulation leads to the ownership of capital and thence to exploitation. Soviet inequalities, on the other hand, are the degrees of difference between several groups of wage earners. No matter how much a Soviet citizen earns he cannot become a capitalist or grow rich on the work of others. The system debars capitalism.

This is the theory. But life is complicated and evasive, and though the Soviet press seeks to explain inequality as normal, the Soviet public does not like the forms it takes. Inequality has of late become a topic of frequent and exacerbated discussion. It is likely to occupy Bolshevik minds for a long time to come.

The other day, several wives of workingmen were in our kitchen bidding farewell to my maid who was preparing to leave for Leningrad. I came in to urge Niura to be sure and see the palaces. She would know then how the Czars used to live.

"And doesn't Stalin live as well as the Czars?" a woman interjected.

She obdurately refused to believe when another woman told her that Stalin occupied three modest rooms in the Kremlin. It was easy to see why. For in the next breath she referred angrily to the parties given by one of her well-paid neighbors, a petty government official. She must have reasoned in this wise: if that tiny "Stalin" who is one-thousandth as important as the big Stalin lives thus, then the big Stalin lives a thousand times better. What could be more natural for a primitive mind?

The little peep into Soviet reality reflects an emerging

state of mind. When a Soviet citizen complains of inequality he forgets those below him and proceeds, with much self-pity, to compare himself with the strata above him. It has become commonplace to speak of the wealth and immense royalties of Soviet authors and journalists. Yet I have heard Soviet authors justify their large incomes, and protest that they live much worse than first rank government commissars. The non-collectivized peasant dislikes the favoritism shown to members of collectives; the collectivized peasant resents the special advantages given to the workingman; the workingman looks askance at the privileged position of the "udarnik" or labor enthusiast; the "udarnik" cannot understand the huge discrimination in favor of the technician; the technician thinks he ought to be on a par with the engineer; the engineer is jealous of the foreign specialist and sees no reason why certain doors open to the scientist are closed to him; the scientist dreams of the luxuries which the writers enjoy; but the writers say that some scientists and inventors and all cabinet members are better taken care of than they.

What are the privileges which are being discussed by Soviet citizens with so much venom? A small open Soviet "Ford" now produced at Nizhni Novgorod in thousands calls for Comrade So-and-So in the morning and brings him home after working hours. Under normal conditions in any other country, a similar official would jump on a bus or trolley or even take a taxi. But in Leningrad and Moscow the buses are irregular, street cars can usually be boarded only by acrobats, and taxis are a rare and fleeting sight. A new house is completed. Certain workers, certain officials, certain writers are assigned apartments in it. They immediately become a privileged class, for there are not yet enough apartments to accommodate everybody. In the Putilov factory, as in most plants, there are separate restaurants for "udarniks" and non-udarnik workingmen. The difference usually is that the "udarnik" restaurant serves a dessert with the dinner, and the other does not. The "udarnik" restaurant, moreover, probably changes its tablecloths once a week while in the other they are even dirtier.

The margin between privilege and its lack may be so narrow as to comprise nothing more than a pair of shoes or an extra room. Yet the value of these simple benefits is greater than elsewhere because of their scarcity. A few years ago, there was the same stratification of the population according to privileges, but it meant next to nothing because so few comforts and necessities, much less luxuries, were available. The recent increase in the supply of goods and perquisites has invested these privileges with considerable importance. Hence the sudden interest in inequality. But a still further increase will wipe out many privileges altogether: when there are enough apartments it will not be a privilege to get one. Privilege is the product of scarcity. Yet it also marks the beginning of the end of scarcity and therefore the beginning of its own end.

The tendency away from privilege has already set in. Here is the core of the problem: scarcity produced a many-price system in the Soviet Union. A pound of vegetables could sell at three prices along the same Moscow street. The closed coöperative of a factory or commissariat asked x kopeks for them; a commercial store open to all $3x$; the peasant market $4x$. And they all got what they asked because no one or two of these institutions could satisfy the entire demand. If, in a condition of scarcity, there were one low price, the high-salaried man would be dissatisfied because he could not spend his money, and because the poorly-paid might anticipate him and buy what he needs.

If there were one high price, the low brackets would protest and demand higher wages; to satisfy this demand would mean to print more money and inflate. The Soviet government, however, wishes to deflate so that money can buy more.

As supply slowly approximated demand, the authorities endeavored to establish a unified price. Often this was done by gradually depressing the commercial and market prices and lifting the coöperative price so that they would meet at a golden mean. The goal was one price, a one-value ruble, and death to those privileges which grow out of scarcity. Concretely: when there are three prices, it is a privilege to buy at the cheapest price. When there is one price, privilege is precluded.

The new trend is obvious. In 1931 and 1932, a number of commodities such as men's suits, underwear and kitchen utensils were sold only to "udarniks." But today anyone who has the money can buy these articles because there are enough of them. More and more shops display signs which read: "Open to All Citizens." Until a few months ago, the persons who were lucky enough to receive money remittances from abroad or who had been providential enough and once rich enough to have gold trinkets or coins could get almost anything they wanted in special "Torgsin" shops. But already some of these shops are being closed, and the goods of which they had a monopoly—imported woolens and shoes, for instance—can be acquired by the ordinary citizen in ordinary stores. In general, the crass demarcation between the "Torgsin" public and the rest of Soviet humanity is no more.

The movement against inequality is really tantamount to resentment against a miserable standard of living. This is a healthy phenomenon when a reasonable prospect exists that the yearning for better conditions can be satisfied. I have heard, and participated in, many private discussions of Soviet citizens on the subject of inequality and privilege. Nobody ever suggests that equality is desirable. The target of attack is always the excessively wide hiatus between uppermost and nethermost. Nobody ever suggests that this evil should be cured by lowering the upper level. The desideratum is the raising of the lower level. This conforms with the Soviets' chief aim.

Something very human has happened in the Soviet Union. Having been starved for years for comforts and luxuries, there was a mad rush for them the moment the factories began turning them out. People began to attach an inordinate importance to material goods, and grabbed whatever they could reach. Those with the highest positions often proved to have the longest arms. Here was a loop-hole for abuse. Party and government officials commenced banqueting one another, and sending one another on trips with fat *per diems* attached. The heavy hammer of the Kremlin has cracked down on the thick skulls of some of these sinners, but a lot are still intact.

Actually, the "backsliders" are claiming much less than would, abroad, constitute a decent life for a below-average middleclass citizen. But here, against the universal background of bad standards, they appear as so many Lucullan revelers or perverted millionaires. Without this perspective the picture becomes distorted. And another factor helps towards an understanding of the situation: the privileged groups are of very irregular composition. If the front rank commissars, army commanders, what was formerly the G.P.U., the militia, writers and the best scientists constitute the first class, many workers follow closely, and certainly many workers are better off than many officials. Some physicians are well-situated, others poorly-situated. A factory can put its entire staff on a privileged basis simply by establishing an excellent dairy farm of its own, or by building a few blocks of houses for its employees.

There are millions of privileged citizens in the Soviet Union. In fact, almost everyone enjoys one privilege or another. But as distribution of necessities and comforts is normalized, the number of privileged people decreases. Citizens need no privileges to live. A greater volume of production eliminates some privileges which are altogether unnecessary. But it creates others. Today inequality may be the difference between having one suit and two suits. Tomorrow it may be represented by an automobile; the day after by the difference between a Soviet "Ford" and a Soviet "Buick-Chrysler." Since the Soviet system does not prohibit the holding of private property—it objects only to private capital, that is to wealth which can produce more wealth—and since it encourages a graduated scale of income according to ability and training, there will always be inequality under the Soviets. Personally, I do not believe that inequality in the form it may ultimately take in the U.S.S.R. is a cardinal sin. Whether inequality must lead to a permanently privileged class is a far more serious issue.

The Bolsheviks assert that the end of the second Five Year Plan, in 1937, will see a classless society. This is an exceedingly attractive prospect. But I think we will all be much older before we see it. Perhaps, in fact, a new class is being born. The Soviets destroyed the capitalist class. Workers and peasants remained. Now a third class is emerging—the "white collars," the bureaucracy, the engineers, officials, scientists, writers, in a word, intellectuals. A few years ago they were persecuted and arrested. The wheel turns quckly, however, in the Soviet Union.

According to Stalin's formula, expressed in an interview with H. G. Wells which enhanced the reputation of neither as a theoretician, the intelligentsia serves the proletariat. Very good. The proletariat pays for the services. But what if the intelligentsia begins to determine its own compensation? What if it begins to take so much that too little is left for the workers? This is the real menace in the U.S.S.R. today.

The danger that inequality will breed vested privilege and that privilege will incorporate itself undoubtedly exists. There is this caveat to be added: all noted the demoralization induced by the New Economic Policy (NEP) period between 1921 and 1927. Most observers darkly prophesied the impending reëstablishment of capitalism. Then suddenly the NEP was banished. The Soviet regime possesses great reserves of administrative action and moral strength and I trust it to make at least an effort to cope with the inequality-plus-privilege situation before it weakens the social fabric.

And so to Moscow in the "International" car, first class.

Chapter V

DYNAMO

A capital is important. But Moscow is a thousand times more important to the Soviet Union than London to England or Paris to France or Washington and New York to the United States. Moscow is heart, brain and purse. Moscow is master, father and teacher. A business enterprise in Manchester or in Chicago or in Lyons may have an agent or two in the capital of its respective country, pay taxes to the federal government, and that is all. But Moscow builds, operates, finances and controls every big and even relatively small factory, railroad, bank, mine, scientific institute, oilfield, etc., in that vast country which covers one-sixth of the earth's surface.

Not only the army, the taxes, the foreign affairs, the post-office—that is, what usually goes as "government," centers in Moscow. Every economic unit, social organization, cultural enterprise, and political office has a lifeline which connects it with Moscow. Moscow is the heart which pumps blood, the brain which sends messages, the dynamo which lends energy to every corner of the Soviet Continent. In its turn, the body keeps the heart alive, enriches the brain and replenishes the dynamo.

Moscow throbs. Human electricity tingles in the streets. Moscow's tempo is racing, staccato, mad.

Green and yellow trolleys, red and yellow trolleys, green buses, yellow and red buses, green giant trolley buses. Flat horse carts with rubber balloon tires. Crowds at stops, crowds in the trolleys, crowds in the buses. Young women driving trolleys. Sleeping heads on trolley window sills. Reckless driving around curves. Little traffic but much danger. Much more traffic each year. An empty taxi races by. Some hopeful Moscovites raise their hands to stop it. No use. And when it is standing still: "Are you free?" "Where do you want to go?" "To such-and-such a street." "I have no gas," or "I must go to the garage," or "This is my lunch hour." You entreat. Offer an extra tip. Your child is sick. You will be late for an important conference. He shakes his head. "I am going the other way," repeats the adamant chauffeur. At night these counter-revolutionaries collect outside the better restaurants waiting for gay couples or drunks. No ordinary passenger can entice them to leave such a post. "Engaged." Engaged to the hope of a good fare. . . . Blue kaftaned droshkie drivers. There were once many hundreds. Now a few score remain. Agrarian collectivization and more socialism sent them back to their villages. Once it was one of the pleasures of Moscow to bargain with them. He asks 12 rubles. "I'll give you three." He says nothing. You walk down the street. He follows at a crawl pace. You turn your head. "Eight," he calls to you. "Five," you yell back. He stops. You slow down. "Six and that's all I will pay." "Take your seat." On the way he fills you with his tale of woe: oats have gone up, harvest prospects are bad. And when you prepare to pay he urges: "Nu, citizen, add another ruble. . . ."

Numerous trucks of Soviet and foreign manufacture. Will Rogers, the American sociologist who visited Russia recently, said: "When there are more trucks than touring cars in a city, it's a good sign." He accorded Moscow the best sign. But no truck driver would ever allow a passenger car to pass him. His truck-driver pride would suffer. All

Moscovites have a lucky star in heaven. If they did not,
they would be in heaven themselves. What though felt-
helmeted militiamen in white gloves execute right-turns
and left-turns and bend their arms in the manner of Balieff's
wooden soldiers. What though red-yellow-green sema-
phores, hand-operated and automatic, guard the street
crossings. There are long distances between crossings where
the big "30's" on the speed-limit discs remind the driver
that it is beneath his dignity to travel less than 30 kilometers an hour. The street cars join in the race. In
trains of two and three trolleys, the motormen rush fiercely
forward sounding their electric alarm bell uninterruptedly.
The cars sway and roll; the wheels roar. The passengers
hold their seats or their straps and their breath. The pavements are narrow. Pedestrians overflow into the streets; the
speeding vehicles dash in and out among them. Besides,
Moscovites have bad ears, and the auto honk usually reaches
their auditory nerves when the tires are three feet from
their heels. Then they scatter like geese. . . .

Along the whole length of one trolley runs a wooden
sign with the inscription: "Tezhe Cream to Make the Hands
Soft"—that in the capital of the horny-handed proletariat.
It is the Soviet government which manufactures that cream.
It also manufactures needles, lead pencils, button-hooks,
underwear, tennis balls, everything. And sells everything.
There is not a single private store in Moscow; all owned
and operated by the community. The kiosks are owned
by the state. The peddlers in white jackets work for the
state. Young boys whisper to you as you pass. They hold
paper cigarette boxes in their hands. You may buy one
cigarette or four or the entire lot. Which means that there
are not enough cigarettes. Women carrying market nets
bulging at the bottom, carrying baskets, carrying bread

which is naked on account of the scarcity of paper; a woman has bent her arm at the elbow and holds a large dripping carp. Men carrying leather portfolios. This is the badge of the official's tribe, and even if the brief case contains nothing more in the morning than a single sandwich for quick-lunch, and in the evening the empty bag in which it had been wrapped, a portfolio is his inseparable encumbrance. Through a window—women shaving men, women spraying water on men's faces, women combing men's sparse hair. Is it any more queer than women manicuring men's fingers? The male barbers are building steel mills. "Six Month Permanents," reads the tonsorial parlor sign. "For Jesus' sake, give me a kopek," a peasant woman begs. A shoe store. Galoshes, baby galoshes, badly finished shoes, rubber-soled shoes (70 per cent of all Soviet shoes were rubber-soled in 1934 because peasants slaughtered their cattle needlessly in 1932); women's felt overshoes, knee-high felt boots which the city has borrowed from the village—and a black-and-white placard which explains how shoes can be made to last longer. Nearby, a shoe repair shop displays the same rules. Apparently they want less business. . . .

"The Bolsheviks Must Master Technique" says an electric sign on top of the ship-like building of the Moscow daily "Izvestia." "In the period of reconstruction, technique determines everything (Stalin)," reads the electric sign on top of the twelve story Government House on the river quay which, in addition to 10,000 persons, houses its own retail stores, restaurant, post office, savings bank, laundry, lecture hall, cinema, theater, kindergarten and nursery. "Dancing in the Foyer," reads the electric sign. Above it, a much bigger moving electric sign announces the name of the cinema. "Jazz in the Foyer," shivers a Neon light in front of another film house. Inside, the spectators waiting for the seance to end—nobody is admitted while the picture is reeled off—sit in their hats and overcoats listening to a big orchestra play the latest American, German and British "hits." In a second room, citizens with a penchant for calmer entertainment play chess and checkers or read magazines borrowed from the free kiosk. Slogans by Stalin and Lenin serve as decorations. This cinema stands in the central Theater Square, now Sverdlov Square. In the same square: the Big Theater or Opera House, the Little Theater, and the Second Art Theater; and also a corner of Moscow's biggest department store, Mostorg, whose radio announcer's voice telling where and what to buy overflows into the street. . . .

"Hunter's Row." The name is an anachronism. One side of this wide avenue radiating from Theater Square once consisted entirely of one-story stores selling game, meat and vegetables. The pavements used to be packed as tightly as a Moscow street car with sellers and buyers. Now the whole block is occupied by the twelve story, marble-faced hotel of the Moscow Soviet. Opposite was a church that stood right out in the center of the thoroughfare, fish stores, little huts, etc. Now almost the entire block is a new skyscraping office building. There is much building going on —it has been going on for years, and will continue to go on for years. Today I was listening in to the radio. A Moscow factory broadcasted an appeal for workingmen. On construction projects one sees permanent announcements like this: "WANTED: bricklayers, plasterers, carpenters, plumbers, and black laborers (unskilled day laborers)."

Moscow has 2,500 streets and 51,000 dwellings. Of these, says Lazar Kaganovich, the city's Haroun el Rashid, 23,000 are one-story and 21,000 two-story. Now, he boasts, they

A girl surveyor in the Theater Square in Moscow. Note the necklace. The Grand Opera is in the background.

are building new six, seven and eight-story houses. This is very nice. But there are other figures. Only 1,178 houses in Moscow have elevators or "lifts" as the Russians say, borrowing from the English. And of these 1,178, only 475 are working. I live in an eight-story building. There is a shaft for a lift but no lift. Occupants of the upper floors are not to be envied, especially when they are women carrying heavy baskets of food. Moreover, what is higher is not always better. Now Stalin has said that Moscow dwellings must not exceed six stories. There is a Soviet sketch juxtaposing the Eiffel Tower, the Chrysler and Empire State Building of New York, and the plan of Moscow's Palace of Soviets—proudly indicating that the palace will exceed the height of the Empire State by the length of the fingers of Lenin's upstretched hand. The comedians laughed at Mr. Chrysler for mounting a thin spire on his skyscraper in order to increase its official stature; they poked fun at Mr. Al Smith for equally puerile behavior. And now the Palace of Soviets, with its assembly hall for 16,000 auditors and another for 8,000, and nobody-knows-how-many offices and club rooms spoils its classic lines with a huge statue of the dead leader which promises to be Moscow's outstanding abomination. The Bolsheviks worship the big. They have taken over this frailty from the Czarist Russians and, needless to say, surpassed them. In the Kremlin, the Czars placed the "Czar Cannon," the biggest in the realm, and also the "Czar Bell" which broke under its excessive weight. Is it bigger than the Place de la Concorde? the Kharkovites asked when they laid out their parade square in front of a modern office skyscraper. "We are erecting an eighteen-story building," the go-getters of Rostov dinned. "Will there be enough water pressure for the upper floors; could your fire department cope with a fire in the upper floors?" They had not thought of that. Skyscrapers, yes, where land is costlier than air. But where land has no price because it can neither be bought nor sold? Moscow has many blocks of multi-story gray barracks which are comfortable enough within but cannot possibly be a foretaste of the Socialist metropolis of the future. In many respects, the Bolsheviks are children, just like so many adult Americans. This is one of several reasons why Americans are usually better equipped to understand Soviet Russia than most other nationals.

The Russians love a show and the Bolsheviks know how to stage one. The Bolsheviks are endeavoring to change the core of life, but they pay much attention to outward appearances. They have decided to make Moscow "the city beautiful" and now nothing must interfere with that goal. The Palace of Soviets probably will, but it is the biggest feature of their plan. In the courtyard of the house where I live an additional wing was started, the foundation built, piles of bricks brought to the scene; building operations, however, have stopped on account of the lack of workingmen. Home building at the Frezer factory just outside Moscow has ceased because of the absence of materials, and the brick walls with yawning holes for windows stand there like gaunt skeletons while workers live in the barracks nearby. These are two instances of many. Yet the Palace which might have been started five years from today without anybody missing it absorbs endless numbers of laborers and infinite quantities of material.

This is true. Nevertheless, the Bolsheviks are not interested in façades. In Warsaw, Madrid, Athens, even in some French and British cities, one need only walk ten minutes from the fashionable streets of the metropolitan hub to be in dirty slums. But the Soviet revolution mixed things up completely. Workers live in the aristocratic quarters. Sometimes the best houses are erected in the factory suburbs. Walk ten or twenty or thirty minutes in one direction from the Nevski in Leningrad, from the Tverskaya in Moscow, from the Kreschatik in Kiev and you do not fall down any social precipice. In fact, one may have some climbing to do on such a promenade. If the central streets of Moscow are all asphalted or being asphalted, so too are distant wards. Stores an hour away from the Big Theater may be better supplied than stores around the corner from it. The fact that not all fine Moscow buildings are in the center of town detracts from the impression the city makes. And so too does the circumstance that many new structures are hidden away in deep courts while the ugly one-story boxes dating back a century or more face the street. Some day they will be torn down. Not a few have already been torn down in connection with the tunneling of the subway and the widening of squares and avenues. In this demolition process, the Bolsheviks respect only utility and history. Old landmarks are not spared just because they are old.

Appearances count but principles are not always sacrificed to them. The Moscow Soviet could round up the beggars of the city just as easily as Mussolini is said to have done. That would be window dressing. Instead the regime goes about improving living conditions. When the peasants are really well-to-do, Soviet cities will know no beggars except the professionals who can then be re-educated. This is the attitude towards prostitution too. Where there is no unemployment and a lot of amateur competition there are few street-walkers. Moscow, with tens of thousands of transients, a garrison, etc., has only a few hundred, perhaps 500, prostitutes. Most of them are house maids in search of careers or peasant girls who had come in to find work and were intercepted at railway stations by adventurers. Soviet cities have prophylactoriums where such girls are segregated and taught professions.

A hatless girl, in rubber tennis slippers and a silk dress down to her ankles. A young workingman with a girl's blue knitted cap on the tip of his head. A woman stops a man on the street for a light. He draws on the cigarette, gives her the light, tips his hat and walks on. A queue forty people long at a newspaper kiosk waiting for the "Evening Moscow." Its circulation is 120,000, but if the state gave it enough paper it could sell 500,000 copies. The only evening paper in a city of 3,600,000! A queue of twelve people at the bus stop. The bus will probably arrive full and not take on a single passenger. When I first came to Moscow in 1922, there was not one bus or taxi. That day in 1924 when eight handsome "Leylands" arrived from England was a holiday. By 1928, Moscow had 175 buses —all foreign. Now it has 180 Soviet buses too. The transportation problem, however, remains unsolved. The first 12-kilometer line of the subway or "Metro" solves part of it. But the complete subway, 80 kilometers in length, will not be ready until 1942. Then the Moscow trolley system will be abolished as superfluous. Happy day! No more waiting twenty minutes at wind-swept car stops when the temperature is 35° below zero and then traveling in a trolley whose only heat is human heat.

Aproned house janitors sprinkling streets and pavements with long hoses. A few years ago when all of Moscow was paved with sharp cobbles and rounded cobbles, rain and snow converted the streets into rivers of mud; summer winds raised Sahara sand-storms. In summer, therefore, janitors had instructions to water the streets four times daily. The cobbles are gone, but the watering goes on. The effect, however, is very salutary. Occasionally, mechanical sweepers and automobile street scrubbers appear on the central thoroughfares.

Moscow has many wooden houses. Moscow has very few completely fireproof houses. Most housewives prepare their meals on kerosene primuses. Yet one rarely hears or sees the fire engines in Moscow. Moscow has few fires. Probably because there is no commercial fire insurance. . . .

A young woman jumps out of a light truck, runs across the pavement, empties the letter box and rushes off to the next letter box. A girl in overalls and beret stands smoking a cigarette. She and her comrades are laughing; they are resting from the arduous work of building Moscow's first subway. "Moscow's subway must be the best in the world," say the placards. Everything Bolshevik must be best; Bolsheviks were never much troubled by inferiority complexes. A girl with high-heeled leather shoes inlaid with snake skin, a crêpe de chine dress in the latest fashion, kid gloves, extending over her cuffs and a cloth beret cocked at the regulation Paris angle of 31½ degrees. A woman with epaulette shoulders on her dress; a woman whose clothes, coiffure, facial make-up and manner reveal a painstaking effort to ape the Western world. Feminine clothes are an intimate thing and the revolution has not changed them. Most Soviet women would walk much more than a mile for a foreign fashion magazine: "foreign" is a synonym for good. The revolution has altered much but not women's styles. And men? When there were no collars, neckties and felt hats it was "counter-revolutionary" to wear them. But now that they exist in abundance, President Kalinin, Premier Molotov, and Comrade Kosarev, secretary of the Komsomol or Young Communist League, have themselves photograpned in these "bourgeois" trappings. And Ordjinikidze, Commissar of Heavy Industry, told his engineers in October, 1934—historic date—to shave regularly. Shades of Peter the Great!

A broad boulevard extends down the center of a long and broader avenue. Children play in sand boxes while their nurse maids watch and gossip. Old men play checkers on a bench. There is a crowd around another bench. A young, heavy-handed artist is making a crayon sketch of a workingman who poses with serious mien. "Know Your Real Weight." A bag registers the force of your punch. Ice cream kiosks, mineral water kiosks, kiosks where you buy geranium pots, chrysanthemum pots, aster pots all decorated with pink and purple ribbons made of thin and wide wood shavings. In the evening there will be free "propaganda movies" on the small screen under those trees. Women resting on their way home from the trying task of shopping. Sandwich and beer kiosks, a shoe-shining and shoe lace kiosk, fruit kiosks with fancy displays, book and newspaper kiosks where, if one is lucky, Moscow's numerous morning papers can be bought; where, if one is interested, one can get the radio magazine, the inventors' magazine, a crude fashion magazine, sports' magazine, political magazines, women's magazine, children's magazine, etc., etc.—all printed on bad paper, but all eagerly read.

A felt-helmeted policeman at a street cross-section is directing traffic. His ballet dancer movements attract a crowd. Two other policemen try to move the crowd away. At another spot one may see a policeman smoking on duty. Or he moves away from his post and temporarily transfers his functions to the white-aproned street sweeper who gives signals to passing autos with his broom. If there were fewer peasants and fewer ex-peasants in Moscow there would be fewer accidents and less chaos in the city.

Take a bus or trolley bus at Theater Square and travel fifteen minutes, then walk ten minutes through Petrovsky Park—you are in the midst of quiet village life where even the people are different. Here one finds the old traditional Russian mujhik type, the bearded giant, the little grandmother. But the city, the multi-story tenement and the factory, the paved road and the telephone wire are quickly invading these islands of repose. Moscow is throwing out tentacles and seizing its dozing countryside neighbors. Moscow's mad tempo is infecting the surrounding village area. A few years ago a sprawling village itself, Moscow is now urbanizing its periphery. In this respect, Moscow is merely an example in miniature of the vast process that has gripped the entire Soviet Continent: the gap between the urban and the rural is being narrowed. The Bolsheviks aim to destroy the gap altogether.

East and West used to meet in Moscow. Now East is being pushed out into Asia.

Chapter VI

MAKING MACHINES AND MEN

Moscow is encircled by a broad ring of new factories and housing settlements. Eight miles from the heart of the city stands the Frezer Cutting Tool Plant finished in 1931. On its horizon stand six other new industrial units. In a few years Moscow will grow out to that ring and swallow it. Meanwhile Frezer has fresh country air and its own farms across the street. From the outside it looks like a modern European or American factory, but on its walls, in large letters, slogans have been painted. "Long live the World Revolution." "Make the Soviet Union the Mighty Fatherland of Socialism," etc. In Moscow, too, the side walls of tall buildings are utilized for propaganda: charts showing the growth of industrial output can be seen on many of them.

Frezer produces what the Soviet Union formerly imported, and is thus a valued landmark in Russia's progress towards economic self-sufficiency. Trotzky, its chief engineer (a non-party man who earns 1,300 rubles monthly —the highest salary at Frezer) and Tolmatch, the director, Trotzky's superior (a Communist who earns 600 rubles a month) are enlightened, cultured men with technical knowledge and broad understanding.

Tolmatch has been pondering the problem of wages. The present Soviet method of widespread, almost universal piece-work has its advantages. It stimulates individual effort in a land where laborers have no tradition of hard work. But it has many shortcomings. The fact that workers can, either when stirred by a propagandist's oratory or the promise of special premiums, increase their output, sometimes by 100 per cent; the fact that they can "storm the program," means that under normal conditions they are not exerting themselves to the maximum extent. One would think that since they get paid for each unit they turn out they would try to turn out the greatest number of units. In actual practice they do not. Why this strange condition? Because, as I have explained, the more the workingman produces the more the management expects of him, and it will, when negotiating the new collective bargaining agreement at the end of every year or even in the middle of a year, raise the standard of output required from each individual. Piece-work, accordingly, stimulates production but also retards production. And Tolmatch's problem was: "How can I retain the healthy results of piece-work yet eliminate its drawbacks."

He devised a scheme and laid it before Sergo Ordjonikidze, Commissar of Heavy Industry. Ordjonikidze told him to introduce it. If it worked, it would be adopted more generally. The scheme is simple enough: Tolmatch gives a flat 20 per cent increase in salary to all workers who have been graduated from technical courses, whose work is of good quality, and who are efficient and devoted. This puts a premium on quality instead of on quantity as piece-work does. The result of piece-work is that many electric bulbs spoil after ten days' use and that some shoes wear out in a month. The Soviets now need quality above all, for, as the dialecticians say, quality is also quantity, and quantity without quality is not quantity.

Tolmatch's scheme has another objective: today, when a Russian worker wants to earn more money he tries to be promoted from a simple machine or a simple manufacturing process to a more complicated one. He thus steps up into a higher category and receives higher compensation. His aim is always to get away from his machine to another. There is consequently a constant migration in Soviet industry. Of course, this has its good sides: the spirit of "Excelsior" encourages study and convinces each laborer that no upward road is closed to him. But it also obstructs the accumulation of experience and of expert, specialized knowledge. Under Tolmatch's scheme the worker will earn the 20 per cent bonus if he stays at his lathe and learns to know it.

Tolmatch has moved in the right direction. He has not solved all the problems of piece-work. That would be too much to expect. But he has made a welcome departure from the principle of the monopoly of piece-work. The Bolsheviks are by nature extremists, and it is difficult for them to follow a golden mean. They lean ninety degrees to one side or ninety degrees to the diametrically opposite side, and when they introduce piece-work they would put the janitor and the scientist on piece-work.

Late one afternoon, at the end of my third day at Frezer, Shingarev, the secretary of the Factory Committee or "Zavkom," went for his dinner at the plant's first class restaurant. I went along for a glass of tea. We found Tolmatch, Trotzky, the chief statistician, and another engineer at one of the white-covered tables. Trotzky had made a prolonged journey of discovery through the United States. He had visited most of the cutting tool factories in the Eastern states and praised their efficiency. "Their floors are as clean as our tables," he said. "Every worker knows his job." He had carefully read American newspapers during his stay. And he had kept his eyes and ears open. "In a small town in Pennsylvania," he recalled, "a huge election banner had been stretched across the street. The candidate for mayor was advertising himself as 'Free from Graft.' Can you imagine a situation in which 'Free from Graft' figures as a special recommendation for office." His round face laughed and he showed his golden teeth. He turned to his colleagues. "Can you imagine," he began, "when I was there, two young fellows kidnaped a rich capitalist in California. A mob caught them and hanged them from a tree. That was bad enough; but then the governor of the state, the guardian of the law, declared that nobody must dare to touch a hair on the lynchers' heads. The lynchers actually became public heroes."

"A wild country," Tolmatch commented, "and yet it has such wonderful industrial technique."

"Then there was the Scottsboro case," Trotzky continued. "Ruby Bates, one of the prostitutes who accused the negroes, has retracted her testimony. The whole story is a fake. But the crisis is severe in the land, there have been more lynchings, and the whites find it necessary to sharpen the antagonism between the white and black workers. Think of such a sight: a negro prisoner is 'stolen' from a jail. Actually the sheriff opens the doors for the mob. The negro, suspected of killing a young woman, let us say, is dragged through the town by a rope tied to an automobile. The whole town ecstatically yells its approval. On the outskirts, the negro is soaked with kerosene and strung up on a tree. A match sets fire to his clothes and the howling, frenzied mob watches him fry. Finally, the charred body is lowered to the ground, and people fight, really fight, for the privilege of cutting off an ear or finger of the negro to show to their children at home as a souvenir of this great triumph of capitalist civilization."

"A barbarous country," the chief statistician commented.

The Soviet newspapers have been publishing a long series of articles by engineers and factory directors just returned from the United States on America's most recent mechanical improvements and industrial advances. "The Soviet cutting machine," reads a Frezer sign, "must be the best in the world."

The library of the Frezer factory is housed in a rude, wooden shack. It has 8,000 volumes of which one-third are fiction, and 28 per cent technical books; the rest deal with politics, economics, history, etc. In addition, the engineers of the plant use a special technical library which is accommodated elsewhere.

Belles lettres are in greatest demand. About 2,000 volumes were on the shelves, but only 220 were novels. The chief librarian and her assistant declared that they were too poorly supplied to meet the entire demand, this though many workers live within the city limits and therefore have access to richer libraries in Moscow. The library has 2,500 regular borrowers—out of 4,800 individuals employed at Frezer. The majority of the readers are men, and yet 68 per cent of the 4,800 are women.

Ten per cent of the library's fiction is translations from foreign languages. Upton Sinclair is the most popular foreign writer. The library has four subscriptions to a new edition of his collected works, ten volumes of which have already appeared. These forty books are taken. Theodore Dreiser is represented only by his "American Tragedy"; not one of the fifteen copies of this book is available. The ten copies of Heinrich Mann's "Untertan" are never on the shelves. Balzac is much read too. But only the youth ask for Jack London, and the workers are also graduating from O. Henry. If there were more translations in the Frezer library, more would be read. The same applies to Russian pre-revolutionary classics. Tolstoi, Gogol, Pushkin, Herzen and, though to a smaller extent, Dostoyevsky, all find eager readers.

The library possesses fifty copies of Alexei Tolstoi's "Peter the Great." They are all out. It has 65 copies of Sholokhov's "Virgin Soil." They are all out. It has ten copies of Gladkov's "Energy." They are out. In fact, almost everything is out. No book may be kept by a borrower for more than ten days, and usually the person returning a book arrives with a friend who wants it next. The librarian keeps waiting-lists for certain books. Maxim Gorki, Novikov-Priboi, Seraphimovitch, etc., are read so much and so fast that the paper-bound books soon become unreadable. The librarian buys what she can, not only of new editions—she also purchases old books from workingmen and personal acquaintances.

As I sat in the library gathering data and impressions, Anna Georgievna Vtichieva entered. Anna Georgievna is a young woman, twenty-seven years old, who works as a cashier in the factory restaurant. Her husband is also a Frezer employee. They have a ten year old child, but no maid. Anna Georgievna was returning two books and asking for the second volume of "Peter the Great." I posed a few questions. She knew George Sand, Balzac, all of Sir Walter Scott, Count Leo Tolstoi and the famous Russians of the nineteenth century. She preferred Soviet literature and talked intelligently about a number of new books I mentioned. I requested the librarian to show me Anna Georgievna's reading card. Since December, 1932, when the library was opened, Anna Georgievna had read 188 books. It sounded excessive and unbelievable, but the librarian assured me that this was not unusual. With her permission, I took several cards at random from the box that stood on the table. One worker, twenty-five years old, had read thirty books in the first nine months of 1934. A workingman thirty-eight years of age had taken out sixty-two books since October, 1932. More than half of them dealt with historical and scientific subjects. A third young man of twenty-three who had come to Frezer as an unskilled hand in December, 1932, had read 103 books since that time. It was obvious that Anna Georgievna was not unique.

Anna Georgievna works six hours a day. She earns 108 rubles a month. Her husband is an electrician and earns 220 rubles. She and her husband eat two meals a day at the factory; their daughter has two meals a day in the school. Anna attends the factory's embroidery circle. She and her husband go to theater twice a month and to the cinema twice a month.

"Why do you read so much?"

"I live with books."

"Why don't you study?"

"I am old. I will teach my little girl."

"Do you ever buy books?"

"No, I had never thought of doing that, and besides we haven't enough money."

A young woman came into the library and returned Mike Gold's "Jews Without Money" in Russian translation. I asked how she liked it. "It is easy to read. It is about such a strange world," she said. "The capitalist world."

During 1934, the library had arranged four public meetings with popular authors. They came to the plant, lectured, and then answered questions. In each case, the librarian told me, the first question was: "How did you start writing?" The factory has some of its own poets who print their verses in the newspaper of the plant. The newspaper, "Frezer," appears every third day in an edition of 1,800 copies.

In Shingarev's office of the Factory Committee we talked about wages. "Your workers earn too little," I submitted. It is always productive to irritate a Soviet interlocutor.

"You are accustomed to capitalist ways of thinking," the young man came back. "You take the man's wage and ask yourself whether a family can live on such an income. But with us there is never only one bread-winner in a household."

A laborer, aged approximately forty, entered. Shingarev put a series of questions to him. He was a tool cutter and earned 310 rubles last month. His wife is employed in Frezer as a clerk; she earns 165 rubles a month. His daughter, a girl of eighteen, just matriculated in the university's medical faculty where she receives a monthly stipend of 100 rubles. He and his wife take two meals at the factory; his daughter has a hot lunch at school.

"Do you make enough?" I asked the worker.

"Enough? There is no such thing as enough. But we are comfortable. My father could not give me an education. I graduated from the fourth grade at the age of thirteen and went to work. Now my daughter attends the university."

"Is she a good daughter?" I went on. "Does she obey you?"

"Obey?" he said. "Why should she *obey?* We are three

comrades. I have no authority over her. I cannot put economic pressure on her. She is independent. It is the state which is educating her. But she knows we love her and that what we advise her to do is for her own benefit. Of course, she is of the new generation and her psychology is soviet. We were bred under capitalism. Sometimes we do not understand her." A little tragedy lurked in his words. She was growing away from them. "Life, however," he concluded, "does not stand still."

This worker of forty is an "old man" at Frezer. For the average age at the plant is twenty. The Soviet Union is not only a rejuvenated country. It is literally a young country: according to one figure, 100,000,000 of the U.S.S.R.'s 170,000,000 inhabitants are twenty-five years old or less. This circumstance explains many things: enthusiasm and lack of experience, readiness to sacrifice and gullibility. Youth in this revolutionary is orthodox. Its allegiance is undivided. To what else shall it be loyal? Why should it be protestant? They are doers. If thinking does not facilitate doing, of what good is thinking? There's but to do and live.

A young fellow rushed in. The assembly hall was cold. A meeting of Red Army recruit-conscripts from the factory was scheduled for the evening and the hall was cold. Outrage! Blame somebody! He was himself a recruit-conscript. And a Komsomol. I subjected him to cross-examination.

He was a skilled mechanic and received a monthly salary of 400 rubles. In the army he would receive 6 rubles a month. "Is it efficient," I asked, "for you to be taken away from a machine where you produce and taught the use of arms for a year?"

"But someday I may have to defend that machine against the imperialists," was his ready reply.

"Are non-Communists as excited about being conscripted into the army as you seem to be?"

"It is an honor to be taken into the army. Only class-conscious workers and collectivized peasants are admitted. A bourgeois cannot get in no matter how hard he tries. In the Red Army I will continue my education. The Red Army is not only an army. It is a school of communism, a scientific institute, and a training ground all rolled into one." He was making a speech.

Russians have told me stories of Czarist military conscription. To be marked for conscription was a curse from God. Parents mourned their departing son as if it were his funeral. Men drank vinegar to get thin and become ineligible. Some maimed themselves. But now? In the Bolshevo Commune, one of the ex-thief members bewailed the fact that his flat feet had barred him from the Red Army. "A few years ago," he complained, "they paid little attention to flat feet. But I was not yet of age at that time." The Frezer mechanic was already a Voroshilov sharpshooter. He wore a badge to proclaim it.

During 1934, the Frezer factory committee sent seventy-eight of the plant's workers to sanatoria for a month, and 526 workers to rest homes for a fortnight. The committee's budget for the year was 235,000 rubles, a sum equal to two and one half per cent of the total wage bill of the factory. The management pays this sum to the committee. I went over Shingarev's accounts. Thirty-three thousand six hundred rubles for office expenses. Ten thousand rubles in loans to workers for emergency cases such as theft, accident, etc. Twenty-five per cent of the loan money is a gift. Four thousand rubles—salary to the lawyer who gives free legal advice to the Frezer force. Five thousand rubles to the plant's kindergarten and crèche: each child costs 74 rubles a month; the parents pay 25 rubles, and the management also makes a direct contribution towards upkeep. Five thousand rubles for sanatoria. Six thousand rubles to the school. Ten thousand rubles to the factory newspaper; the management subsidized it with 36,000 rubles. Thirteen thousand rubles for adult education. Seven thousand five hundred rubles for technical classes. Nine thousand rubles for "Pioneer" leaders and other "Pioneer" expenses. Six thousand rubles for children's summer camps. Six thousand rubles for subscriptions to newspapers and magazines which are conveniently distributed in "Red Corners" or "Lenin Corners" where employees can read them in free hours. Five thousand rubles to the library staff; 10,000 for the purchase of books; 1,500 for literary meetings. Six thousand rubles for trade union and political propaganda. Fourteen thousand rubles for radio—the plant broadcasts its own music and news. Four thousand two hundred rubles to the leader of the plant's sixteen-piece orchestra. Ten thousand rubles for picnics and entertainments. Three thousand rubles to the artist who directs their painter's circle. Five thousand rubles for aid to a village over which Frezer has been elected "patron"; the factory repairs its machines, gives presents of cameras, etc. to good farmers and so forth. Three thousand rubles—expenses as "patron" of a Red Army battalion. The rest of the budget goes for the purchase of theater tickets given free or at reduced prices to "udarniks"; Frezer has bought two permanent seats for the whole year at the Moscow Art Theatre, two more at the Grand Opera, two at the Red army theater: these seats are marked with a little metal disk: "Frezer Udarnik," just like an expensive seat in a foreign grand opera.

This affords a partial picture of what goes on in a Soviet factory outside of making shoes, tools and tractors.

Chapter VII

TO BE OR NOT TO BE

To be or not to be born? To be or not to be a mother? What questions could be more important? The Bolsheviks have failed to discover a method whereby embryos can choose their parents, but parents must have the widest possible choice. Some old-style Russian Communists argue that sexual intercourse should be only for procreation. Nobody listens to them. Madame Alexandra Kollontai, Soviet Minister to Sweden, advised humans to take love as bees take sweetness—from every open flower. The "Pravda" called that prostitution. As a matter of fact, the Bolsheviks are rather puritanical in their outlook and quite moderate in their personal lives. License is frowned upon as detrimental to state and individual; but monks are not popular in Russia. I once attended a court-hearing in a case of rape. "How old?" the female judge asked the woman.

"Twenty-nine."

"Were you a virgin?"

"Yes."

"But why were you foolish enough to guard it so long?" the judge scolded.

Sex questions are rarely discussed in Russian company. The problem of the eternal triangle remains, and little progress has been made towards its solution. Jealousy? Of course it exists. Yet with many it has ceased to play a big rôle, and murders for jealousy are scarcely known. These and similar matters, that is, the social phase of sex, are debated. But gossiping is an unpopular pastime. The assumption is that people may do as they please without becoming the subject of conversations which are themselves dangerously near the borderline of erotic substitutes.

If people do as they please, however, they must know. Girls and boys are told in high school. Last summer, I visited the Museum for the Care of Mother and Child housed in a beautiful building not far from where I live. Incidentally, the Tretiakov Art Gallery recently paid Favorsky 25,000 rubles for a copy of a fresco of a nurse which he painted in this museum. The museum has one of the best foetus collections in Europe—one foetus is eight months old. A young woman was examining it. I asked the directrix, Dr. Berkovitch, to talk to her. The young woman was twenty years old.

"Married?"

"No."

"Have you had sexual intercourse?"

"No." This, standing in a large group of strangers.

"And why are you interested in the foetus jars?" Dr. Berkovitch asked in friendly spirit.

"I am a student in the chemistry school of the university," she replied, "and as my social work this summer, I will spend two months in a village. The peasants always ask about these matters, and I wanted to be informed." Dr. Berkovitch commended her. The information is being spread through city and farm. About six years ago, on the Lubyanka Square, I passed a boy of twelve selling pamphlets. "Here you are," he was yelling, "learn about the prevention of pregnancy." I have not heard such cries since then, but enlightenment is easily obtained.

If contraception fails or is not practised out of a distaste which not a few Russian women have for it, there are abortions. Dr. Berkovitch has told me about abortions. "The

Soviet government," she affirms, in her very intense manner, "was the first state to legalize abortions. We did it to bring abortions up out of the cellar of illegality into which capitalist hypocrisy has driven it. Our abortions are performed by the best doctors in good clinics, and a fatal case is extremely rare."

"If a woman lives with her husband," she continues, "if she lives in good conditions, if it is her first child, an abortion is denied. Indeed, most of our women want to have children."

"Does the possibility of having an abortion conduce to promiscuity?" I inquired.

"No," Dr. Berkovitch stated emphatically, "no more than the ease of divorce gives us a higher percentage than many bourgeois countries. We give abortions and at the same time we make propaganda against them." I recalled having seen a scientific film widely distributed on the dangers of aborting. The number of abortions is decreasing. "We encourage births," she proceeded, "by establishing crèches for babies of working and student mothers. The two months' vacation with pay before and after child delivery eliminates pregnancy as a handicap to an economically independent woman." I once visited a large group of new dormitories for university students on the outskirts of Moscow. The first impression I received was of the babble of children.

What with pre-natal instructions to women, clinics where babies are brought regularly for consultation, and a greater diffusion of culture and hygiene (relatively greater), Soviet infant mortality is very low. And the number of births very high. The population of the U.S.S.R., consequently, is increasing by 3,000,000 each year—an increase equal to that of all the rest of Europe. By 1944, the Soviet Union will, it is estimated, have a population of 200,000,000. That is a fact of incalculable political importance. Meanwhile, however, a lot of economic improvement, industrial progress and construction is being canceled out by the tremendous annual excess of births over deaths. And yet the Bolsheviks never mention this problem. An army of effective Soviet Margaret Sangers would do much good.

All Soviet children are legitimate. Illegitimacy does not exist. Why should a child be branded at birth? To give birth to a child out of wedlock is neither a disgrace nor a handicap in the U.S.S.R. Dr. Berkovitch states that anything else would be an attack on woman's freedom to be herself. A woman may want a child but not a husband. Not a few women, the doctor declares, are too proud and independent to accept alimony. "Child bearing," she says, "is woman's highest right, and to deny her that right either through the pressure of public opinion or by definite regulations— against teacher-mothers, for instance, as in some places— is part of the slavery of capitalism."

"We do everything to enable woman to be economically independent. If a woman suffers pain during menstruation, she is excused from work for three days. In bourgeois lands," Dr. Berkovitch continues, "especially in Fascist Germany and Italy—but it will come elsewhere too— women are being pushed out of gainful employment. This measure is clothed in a cloak of chivalry. But it is simply a reflection of the economic crisis. You haven't enough work for everybody so you bar the 'fair sex.' " Dr. Berkovitch dropped into English. "You are unfair to the fair sex," she said. "We, on the contrary, have plenty of jobs for both sexes."

An exhibit in Dr. Berkovitch's museum deals with wife-beating. That was a universal and honored practice in Czarist Russia. "My husband does not love me anymore," the Russian woman used to say. "He has stopped beating me." Now women know their rights, and men know women's rights. Moreover, womanhood has been invested with a new dignity.

In a situation where women are being offered all sorts of inducements to take jobs, there is a strong incentive to accept them, especially when the supplementary income raises family living standards to a decent level. But the dilemma: To Work or Not to Work has not disappeared, and not a few women choose to be household decorations. Employment in a Soviet office is not exactly a nerve cure and, besides, the beauty parlors are crowded after office hours. Soviet women have a great craving, after the hard years that have passed, to become the fair sex. Yet to quit work also means to cut one's self off from social activity, to retire into a backwater, to become a "parasite." The choice is a difficult one, and I know women who waver from one alternative to the other, now taking a position and now preferring to take care of home and children. Superficial observers may be prone to believe that this deep personal problem has been solved by the Soviets. Such a judgment would be premature. Soviet men make excellent fathers, and in the absence of baby carriages, one often sees them on late afternoons and on free days tenderly fondling their offspring in parks and boulevards. Household burdens, nevertheless, fall chiefly on the housewife's shoulders and when she has a salaried task to boot, her lot is not easy. The institution of maids, to be sure, is very widespread, and many workingmen's families employ servants or "home workers" as they are called. But usually these girls regard their careers as domestics as a stepping stone to the more honored rôle of factory laborer. If they had rooms of their own, most of the maids I know, including my own very restive "worker," would long ago have joined the industrial proletariat or gone to school. The Bolsheviks' solution of this problem is the maximum extension of communal feeding, communal laundries and communal pre-school education which will relieve the woman of the larger duties and responsibilities.

Dr. Berkovitch's Museum for the Care of Mother and Child is accommodated on two floors. The first floor is devoted to mothers. "On the foundation of a healthy, cultured, free mother we build the superstructure, the second floor, the child." Here are graphs, charts, pictures, diagrams, models of perfect nurseries, specimens of children's toys which can be made inexpensively in the most backward village, samples of the free layettes which every Soviet baby receives from the maternity clinic, figures on children's diseases, crèches, kindergartens, etc. This second floor was originally so constructed—it is a pre-revolutionary private villa—that one of its rooms is reached by descending three steps. In this room, a comfortable model children's room in a private family has been furnished in faithful detail. Thus the child should live at home. "You see," Dr. Berkovitch triumphantly points out, "these three steps downward are symbolic. The home is inferior. No matter how well cared for the child is at home, a public nursery or kindergarten is better, not only because it has richer means and better pedagogues at its disposal, but also because it precludes all those complexes which lovingly-nursed youngsters acquire at home. The problem of the single-child-in-a-family does not exist with us because from the age of three our children receive collective training. We are developing a generation in which there are likely to be very few neurotics and people with pathological psychologies." The claim is interesting. If the Soviets succeed, the achievement will be epochal.

Meanwhile, the Soviet mother is taught that her children will not suffer, that on the contrary they will benefit if she sends them to the nursery and kindergarten. Certainly today the average Russian institution offers far better conditions than the average Russian home.

When shopping becomes easy and when there are enough good crèches, public kitchens, communal laundries, etc., women will not want to stay home and be bored. Soviet social life has its hardships but it also has its attractions, even its romance. It is exciting to be a dynamic part of a great creative process. The Bolsheviks, moreover, have readier access to the minds of those women who work, and the government and party, therefore, are certain to strive towards a maximum participation of women in gainful employment for many years to come. "Work emancipates."

The task of mothers, and of fathers, is both facilitated and complicated by the training which Soviet children receive. The children are thrown on their own from the very beginning. They too are taught a new self-respect. "A child is a human being," and at parents' meetings in schools, parents are told that this principle is the key to friendly relations with their children. Children demand to be treated as human beings. They are told by their teachers and "Pioneer" leaders that it is not enough for parents to give them orders; they must explain those orders. It naturally follows that corporal punishment is unheard of in schools —and it is disappearing in the home. Some years ago, when my younger son Vitya had annoyed me till I lost patience, I smacked him where I remembered having been smacked myself and pushed him out into the corridor. By the time my wife came home, a neighbors' revolt had been organized in our former communal apartment, and she was instructed to tell me—they apparently did not undertake to do it themselves—that perhaps such practices were proper abroad, but they offended here. Now we have a private apartment.

Once both my boys contracted the measles in Moscow. My wife was confined to the house with them for a long period and both they and she were irritable. For good reason, no doubt, she rapped little Vitya on the knuckles. Both kids burst into tears, and Yura, Vitya's senior by exactly 365 days, exclaimed: "There is no Soviet law which permits parents to strike their children." Whereupon Vitya promised that when he got well he would go out into the cold and try to die. My wife apologized and immediately commenced the slow process of winning back their affections.

Soviet children are self-reliant and spend a great deal of time outside the home. Early in the revolution, the authorities considered this a boon. Strict discipline in schools was regarded "bourgeois" and reactionary. Primary and secondary school teachers, as well as university professors, had little or no authority. Classes were ruled by their members. The young generation was subjected to practically no control from above either within the family or in educational institutions. All this was in the spirit of a rather un-Bolshevik revolt against authority. Youth grew up in an atmosphere of anarchy and ignorance. Pupils behaved like so many ruffians, especially on the streets.

Then, in the first flush of enthusiasm over the possibility of quickly establishing the communist millenium during the first Five Year Plan (1929–32), collectivism was grafted on anarchism. Group study was introduced. Lectures were derided; homework was sinful. The students performed laboratory experiments, studied lessons and prepared for professional work in groups or "brigades." A premium was put on "collective responsibility." But "collective responsibil-

ity" became a euphemism for collective and individual ignorance. No examinations, no marks, no diplomas, no
degrees, no doctors' theses. That was also "bourgeois." It
was really the glorification of chaos. Soviet educators were
conducting "leftist" experiments on a student body that
could ill support them. For the whole Soviet youth has
passed through terrible ordeals. Men and women who are
twenty-one years old in 1935 were born in 1914, the first
war year. Their childhood consisted of three years of World
War and three more years of Civil War, foreign invasion,
destruction and revolutionary turmoil. Food was short. Life
was wild. Babies were delivered in houses with frozen water
pipes, in houses unheated when the outside temperature was
thirty-five degrees below zero. Pregnancy in conditions of
extreme malnutrition. What parents could pay much attention to the health or the education of their children before 1920? In 1921, famine. Between 1922 and 1927, the
New Economic Policy (NEP), marked on the one hand by
revolutionary depression, social demoralization, the rise of
a speculating, petty bourgeois class of *nouveau riche*, and
on the other hand by a wave of sex license—the reaction
against the social and economic stagnation of the revolution.
The rising generation either felt these phenomena, or wit-
nessed them or participated in them.

Every Soviet man or woman under thirty-five is the complicated product of this checkered career of the revolution.
Privations, mad gyrations of policy, and the kaleidoscopic
unfolding of world-rocking events under their eyes have
made them adventurous and un-self-seeking in some circumstances, but pleasure-loving in others. It gave them a
taste for the heroic. They were sure the world could be
changed because they had seen it turn upside down several
times. It smashed traditions—they had, indeed, never known

any. Death was a daily occurrence. Difficulties came and went. In this insane epoch, the individual was nothing—only collective effort achieved results. Misery spared no one, even as exaltation lifted everyone. Life was rich, hard, exciting.

Came the Five Year Plan in 1929. Industrial giants rose from the earth of Russia's flat, vast steppes. Capitalism was being butchered in the villages. It was for this that the revolution of 1917 had been made, for this that Czarism and the bourgeoisie overthrown. Endless possibilities of advancement to the youth. Imagination was fired. People saw visions of a different future. A new world was in the making. As one looks back, one can laugh now at the foreign observers who failed to notice the opening of this new chapter in the revolution's history. It was not only economic planning; history was being planned. The revolution and its heavy cost were being justified.

The billions of units of human energy which the revolution had created and released now found constructive application for the first time. The period between 1929 and 1932 was trying because all the nation's wealth was thrown into the construction of new industries. Citizens had too little of everything. But it was also a period of joy and exhilaration. Youth felt its power. For without the Komsomol and the rest of Soviet youth, those giants could not have been built. Youth showed itself capable of tremendous sacrifices, self-effacement and devotion to a big cause.

The country went to work remaking itself. Unemployment disappeared. Whoever refused to put his shoulder to the wheel was steamrollered or expressed into exile. The land sizzled with activity. Radical policies were trumps. The revolution had gotten its second wind. The great "Socialist Offensive" commenced—and continues to this day.

And yet, left tendencies at home were accompanied by

right tendencies in foreign affairs and in the conduct of the world revolution. Right and Left, the Bolshevik dialecticians maintain, are never far apart. Similarly, as soon as the Soviets got around to it, which was very late—after much damage had been done, they also introduced conservatism into their school methods.

As the revolution grows older, laws of its action begin to crystallize. Revolutionary policy is like a pendulum. It swings high to one side. It is restrained at this high point artificially. Then suddenly the pendulum is released, and it swings wildly to the other side. The Soviet situation is a strange mixture of perfect stability in some fields and convulsions in others. Economics is in a groove, but cultural matters are boiling in a volcanic crater.

When the first Five Year Plan was finished, school brigades were abolished overnight, just as they had been introduced. Examinations, marks, diplomas, degrees and doctors' theses were introduced. Teachers were clothed with authority. Children were taught to obey and were punished for disobedience. Parents were urged to pay more attention to their children. "The home must have more influence." There is always something new under the Red sun.

The relationship between parents and children has changed for these and many other reasons. In the early years of the revolution, the eternal and universal conflict between fathers and sons was aggravated by the fact that the fathers were likely to be anti-revolutionary and the sons pro-revolutionary. Families split on the Bolshevik issue. Children branded their parents as "capitalists," "bourgeois," "Nepmen." Youths left home out of protest.

But today the new generation of the revolution has its own children. The children of the revolution are becoming parents. There is greater spiritual contact and mental understanding between fathers and sons. The newspapers are mocking the "know-it-all" youth. Family ties are growing stronger. The revolution split the old family wide open. The revolution is cementing the new family together. No principle is involved. The Bolsheviks know that the family at one time did not exist. In some future society, the family may cease to exist. But today the Bolsheviks have no substitute for it and they are not anxious to anticipate coming developments. In fact, the Soviet family is a purer institution than the bourgeois family. For no economic bonds keep it intact. Grown-up sons and daughters are independent and need not tolerate their parents for the opportunities of education and of professional advancement which their parents can give them. The supports of the Soviet family are wholly emotional and social in character. As conditions improve, to be sure, a certain type, a not very pleasant type of Soviet young man and woman begins to live in idleness and to look to "dad" for an unearned money allowance spent at foxtrotting restaurants, at the tailors and in the beauty parlor. But there are few of these, and there can never be many. The social atmosphere is against the unproductive parasite.

Millions of people can rarely be well fitted into a single frame. Generalizations always include a percentage of error. With these reservations, if one were to characterize the Soviet youth, one could say that: it is not decadent, nor degenerate, nor despondent. It has optimism and faith in the future. It is not celibate, nor morally vegetarian, nor ascetic; it lives fully with few inhibitions, but it possesses an inner restraint. It can work very hard and it can play well. It loves the out-of-doors and engages in sports with zest, but it also has, and tries to quench, a great thirst for knowledge. It is not introspective or critical, self-analytical or Dostoyevskian. It is not intellectual. Books to it are a means to action, not an end in themselves. It admires and glorifies heroic deeds. Cynicism and skepticism are strangers to it. Enthusiasm is its outstanding trait. It does not argue much; it decides, and it willingly obeys the decisions of superiors. It can lead but it also gladly follows.

Eighteen is the age of maturity in Soviet Russia. Ten years from now, the generation that knew capitalism will have been pushed aside, and this new youth, the generation born after 1910, will be the master of Russia.

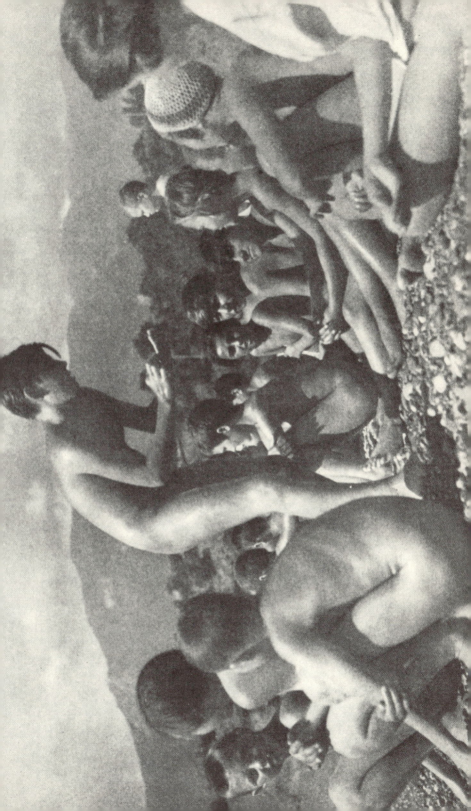

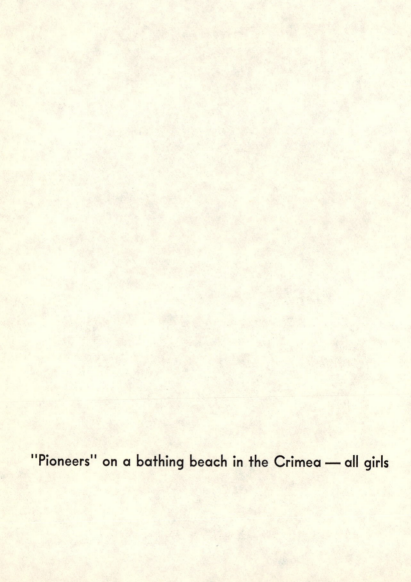

"Pioneers" on a bathing beach in the Crimea — all girls

Chapter VIII

HEALTH THROUGH LABOR

In 1924, Felix Dzerzhinsky, the chief of the G.P.U. and one of the most interesting characters among the old Bolsheviks, decided that it was not enough simply to clap people into jail and let them serve their sentences and rot. The Communist conception demanded something different and better. He would try an experiment.

Dzerzhinsky chose a few wooden huts on an old estate near the village of Bolshevo, fifteen miles from Moscow. Eighteen young thieves were taken from the Butyrki prison and sent there with several instructors. That evening the thieves crept out of their bunks to see who was guarding them. But there were no guards either inside the houses or in the fields. There was no barbed wire or fence or gate. They therefore could not escape. They were free.

Thus began the Bolshevo Labor Commune which is now a small town with 12,000 inhabitants covering an area of two square kilometers. Of the 12,000, 3,200 are ex-thieves. Those 3,200 are the members of the commune. But there is no way of telling the former criminal from a voluntary worker who has won the privilege of living with the commune. When the commune started, there were many kinds of work which the members were not fitted to do, and other kinds, unskilled labor, for instance, which nobody wanted them to do, because the purpose of the settlement was to teach them professions. Outsiders were accordingly employed. Since then, the inhabitants who never served in prison have become a permanent feature at Bolshevo, and

their presence helps to create a normal atmosphere at Bolshevo.

The principle of the commune is very simple. Every now
and then, as its absorptive capacity grows, a committee of
its own members visits Soviet prisons or detention camps
and picks out new recruits ranging from sixteen to twenty-
six years of age—male and female—for the Bolshevo settlement. Usually they take only confirmed convicts who have
committed several crimes. The recruit may have served
only six months of a five year sentence or no more than
two weeks of a two year sentence. He is asked whether he
wants to join the commune. He will have to work. He will
have to start a new life. There are few refusals. He comes
to Bolshevo and is immediately given a job in one of the
commune's factories. The roads are all open. The new electric train to Moscow stops at a station nearby. He may
leave. But then he cannot come back. Of course, a prisoner
can conceive of Bolshevo as the easiest way of shortening
his sentence, for the moment he enters the commune, his
crime is erased and the police cannot touch him. Such cases,
however, are rare. One reason is that living conditions at
Bolshevo are so very good. A few years ago I accompanied
George Bernard Shaw to Bolshevo. He said: "Your commune puts a premium on stealing. If I were a Soviet thief I
would try to get arrested." But only the chosen few get
admission to Bolshevo. Incidentally, Shaw told a group of
members that as a boy he, too, used to pilfer. On that occa-
sion, the members of Shaw's party—Lord Astor, young
David Astor, the Marquis of Lothian, Mr. Tennant and I
played volley ball against a team of ex-thiefs and, of course,
lost. Lady Nancy Astor chose to play on the side of the
former criminals.

In the beginning, the new members are told to stay on the

territory of the commune. After a while, however, they
may obtain permission to visit Moscow or surrounding villages. They go on their honor and not many fail to return.
They may marry. Eight hundred commune members have
wives. The commune counts 570 children.

After a preliminary period—normally three or four years
—during which the ex-thieves become finally confirmed
in the new mode of life, they are reinstated in Soviet citizenship. They may then serve in the Red Army; they are
free to leave the commune and work wherever they please.
Yet the vast majority still prefer membership in the commune to life outside of it. One-fourth of the commune's
3,200 members are full-fledged citizens who do not wish to
quit. Many of them have told me that they love the place
too much to give it up. They want to see it grow.

On five or six visits in the course of the last four years, I
have discussed the work of the commune with the director,
himself an ex-thief, and many of its members. They all insist that no one fails to yield to their method of "cure
through labor." Last autumn, for instance, I asked one of
the commune-ists, Ratnikov by name, what he thought on
this question. "There are no incorrigibles," he replied. "The
only difference is that some require more treatment and
some less. Those who desert—and they are isolated cases—
have merely not remained with us long enough to be re-
formed." Often, criminals at liberty apply for admission to
the commune. I spoke to such a man yesterday. "I knew I
was going to steal again," he said, "and I realized that sooner
or later I would be caught."

The commune's "cure" has three features: 1) obligatory
work, 2) self-government, and 3) freedom. Four factories
stand on the territory of the settlement, a sport shoe factory,
a tennis racket and ski factory, a knitting mill which makes

athletes' sweaters and other sport wear, and an ice-skate factory. All are well-equipped, in some cases with foreign machines. The value of their output mounts into millions. I have inspected these enterprises many times. How intensely the young men and women work! How well organized and efficient these industrial units appear. In addition, the commune has small undertakings which supply its own needs: a cider press, a bread bakery, a big kitchen, and a shoe-polish shop. Round about the factories and the houses one sees the commune's farms from which it receives vegetables, potatoes, dairy products, poultry, etc.

Every worker at Bolshevo is paid wages just like any other gainfully-employed person in the Soviet Union. If an untrained ex-thief earns too little in the beginning for his upkeep, he receives credit which he later returns. Each individual in the settlement pays his own expenses: food, clothing, rent and little comforts and luxuries. This is part of the system whereby he is weaned back to normal life: he is self-supporting. I have talked to many of the commune members. Most of them are children of workers and peasants —ninety-five per cent probably. When they relate their autobiographies, it is practically always the same tale: "We were extremely poor," or "my father and mother died," or "my father died and I became a homeless waif." Most of them started stealing at a very early age. Yesterday a boy of seventeen told me that he began at ten and had been in innumerable correction homes since. He has been in the commune six months and proposes to stay there. "I'm through with the old life," he said to me with emphasis. I asked him whether he did not see his old "pals" when on leave in Moscow. "That is the very reason why I have not requested leave ever since I got here."

The commune member's first achievement is the acquisition of skill. He learns a trade, and they all like the idea of being connected with sport. He becomes a worker. "You are qualifying for admission into the class which rules this country," they are told at meetings. The example of older members has a powerful influence on them, the instructors declare. The factory directors are ex-thieves. Some of the administrative officials are ex-thieves. The editor of the five-day newspaper which this commune, No. 1, publishes in conjunction with Commune No. 2 at Lubertsi, near Moscow, is an ex-thief. The factory watchmen are ex-thieves, so are the cooks, many of the teachers, and, in recent years, some of the engineers, architects, physicians and nurses. The commune has an excellent hospital with fine equipment, a beautiful brick school building with spacious gymnasium hall, chemistry and physics laboratories, lecture rooms, elementary and secondary school rooms, etc., a big department store, a bathhouse, a library, an office building, a theater, a cinema, and a very good restaurant. All these were erected with the commune's own labor. In the early years, the commune walked warily. But since 1929, its growth has been truly phenomenal. "We wanted to be sure our method was right before building for permanence," an official stated.

In the room in the office building where I talk with this official, there is a blackboard. On the blackboard I read, "Proudhon," "Bakunin," "1848." Apparently it is used as an evening class room. In October, 1934, the commune inaugurated a "University of Culture" which holds sessions four evenings a month. Members of the Soviet Academy of Science came to its official opening. On its printed poster, it announced, among others, courses in Darwinism and Marxism, physics, chemistry, astronomy, economics, history, history of art, literature, history of the theater, music, foreign affairs and geography. A large chamber in one house has been given to the artists. In it I saw some excellent male nudes. The commune recently rewarded five of its members with scholarships to the Leningrad Academy of Fine Arts. Bolshevo has a choir, a jazz band, a string orchestra, a brass band, a drama circle, a chess club, a literary circle—some of its members have published their works in Moscow journals—six football teams, a physical culture circle embracing 900 members, a basket ball team, several volley ball teams. There are six tennis courts. Life is rich and full.

Ratnikov walks around and shows me these things. He tells me his story: he has been in the commune since 1927. He is twenty-eight. Started stealing at an unripe age when both his parents died. Has had six prison sentences. His brother is also a member. He brought their sister to the commune to live with them, though she had never committed a crime. I inquired whether the fact that he and his brother had been thieves did not point to a family congenital inclination. "Nonsense," he said. "We simply lived in the same poor circumstances and reacted in the same way." Now Ratnikov is studying at a Workers' university in Moscow and comes to the commune irregularly. He was beginning to talk a broken German.

Twenty-one years ago an American freighter docked for a day at Novorossisk on the Black Sea. Its crew went on land. Now there is a twenty year old negro at Bolshevo who speaks Russian with a Mississippi accent. His mother was a Cossack.

I go into the girls' dormitory. The beds stand very close. Some are covered with lace. Some girls have had their portraits painted by members of the art circle. One girl has a tattoo on her forearm which reads: "There is no happiness in life." The tattoo was made in prison. When I asked another girl to let me see the tattoo on her right hand she blushed and hid it behind her. Finally she yielded. It read: "This hand will avenge the act of Kolya Svertkov." She would not tell me what the act was. She was ashamed of the whole affair. She was glad to announce, however, that Kolya had been shot.

Outside, a group of children was playing. I asked a little girl who her father was. She said he worked in Moscow. She was on a visit to an uncle who was a member of the commune. Obviously, no stigma attached to being at Bolshevo. I went to a class room. The boys and girls were between eleven and thirteen years of age. Some were children of ex-thieves and others of voluntary workingmen who lived in the settlement but were not former criminals and were therefore not eligible to membership. I posed a number of questions. In most cases the children did not know who was a member's child and who was not. They all testified that it made no difference. Later, in the corridor during a recess, I tried to make a boy admit that he was oppressed by the fact of being an ex-thief's son. But he insisted that it did not mean anything to him, that he knew it, but never thought of it. "Why, he *was* a thief," he said. Nevertheless, a mother in the married folks' apartments subsequently assured me that she would try to keep secret her husband's past when her five-year old boy grew up. I think she was not typical. She belongs to the old generation.

A young man whom I stop had spent eight months on the Solovetz Islands in the White Sea and seven more years in Siberian labor camps. He is twenty-six. He came to the commune from Siberia four years ago, has since become an expert ski maker, earns 320 rubles a month, is now reinstated in citizenship, and has no intention of quitting the commune. . . . Another young man presented himself at Bolshevo two years ago when all Soviet citizens were required to apply for domestic passports. As an escaped convict, he knew he would never get a passport. Life here is good, he felt.

Life, indeed, is much better for commune members than for many a Moscow workingman. The commune still enjoys the valuable guardianship of the G.P.U. or Commissariat of Internal Affairs which founded it under Dzerzhinsky and which helps it to obtain materials and privileges. I asked one woman whether she ever went to a rest home. "Isn't Bolshevo a good rest home," she replied. And in fact, conditions are ideal when seen against the Soviet background. The 12,000 inhabitants of Bolshevo are comfortable, they earn good salaries, they have easy access to culture and higher learning, and they feel that they are their own masters. The two important organs of self-government are the Conflict Commission and the Certification Commission. The latter watches over the activities of each member and determines when he can be reinstated in citizenship or when he can be sent to an outside institution for further education. The Conflict Commission sits in judgment over offenders. The usual misdemeanors are drunkenness, swearing, leave without permission, refusal to work and stealing. There is little stealing.

The general meeting of the commune is the highest authority. It may expel members, admit new members and return malignant offenders to prison. It elects the commune's officials, and adopts regulations and rules for the settlement. The active social leaders of the commune are the twenty-five Communists and the 125 Komsomols. Their past criminal records are no bar to acceptance into the party which dominates the Soviet Union.

The commune is no longer regarded as an experiment. Members of Commune No. 1 have gone out as instructors to other convict communes. There are now eleven in the country. Recently three Bolshevo communars went to Leningrad to start a new commune. They report back to their newspaper that their settlement has 273 members and is making progress in industrial production. A year ago, I asked the assistant director of the Bolshevo Commune, himself a reclaimed thief, whether there are any other communes like this one. He replied proudly: "There is no commune like this. There are only communes patterned on this."

Driving back to Moscow, the car passed a large group of men digging the Moscow-Volga canal. They wore short, cotton-padded lumber jackets and heavy working shoes. Red Army guards stood about with fixed bayonets. Those were "kulaks" or recalcitrant peasants engaged in convict labor. I got out of the machine. A soldier came to me to make sure that I had no evil intention, and then, very warily, two or three convicts approached. A red velvet banner stood in a small hillock of mud. What was that? They said: "Three brigades are working on this section, ours, a free workingmen's, and a Komsomol brigade. We were doing the best work. At first there was opposition to granting the banner to kulaks. Finally they decided to let us have it. We will try to keep it. But the Komsomols are mad, and they have sworn to excel us." Seventy thousand such kulaks, likewise subjected to the "cure through labor," were amnestied in 1933 when they had finished the

White Sea-Baltic Sea Canal. The G.P.U., in fact, has ad-
ministered this "cure" to untold myriads in all parts of the
country. The G.P.U. is not merely an intelligence service
and militia. It is a vast industrial organization and a big
educational institution.

Chapter IX

CIVILIZED REST

"Labor." If any one word reflects the essence of Bolshevism it is "labor." The Soviet government is a "dictatorship of the working class." Russia is "the republic of the toilers," etc. Communism has concentrated maximum attention on questions of production and on easing the burden, shortening the hours, and raising the effectiveness of the workingman.

But in exactly the same degree as it solves the problem of labor, Bolshevism creates for itself a much more difficult problem: the problem of leisure. How the Soviets will cope with this problem will be a test of their success.

Leisure denotes something more than idleness. It is not merely the opposite of labor. A person who is unemployed may have nothing at all to do but he is not at leisure. A man may be perspiring, working hard, lifting weights, losing hundreds of pounds of energy in his leisure hours.

Leisure can have economic utility. A woman may knit at leisure and sell the product. A man may mow his lawn after work and save the fee of a laborer thereby. What then is leisure? It is not simply activity which one loves. A writer, an actor, an inventor, a designer, anybody may love his work. But that does not make his work leisure.

Leisure certainly is not merely a pastime. Pastime! The word is as repulsive as "killing time." To pass the time between two periods of work, to degrade leisure to a bridge which must be crossed as quickly as possible is to rob one's personality.

Leisure must enrich and relax. Its biggest common denominators are culture and rest. Coney Islands and Luna Parks would not meet these requirements. Rest without culture does not answer the definition. The rest must be civilized.

The Bolsheviks are struggling with the issue of leisure. Among other things, they have attempted to mould a single out-of-doors institution which would offer at least a partial solution of the leisure problem. In Moscow, a young woman named Betty Glan has undertaken this important task, and her results in the shape of Moscow's Park of Culture and Rest have already been copied in four of the capital's wards, in practically every city of the country, and in scores of villages.

A "blimp" or aerostat, huge silver sausage against the blue sky, is the park's first distant greeting as one approaches the Moscow river from the city. It descends to the ground regularly to empty and fill its balloon basket. I stand on the Crimea Bridge whose geometric design is worthy of a Louis Lozowick drawing. Left is the outline of the towers of the Kremlin than which, at certain hours, there is nothing more beautiful in all of Russia. Nearer in the foreground, boat clubs of trade unions. Some naked males bathing. Right, the tennis courts, diving boards, grandstand, swimming stretch and pavilion restaurant of the Dynamo Athletic Club, a G.P.U. organization to which, however, many outsiders have access. The quays of the river are being faced with white granite—part of the "Moscow Beautiful" scheme of Stalin and Kaganovitch.

And, now, on the right bank, the park. The entrance fee is nominal—30 kopeks. Red Army members and workers can get reductions from even this tiny sum.

"Parachuting" in the Moscow Park of Culture and Rest

A truncated cone tower 100 feet high with a spiral toboggan running from its crest to the ground. A girl has just jumped off the top. Her skirt is buckled high above her knees. The large silken umbrella of the parachute floats over her. She goes out like a diver, then the wires jerk her into a perpendicular position and she drops to the earth. Two soldiers catch her and break the fall. Immediately the parachute is hauled up and immediately a young man or woman makes another jump. Parachuting is becoming one of Russia's popular sports.

Tremendous flower beds. Big stretches of vari-colored pansies. Asphalted roads. A new steel-concrete cinema with neon light signs and huge paintings of scenes from the current film. Ice cream, fruit water and cream-filled-waffle stands.

A one-story concrete hut housing a fashion show. But a Soviet fashion show is different. I enter. An intellectual-looking woman hands me a blank. Each of the exhibited dresses, bathing suits, waists, pyjamas for men, pyjamas for women, women's slips, etc., has a number. You vote for the things you like and would like to wear. A scientific analysis will be made of this referendum to determine popular tastes in clothes. In an adjoining room, orders are taken for ready-made and custom-made garments. Fifty per cent in cash immediately; the balance is paid on delivery. At the exit a sign: the clothing trust needs dressmakers and models.

Two large legitimate theaters wherein, during the summer months, some of Moscow's best companies perform their best plays.

A flat open-air stand with a motor. A young engineer explains the principles of electricity to all who will stop and listen. . . . Fountains. Benches. Pictures of Lenin and

Stalin made of flowers and moss. Along a bank, in moss and grass, this slogan has been fashioned: "Happy Healthy Leisure for Proletarian Moscow."

A stand with an aeroplane model. A model of the "Maxim Gorki," the biggest land aeroplane in the world. More aeroplane models. An engineer to answer questions. That is his social duty today. "Uncle, are you selling these models?" asks a young boy. The crowd smiles. . . . Opposite, a new self-service cafeteria furnished with American and British equipment. The Russians like it; the queues are shorter.

A high fence painted with monkey-filled tram cars showing how Moscovites behave when boarding and alighting from street trolleys. On the same fence, illustrated traffic rules. A colored drawing of a donkey crossing a street against the lights, and this legend in verse:

> *"Though the light shows red,*
> *The ass marches ahead,*
> *The donkey knows no traffic rule,*
> *The donkey is a stubborn fool,*
> *That ass is color-blind."*

An arbor of electric lights. Vast open spaces used for communal choral singing and dancing in the evening. A teacher, usually a young girl, mounts a platform and sings a couplet; the audience, gathered from the four corners of Moscow, stands in front of the platform and repeats the couplet. Soon they have mastered a new song. Dancing is taught by the same method.

An engineer with a model of a blast furnace explains the operations of that devil's contraption. . . . A board chart of the Moscow subway. About a hundred people have

closed around the technician who answers questions on the
workings of the subway, on the geological difficulties encountered, on the escalators that are being installed for the
first time in Russia, etc. We are in the "City of Science."
Today is Welding Day. Factories have sent trucks-full of
electric welding equipment and acetylene lamps. Specialists
give popular explanations. The listeners come and go.
Workingmen cut pieces out of boilers and sheets of steel
and then weld them. Charts elaborate on the importance
of welding in industry. . . . A chemist on a perch goes
through elementary chemical processes showing rapid re-
actions. . . . A man with a megaphone announces a lecture in a nearby hall on the Moscow-Volga Canal.

An indoor dance school. Lessons to anybody who wants
them on first-aid. A small zoo. A circus. A pond on which
row boats move to and fro; in the center of the pond—the
Island of Dance.

A lonely citizen sits at a table in a quiet corner. The
sign over him announces that he dispenses information on
problems of insurance. I sit down with him. He says there
is collective and individual life insurance in the Soviet
Union. The person insured selects his post-mortem bene-
ficiary. Even the beneficiaries of suicides are paid. Persons
insured collectively in their offices or factories need not
pass a medical examination. About sixty per cent of Moscow's population is insured collectively; about 10,000 persons are insured individually.

Crude sculpture; a group of hollow wooden or plaster
figures of workers and collectivized peasants in heroic pose.
There is very little good Soviet sculpture, and the inevitable statues of Lenin in railway stations are sorry displays.

A young woman sits behind a little counter. Behind her

hang maps. She answers questions on geography. A girl asks about the Japanese mandated islands in the Pacific. The instructor, herself a student at the new geography courses in the university, opens one of her many atlases, shows the islands, and explains their political significance. "What is the Saar?" Again she shows and again she explains. A man walks up. "Where is the Island of Dance?" he demands.

A huge two-story wooden pavilion. Above are large porches with easy chairs and flat canvas couches on which visitors may sleep or sun themselves or read in the open. Below, several sections: an exhibition of modern painting, a model of a Czarist prison where revolutionaries languished, a gigantic reading room which loans out approximately 250,000 books and 310,000 copies of magazines annually to visitors who read during the day in the park, a big meeting hall, and two long rows of tables on which eager couples play chess and checkers.

On a grass lawn—hollow wooden figures of people dressed in the bad output of Soviet factories: a boy wears shoes which would fit a giant; a man wears a pair of trousers, one leg of which hangs below his ankle while the other reaches just to his knee; a shirt without buttons; an overcoat without button holes; eye glasses which extend to the tip of the wearer's nose, etc.

A small wooden sign above a wooden stick: "I. V. Tuckov was fined 25 rubles for speaking indecent words in this park." Another: "V. V. Karmanov was fined 15 rubles for rowdyism in the park."

In the open-air gymnasium, men and women in sport costumes swing on bars, climb ladders, fence, walk on stilts, joust on fixed wooden horses; groups play tug of war without ropes; two persons balance themselves on a

Old and young taking "setting up" gymnastics at Moscow's
Park of Culture and Rest

horizontal pole and try, by striking their opponent's extended hand, to unbalance him—a woman, to the spectators' delight, brings a man to the ground.

An electric merry-go-round. Pony carriages and camel-pulled carriages for children. A shooting gallery. A military symphony orchestra. "Flying people": a man or woman (as many women as men), allows himself to be strapped in on a seat at the end of a long stout pole; a machine lifts the pole so that it describes a semi-circle and brings the victim to the other end of the diameter head-downward; the pole then returns to its original position and the "flyer" is released. This is a new and very popular attraction. One woman who was at least forty "flew" back and forth seven times without intermission.

Row boats. Baskets containing people chute from an elevation down almost to the water and then over to the opposite bank. Hammocks strung up in a quiet area where one can rest or sleep; they cost 40 kopeks an hour; workers can rent them out of turn. A kiosk at which the visitor can consult an expert on latest publications and on the right kind of books to read. A stand where instruction is given in behavior during a gas attack. A suspended yellow oilcloth cylinder; the curious person bends under the cylinder, inserts his head into it and gets a taste of tear gas; they all come out in a second crying bitterly.

An immense open-air "Green Theater" seating some 3,000 spectators. Extra admission charged. I have seen evening opera performances here with actors from the Grand Opera and Ballet participating; stage hands change the lofty scenery with astounding agility and speed; powerful search-lights illuminate the scene.

The Radio Theater. Several hundred people sit in an enclosure listening to broadcasted music; "Art Must be Saturated with the Spirit of the Proletariat and of the Class War—Lenin," reads a streamer across the platform.

More cafés. Women sitting on little stools sell sweets, cakes, etc. Groups pass with their own accordions.

"The Economics of Japan." A teacher sits at a table marked with this sign. One old woman is standing by him. I approach and listen. Her son left Moscow for Manchuria six months ago and has not written. She is inquiring of the lecturer how she can trace him.

Volley ball courts: men and women in the same teams. Tennis courts. A meteorological station with a specialist to explain its operations. Machines to measure the strength of punches and pulls. Newspaper and book kiosk, also sheet music. Another shooting gallery. I have reached the "blimp." It is a tremendous balloon with a gondola for four passengers suspended from it; it is attached by a powerful cable; a motor draws it to earth again; it ascends to a height of 400 feet; an ascent costs 5 rubles to a Red Army man or Civil War veteran, 7 rubles to an "udarnik" and 10 rubles to an ordinary mortal, but the queue is too long for me to wait.

Billiards. Showers. A school for oarsmen and swimmers. A vaudeville theater. A children's cinema. A vast cement roller skate rink—this is the only place in the U.S.S.R. where I have seen roller skates; in the winter, it is flooded and used for ice skating.

So I cross and re-cross the Park of Culture and Rest. I have returned to the two-story pavilion. Two tables at the entrance. At one sits a poetess. By her side sits a working-man in his best clothes. He reads from a typed manuscript. It is his novel. He has commenced to write, and the poetess is criticizing his work aloud. A score of people hang over the table and listen. The poetess whose surname is Taine comes there regularly; I have seen her many times. Once a burly peasant brought his verse to her. "Were they any good?" He read them to her. She promised to have one printed. He kissed her hand. . . . At the second table, a writer was organizing a literary circle. Again at Comrade Taine's table. She is still reviewing his first novel. "Your language is too flamboyant. . . . This word does not exist. . . . Simple language would be better." At the same time, she encourages him.

Inside the pavilion, in the big meeting hall, a discussion on literature is taking place. Two Leningrad authors have opened the debate with short speeches. No admission fee; people come and go as they please. The subject is American literature. One author recommends Pearl Buck and Agnes Smedley on China—both have been translated into Russian. Members of the audience take notes. The author asks visitors to report on American books they have read. A man of forty speaks from his seat: His favorite is Dos Passos. He disagrees with those who think he is hard to read; one can omit the "Cinema Eye." Whereas Dos Passos is a real revolutionary, Upton Sinclair is a "political charlatan." . . . A young workingman rises. He is surprised that Upton Sinclair tried, unsuccessfully, to become governor of California as a representative of the bourgeois Democratic Party. But "it would be wrong to brand him because he made this mistake. Maxim Gorki also made political mistakes. Once he was against us. Now he is with us." It is interesting how many simple, scarcely-educated Russians possess the gift of facile expression. The revolution has trained many orators.

The literary discussion is closed. A man steps to the rostrum and announces that a vaudeville artist will now recite his *feuilleton* or sketch on bad production in Soviet factories: The day begins. He had set the alarm clock which he had just bought. It failed to wake him. He must hurry to work. He wants to make himself some tea. He lights a match. It breaks. He lights another. The head flies off and burns his sleeve. Finally, he succeeds in getting a light. The primus stove, however, refuses to work. The needle with which he wants to clean it is dull. He gives up all hope of getting breakfast. He jumps into his clothes. The laundry has burned his best shirt. He is getting nervous; he pulls his collar just a bit; it rips off. Finally, he is ready to go. He leaves his apartment and wants to lock the door. He cannot extract the key from the Soviet "Yale" lock. There is no time to wait; he leaves the key in the door hoping that a thief will not be more successful than he. He races to the trolley. Fights for four square inches on which to place the sole of one of his feet. Nearer, nearer to his office. He begins to dream; he will get tea there, and buy a bun. Why doesn't the trolley move? "The motor is out of order," the conductor announces. "We must send for the repair wagon." He runs to the office. On the elevator shaft hangs a sign: "Lift Out of Order." He hops up the eight flights. The office manager reprimands him for being late. . . . Throughout, the audience rewarded the artist with rich appreciation.

On an ordinary summer's weekday, 80,000 to 100,000 people visit the Park of Culture and Rest; on a Rest Day or "Red Sunday"—between 200,000 and 250,000. The park covers 197 hectares. Behind the area filled with special attractions, is an old wood extending along the bank of the Moscow River. There one finds picnic grounds with tables and benches.

Most visitors come to the Park to spend an entire day. If they feel that their children would bother them or require too much care on a rest day, they can deposit their youngsters in the "Children's City" which constitutes a part of the park. In the summer of 1934, 384,000 children spent an equal number of days in this Children's City. The City has a division for children from four to seven, and another for older boys and girls. This second section has a small electric railway with wooden trains which is run by the youngsters themselves. It is supplied with the equipment for many games and sports. Restaurant, chess rooms, etc., and very richly-equipped shops. Here boys learn how to make electric bells, how to use motors, how to file iron and steel; they make wooden objects. I noticed that the instructors never do anything themselves; the children must depend on their own knowledge and resourcefulness, and only in extreme cases does the ever-watchful teacher offer his advice.

In the section for the little ones. A mother enters the hut, pays the fee (from 1.50 rubles to 3 rubles, according to the parents' income, for the care and food), delivers the child and receives a number disk. The child is then undressed, given a medical examination, bathed, and dressed in the City's clothes. The children are separated into groups; each group wears aprons of a distinguishing color —its teacher wears an apron of the same color so that they can recognize her and she them. They play, eat, sleep in cots that are daily disinfected, and, at the end of the day, mother (or father), on presentation of the number disk, receives back the child.

This is Moscow's Central Park of Culture and Rest. Does it provide civilized rest? Is this a form which the leisure of the future will take? In Czarist Russia, on Sundays and holidays, the chief amusement was calling on friends and getting drunk. Organized sport was limited to the upper classes, and even they had little of it—some tennis and soccer. The masses had no games and no premises on which to play them. Today every city of any size has a stadium. There are yacht clubs, rowing clubs, swimming clubs and tennis clubs in many factories. Thousands of football teams engage in inter-city and national championship matches. Track meets have become a regular feature of life. Foreign runners have been invited and defeated in the Moscow stadium which seats 55,000. Soviet athletes have won victories abroad. But sport is still so new that it practically has no Russian vocabulary. Thus the Russians use "start," "finish," track, which has been flattened into "treck," "footbol," "vollibol," "chempion," "raketka" for racquet, "tennis cord" for tennis court, "gol" for goal, "training," "khalf-time" and "kvarter-time," "match," "out," etc.

Of course, the Bolsheviks have not yet solved the problem of leisure. But every one of them, from Stalin down, is devoting a great deal of attention and time to it. Leisure to them is synonymous with culture, and richer culture is a main objective of the revolution.

Chapter X

MOSCOW DIARY

On the Tverskaya this morning (I cannot yet call it Gorki Street), I met an old Soviet acquaintance. He seemed happier than usual. The first thing he said was: "My son has come back." His son, a Komsomol or member of the Communist Youth League, left home and parents ten years ago and went to live in a university dormitory. He sundered all contact with his "bourgeois" family. Now he has returned to the no-less "bourgeois" family. He is an instructor in a polytechnicum. He is older, wiser; and the atmosphere of the country is quite different. Sins of the fathers are not visited upon the second generation as much as they used to be. Young men and women are no longer being blamed for not having been born to a ditch digger. . . .

The "Komsomolskaya Pravda," organ of the Communist Youth League, has conducted a campaign for the strengthening of family ties. Komsomols had complained that what with work in their factories, schools or offices plus their social activities as young Communists, and meetings, meetings, and more meetings, they had too little time for love, for their wives and children; in general, too little leisure. Did the "Komsomolskaya Pravda" advise them, in reply, to neglect their families and perform their duties as budding Bolsheviks? Not in the least. It denounced the plethora of meetings. There is too much talking. Too much time wasted. No time left for papa and mama; no time left for dancing. A few years ago jazz was anathema. It reflected "bourgeois demoralization." Now the newspapers censure a workers' club which has no jazz band. Nothing is final in the Soviet Union. Life is fluidic and dynamic, and therefore very interesting and very tiring.

In the Pushkin Café this evening, I met a woman lawyer whom I have known for years. She is employed as legal consultant at a Moscow district Institute for the Care of Mother and Child. Most Soviet lawyers work as legal advisers for trade unions, factories, institutes, etc., where they dispense information on the law free of charge. But when a citizen wishes to be defended in court he goes to the Collegium of Defenders which assigns him an attorney. He may also chose his own attorney. The fee, which goes to the Collegium (lawyers are paid varied salaries by the Collegium) is determined according to the income of the given citizen and the gravity of his suit. The abolition of private property, which is the source of most litigation in capitalist nations, has eliminated much of the ordinary work of lawyers and courts, and most Soviet court proceedings involve either family relations or disputes over apartment space. But the "liquidation"—favorite Bolshevik term for suppression—of the G.P.U. and the transfer of some of its functions to the courts, will result in more public trials and more work for lawyers. The law profession, however, remains the least popular in the Soviet Union.

My woman lawyer told me of an interesting case. A couple had been living together for eleven years without registering at the marriage bureau. They had a child of seven. Now they had both agreed to separate because the wife wished to marry again. She was taking the boy with her; the father had agreed to pay alimony. Everything was settled amicably. But when the woman and her new husband appeared at the marriage desk, she was told that she could not marry until her first common-law marriage was annulled. Under Soviet law a common-law marriage has all the validity of a registered union, and a second marriage would therefore constitute bigamy, which is a crime. The wife, accordingly, had to obtain a divorce from a man to whom she was never married.

Hundreds of thousands of Soviet couples never register their marriages. But more do because they cling to tradition; because, since the government allows the institution of registration to exist, there is no reason for not registering; because a registered wife can more easily enjoy the privileges accorded to her husband, and because a registered marriage is officially recorded whereas, in the event of a dispute, it is necessary to establish the existence of a common-law union through witnesses.

I felt someone looking at me. I turned around; he seemed very familiar. I felt my brain go back over its files: it was not in 1934, nor 1933, nor—no, still further; 1924? Ah, 1923. He had been thinner—in uniform. I had it. I smiled. He smiled. He came over to my table.

It used to be a custom here, when foreigners left the country, to have any papers or documents they wanted to take abroad examined by the G.P.U. By previous arrangement, one day in June, 1923, a G.P.U. official came to the Foreign Office to examine my copies, letters, etc. He was young, tall and blond. He spoke perfect German. His father was Russian, his mother Austrian, and he had received an excellent education in Vienna. His perusal of my papers was most perfunctory, and while he paged through them, we talked. It was my first intimate contact with a member of that dreaded three-letter organization. I would learn something about it. I carefully prepared the way, and then I said: "Have you ever executed anybody?"

"Yes," he quietly replied.

"Shot people with your own hand?"

"Yes," he repeated just as quietly.

"I understand," I began, "how a man can kill in battle. Bandits also kill. But for a government official to walk up to a defenseless person in prison and drive a bullet through his medulla oblongata—how could you do it?"

"Listen," he said, "I will tell you a story. Four years ago, in 1919, I was in the Siberian Red Army fighting against Kolchak. Fifteen hundred of us were taken prisoner. The counter-revolutionaries divided us into three groups of 500 each. The first group was given shovels and ordered to dig a long trench. Then they were stood in front of the trench, a battery of machine guns poured lead into them and they fell into the grave. The second group received the shovels. They covered their dead comrades with sod, and then dug a second trench. They were stood in front of it. The machine guns mowed them down and they collapsed into the trench. I was in the third group. They gave us the shovels. We had not talked. But we all knew what we would do. We rushed the gunners. We hacked them with the sides of the spades. We were mad with hate. The gunners pulled their revolvers. We seized some of their weapons. One hundred and forty-two of us were killed. With the rest I escaped into the woods. Do you imagine that after that I would ever hesitate to execute a condemned enemy of the revolution?"

He was visibly exhausted when he finished the account. He had lived through the harrowing experience once again. We recalled that conversation now, in the Pushkin Café.

"Are you still interested in why we shoot Whites?" he asked. "The G.P.U. is shooting very few people these days. This is the period of economic and cultural progress." He was building a huge factory in Central Asia. Was he glad to have transferred his energy to construction? "I am a soldier of the revolution," he retorted.

The Pushkin Café is fitted out with modern tube furniture; it serves good food and drink; a uniformed jazz orchestra pleases some guests and irritates others who come to chat. Its men's room "is so advanced culturally," as a Russian would say, that it has a Soviet-made electric towel which dries wet hands with pleasant streams of hot air. But the last visitor had not mastered technique sufficiently to know how to go through the complicated process of pulling a chain.

P.S. A week later. Three days ago, Demyan Bedni published four verses of poetry in the "Pravda" inveighing against the blasphemy of naming a café after Russia's most beloved poet, Pushkin. Today the word "Pushkin" was removed from the outside façade. In Bolsheviks, apparently, hero-worship is blood-brother of stupidity.

In a street car which, this once, was only moderately crowded. A father sits with a six year old. "Papa," the boy says, "can there be another Lenin?"

"Of course. Why not?"

A woman nearby joins the conversation. "My dear," she says to the child, "you yourself may be another Lenin." The boy is happy.

"Papa," he asks after a long intermission, "who builds subways and factories in capitalist countries?"

"The workers."

The boy turns his head to have a better look at his father's face. He cannot believe it. "The workers?" he doubts. "But there are no workers in capitalist countries."

Passengers smile. "Oh, yes, there are," the father explains. "There are millions of workers everywhere."

"Then why don't they drive out their capitalists?" the boy wonders aloud.

Nine p.m. The streets are dark. A penetrating chill fills the air. Children are coming home from school. They are weary and pale. They drag their legs and bend under their school bags. They are the older children who have just finished the second shift. The Moscow schools are too crowded to admit all pupils in one shift. Moscow has grown and the percentage of boys and girls who attend school has risen sharply. But why are not more schools built? Why are tens of millions spent on the construction of the superfluous Palace of Soviets? Office buildings are very important, but schools more so. The men and materials necessary to erect the ridiculous Palace could suffice to erect fifty schools.

I have heard Soviet parents express these sentiments time without number. But Soviet leadership blundered once when it decided to have its Palace and now it cannot reverse itself. Why not? Bolshevik stubbornness has won many victories. The government has broken through many walls by sheer determination. If they insist they will certainly overcome all the geological and practical obstructions and let the Palace mount to the skies. But it would be wasting will-power not to speak of bricks. To desist requires greater strength, in this case, than to proceed.

In the now nameless ex-Pushkin Café I keep an appointment with a professor of the Communist Academy. "I see," he begins, "that apropos of the Stalin-Wells interview, Bernard Shaw, H. G. Wells and John Maynard Keynes have been tearing at their hair in the London 'New Statesman.' "

"Yes," I say, "boiled down, the issue between them is Evolution vs. Revolution. Wells and Keynes think we are too modern for the class-war theory."

"As a matter of fact," he says, "economic theory has advanced little if at all since Adam Smith, Ricardo and Karl Marx."

"Yes, but economic facts? That is Keynes' point. He maintains that the old theories do not fit the new capitalism. There has been a shift in ownership from the big magnates to the millions of stockholders. The engineers and technicians run industry, and the proletariat is shrinking in size and in importance."

"Technocracy," he scoffed.

"Wells believes the intellectuals are moving towards a new conception of the world which might lead them to try to change it—gradually, without violence."

"The intelligentsia," he says, "has power only to the extent that another class lends it power. It was opposed to our revolution. It attempted to obstruct us. We crushed that attempt. Now it loyally coöperates with us. It has no choice. The technical intelligentsia, the engineers, will always be on the side of their employers. The moment our government was finally entrenched, the engineers became pro-Soviet. As long as the capitalists are firmly entrenched, the engineers will be pro-capitalist. They know who butters their bread."

He continued: "The class war does not disappear because lovers of humanity think it is too cruel. Keynes and Wells are kind men. They see the hardships which the class war brings. They suffer from the sight of those hardships. To comfort themselves they therefore decide that the class war is no more."

A waitress brought coffee with whipped cream. The professor took off his glasses, lowered his eye to within an inch of the table and found the spoon. Stirring, he proceeded: "The class war will not retreat before the magic wand of even the wisest intellectual. Even when the worker owns a house or an automobile, or shares in a company, even were the worker wealthy, he could not own the machinery on which he produces. We say some workers are capitalists. That is a fallacy. The ownership of factories is a monopoly of capitalists. The operation of capitalist factories involves the exploitation of labor. That is the only reason why a capitalist operates his factory. For the profit. The profit is subtracted from the wage bill. No capitalist is in business for his health. To be sure, there are periods without profits. There may be periods of loss. But past profits and hope of future profits sustain the capitalist —otherwise he declares bankruptcy. You speak of the hundreds of thousands of stockholders. How many of them are workers? Do the miners own their mines, the steel workers their mills, the railway men their lines? Stockholders, yes, but the concentration of capital continues, and wealth as well as income in the United States goes into fewer and fewer hands. I have not the statistics with me but the proof is there. Who owns the land in England; who receives the coal mine royalties? Are the 40,000,000 unemployed workingmen of the capitalist world also capitalists? Do you think the proletarians can accept a system as their own which periodically throws them out on the street? Hitler also dislikes the class war. That is why he suppresses working class organizations. Obviously, if the proletariat forswore the class war the capitalists would be pleased. There would be no strikes, no trade unions. Heaven. Is there a need for strikes and trade unions today? Yes. Then there must still be a class war. Or are all the workingmen deluded and mistaken about their self-interests? In any event, they will not listen to Wells and Keynes, and not even to Shaw. In the end they will listen to Lenin and Stalin. Because idealists like Ramsay Mac-Donald and Philip Snowden betrayed the working class and served another class is no reason why the working class should betray itself and supinely submit to the capitalists. Do the capitalists submit to labor when ill-paid workers ask increases in pay? No, they try to break the strike with strike breakers, armed thugs, with constabulary and police. They mobilize the press and public opinion against the strikers. Those are all forms of the class war."

He paused to drink his coffee. "It is really funny!" he suddenly burst out. "To talk of the cessation of the class war today when the workers have taken up arms in Vienna and in Spain and elsewhere—only a great intellectual is capable of such blindness. I hate phrases, but just because Wells and Keynes make such nonsensical statements, our propagandists, not without a certain measure of justice, call them the lackeys of capitalism. Unconscious or conscious agents—that makes very little difference. For to prate about the end of the class war is tantamount to an attempt to persuade the proletariat not to overthrow capitalism."

"But perhaps H. G. Wells has discerned the beginnings of a new economic tendency," I interrupt.

"Where?" he exclaimed. "Only in their own imaginations. Show me the slightest evidence of any capitalists' desire to hand over their wealth and control to the workers. Either the capitalists run the economic system or some one else does. Where is that some one else? The state? The state only takes over what, in this era of capitalism's decline, has become unprofitable to the capitalists. But the capitalists control the state."

"Suppose," I venture, "that the state takes over everything. Then the capitalists would lose their economic power, and the workers could outvote them."

The professor looked at me but I am sure I was only a blur in his near-sighted eyes. "Ja," he said sarcastically, "that is a marvelous scheme. When it happens, please telephone me. Meanwhile we see how tenaciously the capitalists hold on to their capital and social position, tenaciously to the point of shooting down with machine guns and artillery hundreds of workers who attempt to break that hold. See how the big industrialists are resisting the organization of trade unions in the United States, how they create their own company unions to compete with the workers' trade unions. Isn't that class war? See how the kings of steel, automobiles, coal, etc. in the United States are resisting Roosevelt's hesitant encroachment on their preserves. They have already stopped his aggression. They will not let him dictate prices and they will not allow him to reduce profits. Will they then permit him or any other state to expropriate them? That is, excuse me, nonsense."

The theaters had let out, and friends came in who joined us at the table. One Soviet journalist said: "Look, this will interest you," and began to search his portfolio until he found an old clipping from the London "Times."

"It has now been decided (it read) that there shall not be more than 30,000 students at universities in Germany, since it can do only harm to have so many educated unemployed when there is no suitable work for the type of person produced by universities. . . ."

"That's Fascism for you," he commented.

"Capitalism," the professor intervened, "was once progressive. Now it is anti-progressive. It does not need education. We, on the contrary, want more universities, more university graduates. Socialism needs science and education."

Somebody started an argument about dialectics. But the café was filling up, and the noise of conversation mixing with the clang of jazz crowded out philosophy.

I went to see "Personal Life" at the Theater of the Revolution. It is a good comedy, well acted, and the audience seemed to enjoy every minute of the performance. As usual, not a seat was empty.

The play reflects the new policy of liberalism and tolerance in matters of culture. It would have been impossible to stage such a drama a year or two ago. An engineer who is not very soviet in his convictions is the hero. He comes to a meeting of the Komsomol and preaches his individualistic philosophy to them. "The first letter of the alphabet must be I," he urged. This self-centered engineer marries the secretary of the Communist party committee of the woolens factory where the scene is laid. But she reveals her love to him only after he has explained that he really did not have an affair with the director's wife. She was jealous, in other words. The director is criticized for paying too little attention to his wife and step-daughter. He is an old Bolshevik exceedingly devoted to his work. Spends most of the twenty-four hours of the day at the plant. But a good Bolshevik must have, a rich personal life too; he cannot neglect his family. His wife says: "Ah, how wonderful it was before the revolution when men loved women as they now love their work."

The butt of the playwright's ridicule is the secretary of the Komsomol, a pedantic bureaucrat. His official clichés are mocked. His ugly girl assistant declaims: "In Africa there are insurrections, in Germany oppression, and shall I dress well?" The audience laughs at this foolish sentiment. On the other hand, Marusya who wants to drop her simple Russian name for Ramona is taken to task for starving in order to buy silk stockings. However, says the party committee secretary, Marusya-Ramona needs not censure, but friendship. The Komsomols were only comrades, not friends. And they should be friends. Comrades do not talk any more. They come to a meeting, debate, adopt resolutions. Everything is so cold, heartless, and official. A little personal warmth, she demands.

The factory is trying to develop a new knitting machine. Three Komsomols are assigned to the task. They constitute the "brigade." One of their number is sent to Berlin to study foreign models. The other two are given every advantage too. But nobody assists the engineer-hero. Yet the Komsomol brigade, in the end, wastes a lot of money and time, and produces nothing, whereas the engineer invents the machine.

The isolated engineer wins. But it is the collective which makes the individual possible, his beloved party committee secretary teaches him. The collective lifts the individual. The collective gives the individual education, books, the factory, the experience of the past. There is no conflict between the individual and the collective. They supplement one another. In the collective the individual is strong. He is not alone. And in the end the engineer, like the Hairy Ape, rejoices that he now "belongs." He is no longer alone. . . .

Several years ago, I think it was in 1931, I toyed with

the idea of writing a long article on "What is a Bolshevik?" How does a typical Bolshevik behave; how would he react to love, art, war, friends, difficulties, illness, etc.? In that connection, once when three Russian Bolshevik friends were visiting at my apartment, I quoted these words to them: "The theater is necessary not so much for propaganda as to give people a rest from daily work." I asked them whether that was a Bolshevik sentiment. They all answered "No."

"Well," I said, "that is a quotation from Lenin."

The Soviet theater is going back to Lenin.

In a sense, it is also going American. A Soviet cinema producer who took lunch with me the other day said, *apropos* of a picture which a colleague was just completing: "If he can give it a happy ending, the censorship will pass it." The country is optimistic because material conditions are improving and because future prospects are good. But the Kremlin is forcing the pace and insisting on more comedy, more music, more dancing, more gaiety, more leisure, more laughter. The Kamerni Theater has staged "The Optimistic Tragedy"—tragedies must be rosy; and "Chapayev," the most popular Soviet sound film since 1931, receives extra praise from the newspapers for lending a touch of comedy to the gruesome events of the Civil War.

There have been a large number of scarlet fever cases in town, and since Vitya looks pale I overruled his violent protests, kept him home today, and invited a doctor. He came after working hours. He holds a position in a clinic, but he practises privately too. Gregory Kaminsky, the new Health Commissar, has vigorously encouraged physicians to extend their private practice.

"We are overworked," the doctor complained. "More

clinics are being opened every month but doctors cannot be manufactured like tractors. Men do not want to study medicine because we physicians are paid so little. Men take up engineering."

"That is natural," I suggest, "in a country that is building."

"Yes," he replied, "but if physicians received higher salaries some of our young talent would go to the medical faculties. Besides, you have no idea of the difficulties we encounter every day. We prescribe a diet. The patient laughs sadly. And I myself know that he cannot buy the food I order. And medicines? Are there enough medicines? People are worn out after the lean years. You have no idea how anxious Russians are to cure themselves. Life begins to grow brighter and they want to have the health to enjoy it. But our resources are limited. It is really fortunate that the revolution occurred in a country whose population is as fundamentally healthy as ours is. What other nation would have borne such hardships so patiently?"

"Patience," I said. "Patience is one of the worst curses of this land. If the crowds which stand in queues would break a few windows and heads the queues would grow shorter. I watch them selling bread. Every customer's bread is cut with a knife and weighed. That's insane. Why not bake a standard loaf? Elsewhere the population would insist on such a simple innovation. Here they accept the *status quo* with bovine equanimity. The Russians are a queer combination of revolution and submissiveness. I go into stores. Recently I walked into a shop where the salesmen were standing idle. The whole place was empty except for the line of about twenty customers at the cashier's box. To make a purchase, one stands in one queue to choose the article, one stands in the cashier's queue to pay and get a check; then one stands in a third queue to receive the article. If you trusted your salesmen and had cash registers there would be a tremendous economy of time. Now that the volume of commodities is growing, queues are a crime."

"I have to stand in the queues too," he said wearily. "I cannot leave the entire burden to my wife. She is a physician and has two positions." He looked at his watch and prepared to go. I pressed a fee on him. He refused. "Of course," he explained, "it would do no harm if we earned more. The government ought to pay us more. Then if we had more time for each patient in the clinics, we would reject private practice altogether. It is only a means of somewhat relieving the clinics. But we have to resort to the chemical laboratories, electric and Roentgen apparatus of the hospitals anyway. I haven't the time, moreover, to come every day to a patient who contracts pneumonia, say, or diphtheria. Private practice gives us no satisfaction. The physician assumes the rôle of merchant; he sells his knowledge to a customer. This is unpleasant and contravenes the Soviet physician's ethics. There is no doubt that in a few years all medical practice here will be socialized."

"Meanwhile," I said at the door, "you will take your deserved fee," and put the bill into his pocket.

This warning from Marx and Engels is permanently on my desk: "Although in everyday life any shopkeeper can easily distinguish between what a man says he is and what he really is, our history writing has not acquired this banal knowledge. It takes every epoch at its word, and believes what it says and imagines about itself." When I read Soviet newspapers and magazines, when I read Stalin, Kaganovitch or Postishev, I keep this Socialist admonition constantly in mind. No one can be altogether objective about the Soviet Union; it is too alive a subject. Only a jelly fish has no attitude towards it. Most people either hate it or approve of it. Most observers see it, as human beings see everything, through the prism of their own limited selves. Nevertheless, detachment and critical attitude, some skepticism and the perspective acquired by being outside, contribute towards a better understanding of Bolshevism. Yet if one is outside and too far away one does not see it, much less understand it. One or two foreign students of the U.S.S.R. know the country without understanding it. One or two understand it more than they know it. The combination of understanding and knowing is rare.

Marx and Engels notwithstanding, however, the Bolsheviks tell many truths about themselves, often many unpleasant truths. Being the heirs of Dostoyevskian Russia, and delighting in occasional self-flagellation, the Soviets exalt as a primary virtue what they call "Samo-Critica" or self-criticism. "Samo-Critica," to be sure, usually means criticism of someone else, but now and then a wise man confesses his own errors too. Lenin did it publicly on numerous occasions. Since then a strikingly un-Bolshevik code of infallibility has been introduced. Yet the little fellow is expected to appear regularly in the nude and make a public statement of his weaknesses, faults, and mistakes.

In the same spirit, the newspapers fill column after column of revealing criticism. The Soviet press is the best source of anti-Soviet data. (Why, under the circumstance, foreign "lie factories" bother inventing anti-Soviet canards is more than I can understand.)

The "Komsomolskaya Pravda" often justifies its name: "Pravda" means "truth." A recent article about conditions

in Gorki (Nizhni Novgorod) stated that many Komsomols
were leaving their Young Communist League in disgust.
"Dozens of Komsomols deliberately do not pay their membership dues in order that they be mechanically excluded
from the League." "The youth at the automobile factory
is gradually losing interest in the Komsomol organization."
Why? The Komsomol officials are interested in their members only when there is some work to do. But why, asks
the daily, do they not concern themselves with the leisure
and living conditions of the Komsomols? The houses in
which the Komsomols live are ridden with bedbugs. The
wooden homes should be stuccoed with plaster. The
officials reply that they cannot find the plaster. Is that an
excuse? demands the paper. A factory which can turn
out automobiles cannot stucco its workers' quarters! The
result is that the men sleep badly at night and produce less
during the day.

Moreover, the Komsomol officials are bureaucrats. They
do just enough to hold their posts. A secretary presents his
report: such a production plan was fulfilled; such a plan
was not fulfilled. "That was all right in 1930 and 1931," says
the "Komsomolskaya Pravda." But not now. Now we want
to know "how the youth lives at home." It is not enough
to be informed about the youth at its machines. What
about evening hours? Dances? Leisure? You want to ride
down to the Volga to take a swim. "But a factory which
manufactures automobiles hasn't enough buses for its
force." You want to play volley ball. There are only two
courts and a waiting list a mile long frightens you off. Well,
you finally decide, the simplest thing is to borrow a book
from the library and go home and read by an open window. You are told in the library that you are ninety-third

in the list of those waiting for "Virgin Soil" by Sholokhov, and 89th in the list for Sobolev's "Capital Repairs." And so on.

Leisure?

On Nov. 11, 1934, I asked Commissar of Internal Trade Weizer, a member of the Soviet Cabinet, for an interview. He told me to telephone on the 13th. I telephoned on the 13th. He told me to telephone on the 19th. I telephoned on the 19th and he gave me an appointment for 1 p.m. on the 23rd. I was in his office ten minutes before one on the 23rd. I waited forty minutes but he did not appear. Finally an assistant and a secretary came to me full of apologies and explained that Comrade Weizer was engaged at an important Cabinet meeting in the Kremlin. "And why hadn't he informed me in advance?" Well, they could not say. But he had told them over the telephone that he would get in touch with me on the 25th. Yes, they had my 'phone number. He did not telephone on the 25th and he has not telephoned since then. This is what we in Moscow call "granting an interview in principle."

A very large number of foreign musicians come to Moscow and Leningrad to give and conduct concerts. At the beginning of 1934, this movement assumed considerable proportions. The circumstance tells a story about foreign economic conditions and about Soviet economic conditions.

I asked a popular Soviet author how much he had earned last year. He named a fabulous sum—something like 120,000 rubles. (Writers, journalists and artists are the richest persons in the Soviet Union.)

"Now suppose," I said, "you invested part of this money

in Soviet government bonds, and did the same next year and next. After a time you could live on the income from those bonds. You would be a capitalist *rentier* in a socialist country."

"Y'know," he replied, "I've been buying these state bonds ever since 1924. I must have a fortune in bonds. But I never look at them. Some of them have lottery features attached to them. Occasionally I win a few hundred rubles if the number of one of my bonds is picked. But I never bother about collecting the interest."

This is the attitude of most Soviet citizens. The bonds are a kind of tax, and those persons who do not purchase them willingly buy them anyway for fear of social pressure. The return from these bond issues helps the government to finance its construction programs. Some of the bonds bear interest; others entitle one to premiums in lottery drawings; a few pay both interest and lottery premiums. Most people prefer the lottery loans.

No one buys Soviet internal bonds as an investment. It is considered bad form and unpatriotic to sell them except for a very good reason such as prolonged illness, etc. Since every adult buys another bond each year the certificates usually clutter up a drawer or are stuffed into a hat box as proof, should it become necessary, of a social duty performed but not as a supplementary source of income.

"Some day," the author said to me, "when the ruble is stabilized and returns to gold, all my heap of bond paper will be converted into one bond which may have some real value. But in time, probably, the government will stop this business of issuing bonds. We won't need it. The state will be rich enough without making us buy bonds.

"Anyway," he added, "you can be sure that no Soviet citizen will ever become a capitalist through state bonds.

Such parasitism would not be tolerated. At present, the bonds don't yield much real interest because the ruble is devaluated, and when it returns to normal we won't have bond issues."

I passed the planetarium today. The building is shaped like a huge cannon shell. Inside, an expensive Zeiss machine helps to show the stars, the constellations, the planets, the heavens. Outside is a signboard which gives a list of the lectures held within. One lecture is entitled: "Astronomy and Socialist Construction."

This made me wonder what institution in the Soviet Union has been left untouched by the revolution. The stars are being drafted for the fulfillment of the second Five Year Plan. In the zoo, of course, animals are being cross-bred for domestic purposes; also, special exhibitions on helpful and harmful insects have been introduced for the benefit of collective farmers. The ballet has been affected too. Workingmen's daughters have been admitted to its schools, and it has added the "Red Poppy" and "Football" to its repertoire.

One can no longer even talk about the weather in the Soviet Union without quickly entering the field of politics. "Nice crisp weather today, isn't it. We should be having snow soon." "Yes, we need a good snow. Otherwise the night frost might kill some crops. And we can't afford to have a bad harvest next year" . . . which naturally opens a wide door to a discussion of collectivization, the war scare, the wisdom of rapid industrialization, etc.

"In the Civil War, I built trenches and dugouts."
"I load my cinema camera with a ribbon of cartridges."
Eisenstein speaking, Sergei Eisenstein, the best-known

Soviet film producer. Significant and interesting that the
outside world knows Eisenstein better than any other
Soviet artist; significant of the rôle of the cinema in the
art of the world and in the cultural life of the U.S.S.R.
Yet this great artist loads his camera with ribbons of
cartridges. He fights the battle of the revolution with and
through the cinema. He is a propagandist. But also a great
artist. The crude producer, the artist without art, creates
a sickening effect with his propaganda. The man with taste
and talent and delicacy insinuates his propaganda as the
poets and novelists and playwrights of all ages have done.
Eisenstein's "Armored Cruiser Potemkin" was straight un-
diluted propaganda, but nobody felt it. It was probably the
best film ever made anywhere.

Eisenstein is the only genius I know. A strange person
with innumerable idiosyncrasies. A mind that thinks deeply,
a mind's eye that sees directly ahead and also tests a thought
from above, below, sidewise, edgewise. (He does the same
with his camera.) He absorbs a new melody with his ears
and skin and fingers. He imitates and at the same time cari-
catures the dancers of Harlem with a rhythm that the best
of them would envy. A serious student with a pen that
prefers spirals to straight lines, he is essentially a comedian.
His interests are catholic and his knowledge very broad;
he is the most cultured man in the Soviet cinema. He is
thirty-seven years old.

Eisenstein has not been making films for several years.
He wanted to shoot a quick comedy but was dissuaded. He
has worked on an epic of Moscow—history and present
—without concrete result. Now he is going into the theater.

Eisenstein in the theater. Years ago he used to say: "I
want to destroy the theater." He began his artistic career
in the theater. He graduated from it into the cinema. He

thought the theater was doomed to die. He would fire his ribbon of cartridges into it. The screen would be the curtain rung down forever on the stage. Now he has returned to the theater. After that he will go back to the cinema—that is certain.

"Potemkin" was an epic. It has no heroes. Its heroes are revolutionary pathos and the mass. The individual was missing. The nameless millions made the revolution. The nameless were Eisenstein's heroes. He needed no actors. He could pick them up on the street, on the army parade ground.

But today the individual is coming into his own in the Soviet Union. The mass is becoming differentiated, and each person assumes a face and a character. Eisenstein wants to go back into the theater to study individuals and to recall how to project art with the aid of individuals. Then he will transfer that training to the cinema. Some day he may create the epic of the Soviet individual.

"Chapayev," by the Vasiliev brothers, presents the Soviet hero of the Civil War. But the subsequent hero, the hero of the reconstruction and construction period, is more complicated and elusive. Chapayev, leader of the Red guerrillas, was a finished type. But the modern Soviet type is in the making. He will not pose for the photographer. Will Eisenstein catch him?

Eisenstein is writing a many-volume opus on the theory and practice of cinematography, of which the first volume will soon be ready for publication. Much of it constitutes trail blazing through the thick empiric forests of Hollywood, Potylekha (in Moscow) and Elstree. Eisenstein lectures on these questions in the Moscow State Institute of the Cinema. The government has given him the title of professor, the world's first Professor of Cinematography.

Professor Sergei Mikhailovitch Eisenstein. Or, more simply, as Atasheva, his assistant, calls him: "Old Man." Old young man. A talk with Eisenstein about the movies is a journey of exciting discoveries over a road that one has traveled thousands of times.

Flanders in 1917. The center of Moscow in November, 1934. Houses in ruins, deep caves in the ground. Excavators removing the ruins. Scores of motor lorries race to and fro. Cement mixers and steam rollers paving adjacent already-cleared sections. Two giant buildings on Hunter's Row being released from their scaffolding. Below, towards the Lubyanka Square, another high house showing its new face for the first time. A part the Chinese Wall, a church and some old homes being leveled to make a vast open square. Trolley lines are picked up and straightened. Above, the Lenin Library with its classic lines and marble columns is nearing completion. The subway too is removing all surface obstructions, brushing its clothes, so to speak, in readiness for the first underground train ride. And all these processes proceed simultaneously in a small area in a few days. Thousands look on and marvel. These had never seen such "tempos" and such structures. They may never enter those buildings. But they are proud. It is their subway. They followed its difficult course with tender concern, for all of Moscow dug that subway.

Moscow is getting ready for the two-day holiday which marks the seventeenth anniversary of the revolution. I walk down the Tverskaya. All the store windows display drawings and drafts of new buildings and new cities that are planned by the Soviet government. Beautiful buildings, some bizarre buildings, almost all in the epic, classic style, fronted with marble, heroic in their pose. Crowds look through the glass into the future. I turn away from a window to walk down the street. Right under my elbow is a loaf of bread. A worker who gets an excessive ration is selling it to a woman with a shawl around her head. She sticks her fingers into it to test the freshness, weighs it in her palm, pays him the kopeks, and goes off.

From Moscow to Alexandrovsk by direct train.

Alexandrovsk, or Zaporozhie, is the junction station for the great Dnieper Dam.

Chapter XI

COSSACKS AND DAM

The Dnieper Dam is still the largest in the world—until Boulder Dam is ready—but it has lost its distinction as Soviet Giant No. 1. Since it was finished in 1932, other industrial enterprises, bigger and costlier, have come into operation. Nevertheless, it remains unchangingly interesting.

We learn by comparison, and one of the best methods of observing Soviet conditions is to return, year after year, to the same place and see what has happened to it in the meantime. I saw Dnieperstroi in 1930, 1931, and 1932. This is my fourth visit. A suspicion of yesteryear is confirmed as a fact. An empty field becomes a factory. One walked through a village. One rides high over its ruins in a steamboat.

In 1930, I clambered over the red granite boulders which form the bed of the broad Dnieper. This evening, immediately upon my arrival, I strolled by moonlight 37 meters above those boulders on a smooth roadway—the top of the dam. Trolley and bus lines now run across the dam. In 1930, Dnieperstroi was a blueprint. Now it is a work of art and a producer of current.

This colossal wall of white concrete 110 feet high that checks the broad flow of a turbulent river; the delicate bowform of the dam; the cathedral-like solemnity of the power station where stand nine shining monsters as strong as 810,000 horses—all these are far more beautiful than the rapids and the dirty village which I saw at this point in 1930. Yet utility does on occasions conflict with beauty.

When the turbines and generators are not working, as was the case in October, 1932, at the official opening, the assembled waters rush over the dam and drop in 48 falls to the stream below. White foam, high spray, boiling, churning, struggling river—a thing of joy. Now only two gracefully mad falls can be seen. The remaining fallways are dry; the water that would otherwise beautify them is caught by the maw of the power station, pressed into its mechanical vitals, and ultimately issues forth tamed and tired, with just enough strength to slink down into the Black Sea where it is once more revitalized. The less beauty the more kilowatts.

I am hungry after the long train ride from Moscow. But dinner is delayed. I storm and rage. The delay continues. Finally, an exquisite platter is brought in on which the black of the caviar, the green of the serrated cucumber slices, the red rose that was once a tomato and the yellow of the butter have been worked into an impressive color scheme. I had waited because that design had to be finished. The waiter who had been all apologies and excuses now beams with satisfaction. He is a jolly vivacious person with a very long dark moustache and a big, round, flat face—the face of his semi-Turanian forebears, the Cossacks of Zaporozhie, who once made history where he now serves hors d'oeuvres.

The Zaporozhie Cossacks have been immortalized in Russian literature and song. They combined romance with adventure and a love of liberty. Originally stray fugitives from serfdom in Moscow Russ, they collected and entrenched themselves in the marshes and woodlands of the islands just below the spot where the dam now stands and where, formerly, were the rapids that are now covered by the elevated river. On account of the rapids, no one could easily attack them from the north. This important fact gave them their name: Za-porozhie, beyond the rapids. They lived in tents covered with animal skins and in rude wood huts. By 1450, they were an important community. Fishing, hunting and bee-culture sustained them; but fighting was their profession. They were at the apex of several triangles. North were the Moscovites engaged in wars with the Poles and Tartars and Turks. South were the Tartars and Turks. East were the Poles. The Zaporozhie Cossacks fought them all at different times, and managed to maintain their independent freeman's state for several centuries. They were a border barrier. Only when the harsh winter froze the river and its tributaries could a hostile army penetrate to their island fastnesses and their swamp settlements; but there was no point in invading their territory. They merely retired and harassed the intruder until he went home.

About 1630 the Polish kingdom began pressing the Cossacks and cutting them off from their supporters in the Ukraine. Then there arose the famous Bogdan Hmelnitski —his statue, on a rearing horse, still stands in Kiev opposite the St. Sophia Church. Hero of many legends and folk songs, he drove out the Poles and restored Zaporozhie's autonomy.

Early in the eighteenth century, Sweden was locked in a mighty war with Peter the Great. Hatred of the Czar led Zaporozhie into an alliance with distant Sweden—for which the Russians rewarded them by crushing them. Thereafter, the Zaporozhie Cossacks became an appanage of Czarism. Moscow gave them land; the Cossacks settled down to agriculture. Moscow paid them to protect it against the incursions of the Crimean Khans and Turkish armies. They became mercenaries who guarded Russia's frontier provinces or "okraine" (hence Ukraine).

By this time, the Zaporozhie community had lost its unique social character. But earlier, when their common emotion was the desire to be free from northern slave-owners, these Cossacks had established an almost classless society. They called themselves "the Zaporozhie Brotherhood" and elected their own elders democratically. It was obligatory for all members to eat at a common table. In many respects, these unruly spirits were ascetics. Tradition has it that no women were allowed on the islands.

Today, descendants of those woolly Zaporozhie Cossacks are working in steel mills and waiting on restaurant tables. Their separate community has long disappeared. A new fighting race has succeeded the Zaporozhie Cossacks. It does not give battle to infidel Turks and Polish Pans. It conquers the forces of nature.

But the past is not forgotten. Alexandrovsk, the junction city some 15 kilometers from the dam, has been rechristened Zaporozhie. And the new industrial town on the left bank of the Dnieper opposite the power station is New Zaporozhie. The two names, however, are a temporary expedient. For old Zaporozhie is growing quickly towards New Zaporozhie, and New Zaporozhie is growing quickly towards old Zaporozhie. Soon the suburban tram line which connects them—it was not there in 1932—will be a street trolley.

Between the two towns lies the village of Voznesenska. In their progress, the two towns have gripped the village at either end, and under their pressure, the village is becoming a city ward. Its peasants are working in factories. Wives tend the fields. Some wives have jobs in the plants. Voznesenska plus old Zaporozhie plus new Zaporozhie will soon constitute one big city. Plans of Greater Zaporozhie can already be seen by the inquiring student.

I asked the chauffeur who drove me around New Zaporozhie whether I might visit his home. He agreed, but he himself remained out in the second moonlight night to pay court to a plump Russian maiden. His father was a judge. He had been a judge under the old regime too. He was the typical old Ukrainian intellectual. Two walls of his sitting room were covered with open bookshelves high up to the ceiling. On another wall hung a large portrait of Taras Schevchenko, the Ukraine's great national author of the nineteenth century. When I arrived, the judge's wife was reading the French language weekly published in Moscow.

The judge always had been a Social Revolutionist and as such opposed in principle and theory to Bolshevism. Indeed, during the Kronstadt insurrection in 1920, he was arrested and thrown into a G.P.U. prison. There, G.P.U. officials had tried vainly to convert him to Communism.

Now he was a staunch supporter of the Soviet regime. I tried to probe the psychological processes that had brought about this metamorphosis. Did he live better? Before the revolution he earned 3,000 gold rubles a year; now 5,000 paper rubles a year. Obviously, the 5,000 were less than the 3,000. He had a delightful little apartment of two rooms, with running water, coal range, gas, bath and electricity. But before 1917, he occupied five rooms in a small town near Kiev.

In general, his material conditions had grown worse. Then how explain his conversion? "I live in the world of ideas and books," he declared. "In that world there is more space now, more freedom. We are creating a new human being. In 25 years, all class distinctions will disappear.

"I used to think," he continued, "that the Bolsheviks were self-seeking politicians who would ruin our country and suppress the national culture of the Ukraine, my fatherland. But all about me I see concrete evidence of tremendous upbuilding. We are becoming a modern industrial country. Here in the Ukraine, the Ukrainian language is the official language of the state. Many of our officials are Ukrainians. This was never so under the Czarist regime."

"And is there no oppression?" I demand.

"I feel no psychological oppression," he replied. "On the contrary, I feel intellectual exhilaration. Old as I am, the Soviets expect me to learn and raise my qualification. I have access to a marvelous law library right here in Zaporozhie.

"What I enjoy most," he affirmed, "is that I am no longer lonesome. To be alone is perhaps the worst sensation man can have. I feel now that I am part of a big rich social whole. It makes demands on me. I must conduct classes. That is my voluntary social work—three nights a week. I must give back what society has given me. I am necessary. I am living not only for myself."

His wife concurred. I suspect it was she who brought him to his new point of view. "The Bolsheviks would deserve our support if they had done nothing more than liberate women," she says. "Formerly, we ate well, we slept well, we took care of ourselves, and that was all. The revolution has lifted us out of ourselves and above ourselves. It is exciting to live."

The Dnieper dam was the first gigantic industrial project undertaken by the Soviet government. Part of its usefulness lay in the political significance of that fact. The beginning of operations on this unprecedentedly large task in 1927 was a signal to the skeptical outside world and to millions of hostile and skeptical Soviet citizens that the Bolsheviks could and would rebuild their country along modern lines. The advantage gained by creating this impression

—especially at home—was not nearly as important as creating volts and amperes. But it was very important nevertheless.

It is in this light that the wisdom and waste of erecting the Dnieper dam must be viewed. Stalin and other prominent Bolshevik leaders opposed the project; they said it was too early or too costly. But the contrary opinion prevailed. . . .

The Dnieper dam was conceived as a solution of three big problems: 1) electric energy, 2) river navigation, and 3) irrigation.

1) The maximum energy capacity of the Dnieper hydroelectric power station is 600,000 kilowatts. But the factories in and around Zaporozhie will never be able to use more than half of this amount. To consume the balance, a 200-kilometer-long, high tension line must be built to the iron mines of Krivoi Rog, another, 120 kilometers long, to the Donetz coal field, and still another to the manganese deposits at Nikopol. During the months when the water in the Dnieper is low, however, these remote districts will be dependent on their local power resources, while in November and December when the river is frozen, it is possible that even the plants at the dam will not be sufficiently supplied with current. The problem of electric energy, in other words, has been only imperfectly solved.

2) Where the dam ends, three huge locks have been cut out of solid granite. This makes the Dnieper navigable from the Black Sea all the way to Smolensk, in White Russia. On the Dnieper near Kiev I saw timber rafts being floated downstream from the woodlands of North-western Russia to the treeless prairies of the Ukraine. But that is just the point. The Dnieper is only navigable to timber rafts and river barges. Sixty miles above the dam, the

Dnieper becomes shallow again. To open the river to deep-draught, sea-going vessels, the Bolsheviks propose to construct three more dams along in the Dnieper in the next five years and ten more by 1950. Then the Dnieper will really be navigable. Meanwhile, however, the dam has already affected transportation. Nikopol produced 371,000 tons of manganese in 1927. By 1933, output rose to 1,000,-000 tons. In 1934, it was 1,800,000 tons. All this had to be carried by railroads which are creaking under their excessively heavy burden. But now arrangements have been made to convey the ore from the mines to the river and then transfer it to barges. The economy amounts to eighty-four per cent of the total hauling costs.

3) In the month of May when there is a surplus of water, the dam authorities distribute water which irrigates 3,500,000 acres of land below them. This is of course too small an area to justify large expenditures. When the Ingales power station is built between the Dnieper Dam and the sea, the Dnieper will irrigate all of northern Crimea.

Of course, the Bolsheviks argue that you cannot dam up half a river. A hydro-electric power station must have the capacity of all the harnessed waters at that point. If the amount of current produced is too great for the industries which can profitably be established nearby it is regrettable, but it is nobody's fault. An imperfect solution is better than none. For decades before the Soviets came on the scene, Russian engineers wanted to put the Dnieper in chains. Now it has been done. And a striking achievement it is.

I went to the brain of the station which can produce 810,000 horse power. An operating theater in a good hospital could not be cleaner and quieter. A battery of telephones on a long table, innumerable clocks, meters, and switches. Pull a switch and 90,000 horses go to bed. Three young people, two men and a girl, run the power station from this control room. The girl is a student. She had started at the dam as an unskilled worker. When the dam was being built, huge cranes would lower great tanks of mixed concrete into the belly of the dam, and then brigades of eight with boards tied to their shoes would stamp down the concrete. Colonel Cooper, the American constructor of Dnieperstroi, found that when one of the eight was a woman, the seven men worked better. This girl was in such a brigade. And she has moved up gradually "from concrete stamper to control engineer-apprentice." She went to school evenings, learned the elements of mathematics and physics. Then she was granted a scholarship and stipend and matriculated at a full-time university. I asked her how much she earned and how she lived. She answered politely but impatiently. "The important thing is," she said, "that I am going forward."

The Dnieper Hydro-Electric Station, naturally, is only a means to an end. The end is the new industrial city of New Zaporozhie on the left bank. The residential sections of the city are near the river; the plants are several kilometers further inland. In 1931, the homes were being built, but wheat still grew where the factories now stand. An industrial center at this point enjoys the advantage of cheap local electric power and of its proximity to the coal of the Donetz coal basin and the iron of Krivoi Rog. Besides, there is inexpensive water transportation.

Only a fraction of the plants is now ready, but the city is already a busy metallurgical center. The aluminum group is producing goods which, unfortunately, do not reach Soviet citizens' kitchens. Some mills are being built and turning out alloy steels at the same time. In like manner,

some Moscow apartments are occupied before the scaffolding has been removed and before the stairs have been put
in. Russia is in too much of a hurry to be normal.

On a sizzling hot day, I went to see the two blast furnaces. I had never gone near one before and I never shall
again. No wonder pig iron production in the U.S.S.R.
drops during the summer months. In just thirty seconds I
was choking, breathless, hors du combat from the attack
of fumes and heat and smells, and in precipitate flight. How
can men stand it six hours a day? "They get used to it."
It's like getting used to living on rat poison. "Can't they
wear gas masks?" Under a truly Socialist regime, these
victims will work two hours a day and then be taken for
rides in open aeroplanes. Gas masks, I am told, are not
employed abroad anywhere—and this is one of the youngest
and technically most perfect blast furnaces in the world.
The older ones are worse. I decided that if I ever had to
work in a blast furnace, or a coal mine, I would always
be organizing strikes.

Anybody who must earn a living at a steel mill deserves
the best living conditions civilization has to offer. Perhaps
this motive guided the authorities in the construction of
New Zaporozhie. The streets are broad avenues lined with
trees and lawns. The houses are good, and by Russian
standards excellent; two or one story dwellings with big
windows, much electric light, white inside and out. The
new city—it has a population of about 150,000—boasts a
theater, several cinemas, two clubhouses, a Park of Culture
and Rest, a small stadium, schools, etc., etc. It is well
planned. But there is no planning for the future. No space
for garages, for instance. No consideration for the development of an automobile civilization. This exposes Bolshevik
psychology. They are iconoclasts. Nothing is too daring

for them. Yet Russia's poor past clips their wings, and they cannot imagine that one out of every five Soviet citizens will own a car. Or will New Zaporozhie be rebuilt in fifteen years? Maybe.

Chapter XII

CHILDREN

Kharkov.

Russians usually address one another by their given names and patronymics. Lenin was Vladimir Ilitch; Stalin is Joseph Vissaryonovitch. Paul Petrovitch means Paul the son of Peter. His sister would be Maria Petrovna, Marie the daughter of Peter.

"Dear Paul Petrovitch,

"I am a pupil of School Number 36 first grade A, Lena Alexandrovna Kochanova. Yesterday I was playing in the city park. I was playing school with my girl friend. The keeper came up and said that it was not permitted to play school in the park. Dear Paul Petrovich, I beg you to give the children a place in the park where they could play.

"L. Kochanova."

Lena, to judge from the fact that she is in the first grade, is about eight years old. Paul Petrovitch is Comrade Postishev, the Stalin of the Ukraine, the Bolshevik leader of the Soviet Ukrainian Republic which has a population of some 40,000,000; the richest industrial and agricultural region of the Union. A few days after he received Lena's letter, he wrote:

"Dear Lenochka,

"I fully share your displeasure. The keeper, of course, should not have prohibited you from playing school in the

park. It is permitted to play in the park. That is why the park was laid out. But it seems the doctors say it is not so good to play school. I am not quite sure whether they are right or not. Now, a special playing section will be built in the park, and near it two booths: one where the children can buy ice cream and soda water, the other where their toys will be kept. Besides, we will have a special play square for the smaller tots.

"Comrade Saratnikov, the chairman of the Kharkov Soviet, has personally undertaken to see that the sections and booths are built.

"I only ask all of you not to run on the grass, not to tear flowers, and to look after one another so that no harm is done to the park. You may run on the paths as much as you like.

"Greetings.

"P. Postishev."

No sooner said than done. I visited the new children's playgrounds. Excellent modern equipment, the ablest teachers, flower beds, etc., etc. During the summer, the average daily attendance is between 1,000 and 1,500. And still the children make demands. They have written Paul Petrovitch —this time over a host of signatures—and told him that they want a library, a pavilion, "otherwise we must stay in our apartments when the weather is bad," a leader for their aviation-model section, and, for the winter, an ice-skating rink and skiing hill.

Postishev devotes considerable attention to parks. One sees many trees in the parks and streets of Kharkov to which little signs have been attached. The sign gives the name of the child who is the monitor of that tree. If any harm is done, the child reports it. But of course the chief advantage of this system is that the monitors themselves, of whom there are thousands, acquire a psychology which does not allow them to hurt vegetation.

Many old houses in Kharkov were separated from the street by high brick walls. Behind the wall was a garden and then the house. Postishev ordered that where a garden contained twenty or more trees, the wall was to be torn down. The additional green has changed the aspect of whole thoroughfares. The city now breathes with numerous new lungs. Benches have been placed in the gardens on which pedestrians may rest. Kharkov's example is now being followed by other Soviet cities.

Postishev is the hero of the children of the Ukraine. He receives, on the average, 200 letters a day from children; most of them include requests and complaints. He is also respected by millions of adults. One sees his picture in store windows, offices, and homes. His young face with the short-clipped hair speaks of his energy. He is the doing type of person. This summer he was scarcely ever to be found in Kiev, the new capital of the Ukraine. He spent most of his time on the countryside, stimulating the peasants to greater activity, correcting mistakes of local administrators, giving orders that oiled the machinery of collectives and soviets. Postishev formulates larger policy and deals with details as well.

Lenochka wrote to Postishev because she knew his name and no one else's. But she was guided by a healthy instinct. In the Soviet Union, it is the big man who does things quickly. If Lenochka had applied to a minor commissar he might have pigeonholed her plea and forgotten it. The busy Postishev, however, found time for her. In like manner, Stalin receives thousands of personal requests and answers every one of them. When a writer's play has been prohibited, when an artist wants to go abroad and has been refused a passport, when an official has been wronged and cannot get justice from his immediate superiors, he resorts to the "hozyayin," the "boss" in the Kremlin. By encouraging this sort of correspondence, Stalin, as well as Postishev and other provincial leaders, keep in touch with the temper of the country and enhance their own popularity. No one is indifferent to popularity. Or immune to vanity.

The Kharkov Tractor Factory is called "The Kharkov Tractor Factory in the Name of Ordzhonikidze" after Sergo Ordzhonikidze, the Bolshevik Commissar of Heavy Industry. Then there is the "Moscow Automobile Factory in the Name of Stalin." The Nizhni-Novgorod "Ford" plant has been named after Prime Minister Molotov, and Nizhni-Novgorod has been renamed Gorki, after Maxim Gorki, the well-known author. Dozens of collectives, villages and mills bear the names of Postishev, President Kalinin, War Commissar Voroshilov, etc. The number of schools, universities, collectives, steamships, institutes, factories and libraries called after Stalin probably compares favorably with the number of enterprises in England bearing the title: "Royal." Living Bolshevik leaders also have cities named for them. Petrograd became Leningrad only after Lenin's death, but already Tver has become Kalinin and Vladikavkaz in the Caucasus is Ordzhonikidze. In Tadjikstan there is a Kaganovitchensk. And as for Stalin: the old Tzaritzin on the Volga has become Stalingrad; Georgia has its Stalinir and Stalinisi, Central Asia its Stalinabad, the Ukraine its Stalino, Siberia its Stalinsk, the Moscow district its Stalinogorsk,—and perhaps there are others.

Since Postishev and other big Bolsheviks get things done, since the mails and telegraphs function badly, since people moreover like to believe that their personalities will hasten a favorable decision, innumerable Soviet citizens and sub-ordinate officials appear personally before high officials to plead their cases and causes. The authorities estimate that when Kharkov was the Ukrainian capital, 15,000 men and women from the provinces entered the city on "business" every day. Now they go to Kiev. God only knows how many carry their troubles to Moscow. My guess is 50,000.

A capital is the front and the façade of a country. It tries to create a good impression. The fact that the governmental chiefs live in it helps it to get the wherewithal from the treasury for its upbuilding. While Kharkov was the capital, it lived through an uninterrupted construction boom. I re-member the city from the time I first saw it in December, 1922. The famine had just ended. In clinics I found women and children swollen from hunger. Mud and dirt dominated the scene. All houses were in disrepair. A rickety trolley ground its way through a few central streets. At night, the town was glum and dark. Subsequently, I visited Kharkov almost every year and watched its frown change to a smile until today it is a bright bubbling metropolis with innumer-able asphalted streets, many efficient street car and bus lines, big new parks, a stadium (and another with 100,000 seats in construction), a race track, several new universities, stores filled with goods, and thousands of new homes. Offi-cials believe that the city's growth will continue even though it has lost its position as political center; it is still the great industrial capital of the Ukraine.

Kharkov boasts of what is architecturally the best office building in the Soviet Union. It is a block wide in the form of a gentle curve. Some of its sections are fourteen stories high; others eleven and seven. Cement roads run between the sections, and high above the roads are enclosed bridge-corridors which connect the sections. This scheme gives the tremendous structure an almost fairy lightness.

From the roof of this building, a large part of Kharkov is visible. Here one realizes how much of the city is newly built. Many complete blocks of houses stand out as fresh and modern. And each is like an island surrounded by a band of green. The population of Kharkov rose from 288,000 in 1917 to 380,000 in 1926, to 836,000 in 1934; it is now the fourth largest city in the Union.

Smokestacks indicate that numerous factories operate within the city. But most of the large industrial plants erected by the Bolsheviks during and since the First Five Year Plan are located far from the center of town. Thus the Kharkov Tractor Factory is some 12 kilometers from the city. One reaches it by a smooth speedway sometimes called "The Avenue of Giants," for along its course stand half a dozen immense enterprises, among them the Kharkov Turbine Factory which manufactures machines formerly purchased abroad.

I have followed the progress of the Kharkov Tractor Plant ever since its birth in 1931. On previous visits, I noticed and discussed with the director the excessive number of workers employed. Men seemed to be standing around accomplishing nothing except getting into one another's way. Little of that phenomenon remains now. As one looks over the great assembly room—the eye cannot see its end— each person is obviously tending to business and working with fair intensity. The plant employed 11,000 in 1932 when it was manufacturing fifty tractors a day, and employs 11,500 at present when it makes 145 per day. The problem of internal transport has likewise been solved. Where formerly there was a lot of carrying and walking around for parts, now little electric trucks, manned by young women, move almost noiselessly from place to place delivering raw material and taking away finished products. The necessity of cleanliness, about which Director Swistun talked to me on previous occasions, has become a tradition. I asked the chief engineer where the assembly plant's machines came from. He said fifty per cent were American and fifty per cent German, "but if it had not been for Hamilton Fish, almost all would have been imported from the U.S.A."

The Kharkov plant has reached its capacity and turns out 145 tractors a day, every working day in the year. Last March the conveyor stopped twice for lack of parts, but they soon erased the loss and have been working normally since. Occasionally, the belt is checked even now by the slackness of a department.

A tractor costs the plant 3150 rubles. The Commissariat of Heavy Industry pays the plant 3186 rubles for each tractor. The 36 rubles is the factory's profit and covers cultural necessities. The Commissariat of Heavy Industry sells the tractor to the Commissariat of Agriculture for 3,000 rubles. The loss is a government subsidy calculated to stimulate the mechanization of farming.

In 1935 the Kharkov Tractor Factory will begin work on a caterpillar tractor. Its present wheel tractor cannot negotiate the deep Ukrainian mud of late March, and plowing is therefore postponed till April. The caterpillar will advance cultivation by a fortnight, give the seeds more winter moisture, and enable crops to ripen before danger of drought intervenes. The authorities hope thereby to achieve a fifteen per cent increase of the harvest.

The Kharkov plant has a little recently-constructed town all its own not far from the shops. Here 8,800 of its employees are housed in new apartment houses. But this is

A government employee selling buns and sandwiches in the
streets of Moscow

only about half the force. For the factory employs 15,500 people. This figure reveals an interesting situation which applies to all Soviet industry. Eleven thousand five hundred men are actually engaged in production. The entire staff, however, consists of 15,500. Those extra 4,000 are clerks, bookkeepers, teachers, officials in the plant's coöperative stores, waiters in the restaurants, party and trade union functionaries, librarians, peasants engaged in growing food on the factory's farms, etc., etc.: a large overhead which raises production costs.

"Teachers" is not a negligible item. There must be hundreds of them. For employees of the plant have 11,000 children. Fifteen thousand five hundred adults, many unmarried, whose average age is probably twenty-five,—and 11,000 children. Fifteen hundred of them are four years old or younger. Two thousand are between four and seven years of age. Some birth control, one muses, would not be amiss. It seems that in Russia and in other countries as well the poorer the family the larger the family. The less parents can afford to support children the more children they have.

In a recent interview in Moscow with Gregory Kaminsky, the Soviet Health Commissar, which I attended, Mrs. Margaret Sanger, the well-known birth control advocate, asked not a few questions on her favorite subject. I think she learned that the Bolsheviks had a special approach to the problem. They do not, of course, object to birth control on moral or religious grounds. But they submit that the earth is rich and the possibility of technological progress infinite. Though the world's population is greater now than two or three centuries ago, living standards are also higher. There is no reason, the Bolsheviks accordingly argue, why in a perfect society all the human beings born into it should not be excellently provided for. Every new individual should be able to produce at least as much as he can consume. This is their attitude in principle. On the other hand, the Communists are realists, and they know that conditions in the U.S.S.R. are not perfect. Temporarily, therefore, contraceptive information and paraphernalia are made available to all who may desire them. In addition, there is also birth control after conception. But it is much more difficult to get an abortion in the Soviet Union than many foreigners have been led to imagine. In any case, few abortions are made after the eighth week of pregnancy.

The interesting thing is, however, that Russians marry early and want to have children. And although the two-child family is becoming the type here too, there certainly are enough young ones. Children are about the only article of which Russia has no shortage. In this respect, the Kharkov Tractor Factory is merely one illustration out of thousands.

The factory has three nurseries or crèches for youngsters up to the age of three. These are housed in two-story, stone buildings which one easily recognizes from the street by the U-shaped extension running from ground to roof. Inside, you discover that these extensions provide space for the extra length of an inclined plane of delicate gradient which takes the place of stairs. Thus as soon as a child can walk it also can find its way upstairs. I saw tots of eighteen months, or perhaps even less, resting at various stages of their adventurous solo climb towards the sleeping porch on the roof.

An American pediatrician who inspected the Kharkov crèche with me stated that one would have to look hard in the United States to find one better equipped. There are few better in the Soviet Union, but not a few like it. Every Soviet factory has a nursery, every office of any dimension, in fact practically every urban institution, and, now, almost every collective farm. To supply these crèches with equipment and, what is more important, with personnel, has become a major Soviet industry.

Several hundred children attend the three Kharkov Tractor crèches. In the one I visited and presumably in the others too—the children were divided into groups of fifteen or sixteen. Each group had its own rooms which no other children ever enter, its own toys, beds, and nurses. This arrangement was devised to reduce the likelihood of contagion which is a serious problem in all Soviet nurseries and kindergartens.

The young ones are deposited in the crèche in the morning and taken home by their working mothers after working hours. Since most of the mothers are employed nearby in the tractor plant, those who still nurse their babies come to the crèche three times a day for half hour periods. Before feeding the baby, the mother must wash, don an apron, and partake of a meal from the nursery kitchen.

I was very much impressed by this institution and said so to the acting director of the plant who accompanied me. "Yes," he said, "but it is not enough. After all, our children are our future and they should have the best of everything. But we are still poor." I wondered how it would be when this poor, backward country became rich.

Chapter XIII

MARX AND THE PEASANT

There is farm land between the Kharkov Tractor Factory and the city of Kharkov. And on the other side, the factory settlement merges into farms. This is symbolic of Soviet industry. Most workers are less than a generation removed from the village. Indeed, numberless Russian workingmen are members of agrarian collectives, and desert their factory jobs in summer months to contribute their labor to the fields. This is one of the many problems of a nation which wants quickly to become less rural and more urban.

Marx and Engles, the Moses and Aaron of Socialism, inveighed against "the idiocy of rural life." That so many millions of people throughout the world should be condemned to hard labor in the gamble on weather which is called farming just in order to fill the stomachs of humanity is indeed a bit odd in the days of radio, television and lap dogs. At any rate, the Soviets propose to get as many people as possible out of the villages and into the more comfortable cities. Then perhaps those who remain in the country will be more prosperous.

The London "Times" wrote on August 1, 1934, that "one object of a constructive agricultural policy" in England was to keep as many people as possible on the land by retaining "the existing system of small farms." The Bolsheviks wish the very opposite. Their policy is not to keep men off the urban unemployed lists by letting them raise wheat and peas by hand, but to solve Russia's labor scarcity problem by having machines do the farmer's work. "Back to the Farm" is not a cure. It is an expedient of despair on the part of economists who know that when a country cannot go forward it must go backward. They want the backward movement to be orderly and planned. There was a time when the workers were anti-progressive and tried to destroy the machines which the industrial revolution introduced. Now, Western industrialists have borrowed the psychology of eighteenth century laborers.

Soviet agricultural aims are: bigger farms, fewer hands, more machines, and security against weather. "A day feeds a year," runs a Russian adage. If that day of harvest is spoiled by inclemency, the countryside has nothing to eat. This is man's greatest slavery to nature. But agriculture need not be a game of luck when scientists can conquer the stratosphere and produce lightning in the laboratory.

The vast Volga region has always been subject to drought. "The hand of God," the mujhik said. But part of the Bolsheviks' atheism consists in opposing science and modern organization to such "hands of God." The chief cause of the Volga drought is the hot winds which blow up from Central Asia in the Spring and quickly melt the heavy winter snow. The water then flows down into the Volga and is lost for cultivation. In the last two years this has been done to meet the problem: During the Winter, large fields are divided up chessboard-fashion. Brigades of men and women then remove the snow from one square and place it on the other so that snow pile alternates with cleaned square. When the Spring arrives, the hardened snow and ice at the bottom of each pile resist the heat longer and permit the moisture to soak into the ground. Moreover, the water from the snow which does melt is caught on the cleaned square and cannot rush down to the river on account of the four surrounding piles. The cleaned square is thus saturated. This simple device practically saved some Volga districts from crop failures in 1934. Six million hectares were subjected to the snow preservation treatment. But if there had been fences and ruts separating individual holdings, if, moreover, the peasant had been left, as he had been left for centuries, to his own fatalistic inactivity, the chessboard method would have been impracticable. It was collectivization, which erases individual farms, that made this moisture-saving scheme possible.

I never saw Russia when it was Czarist, but I saw Czarist Russia when it was Soviet. The past of Russia is not dead; there is plenty of Czarist Russia in the Soviet Union. I know exactly how poor and backward Russian villages were before 1917, because they are only now beginning to look slightly different. The Russian village was so unproductive and unprogressive, so illiterate culturally and agriculturally that almost any change would have been a change for the better. The chief cause of the fall of Czarism was its failure to solve the land problem. Nor did Kerensky solve it. Hence Bolshevism. Nor did the Bolsheviks solve it—except negatively by driving out the landlords—until they inaugurated large scale collectivization in 1929.

1917 to 1921. Grain requisitioning to feed the army and the city population.

1921 to 1927. Stimulation of the peasants' initiative by allowing them to sell their produce on the private market. The countryside became more prosperous, but also more anxious to develop little private capitalists.

1927 to 1929. Persecution of the rising little private capi-

talists. Restrictions against ownership of
more than two or three cows, etc., hence
reduction of agricultural yield.

1929 to date. Collectivization.

This is the skeleton record of farming under the Sickle
and Hammer.

With 1921, when Lenin introduced the New Economic
Policy or NEP, begins the peacetime, economic history of
the Soviet regime. The Bolsheviks were immediately im-
paled on the horns of a dilemma. If they gave the peasant
free rein to produce, he would become rich, turn into a
capitalist and passively put pressure on the socialist city
likewise to become capitalistic. Many leading Bolsheviks
were harried by this fear. If, on the other hand, they held
the peasant down and prevented him from becoming a
capitalist, he would produce less and the nation would have
insufficient food. In any case, moreover, his methods were
so primitive that his yield was far below the minimum of
most Western countries. The situation demanded a new
system which would produce bigger crops without producing bigger capitalists. That new system is called collectivization. But the process of weaning capitalists from capitalism was not so easy. For even the most backward peasant
realized that if he lost this battle, capitalism in Russia would
be dead. The Soviet government likewise attached great
importance to the new system. It had tried being Janus-
faced: one face had looked up the red road of Socialism, the
other wore the well-known features of the Russian mujhik.
That had not worked. The task was to make 120,000,000
peasants about-face toward socialism. Nothing like it had
been undertaken in history. Because the peasantry—in
Russia or anywhere else—has so little property, it loves

property all the more. Yet the Bolsheviks were saying to the peasants: You will never again own a horse or a plow. You cease to exist as an individual farmer and join a group. Needless to say, there was plenty of resistance, and needless to say there was plenty of force.

Those peasants who had nothing went into the collectives willingly because they had nothing to lose. They hoped to gain. With these allies, the Bolsheviks rammed collectivization down the throats of the middle-class of peasants and crushed the best-situated "kulaks" who had property and prospects to forfeit and who therefore employed arson, sabotage, propaganda in churches, killing of officials and shrewd whispering campaigns to thwart the state—but in vain.

Today, any discussion regarding the permanence of agrarian collectivization in the Soviet Union is wholly academic. The Soviet regime now stands on two legs: one is collectivization, the other is state-owned industry. The Kremlin has no desire for a return to the days when it had two faces and one leg.

In October, 1932, I went to see Diamant, the assistant Commissar of Agriculture of the Ukrainian republic. After talking to him about current problems, I asked what was the best agricultural region of the Kharkov district. What was the next best? What was the worst? The worst was the Volchansk region. I said I would go to Volchansk. The roads would be very bad. That did not matter. Anything within 50 kilometers of Kharkov would be too near town to be typical. I penetrated deeper into the countryside.

Two years later, I revisited the same Volchansk region. The road, if anything, had deteriorated. For there had been rain the day before. This meant that the dirt was now mud and the skidding was much more perilous. At one moment, I thought I would have to turn back and try another day, but I persisted.

I recognized the "Twelfth Anniversary of October" collective (kolhoz) immediately, and it was pleasant to have some of its members recognize me. That establishes personal contact and confidence right away. I recognized the kolhoz because nothing had changed in it. In the last two years, there had been no construction. But a highly important change had taken place in the organization of the village. In 1932, it was a commune. This is the highest social form. It is the highest ideal of Communism. Yet this backward village had voluntarily established that form long before collectivization started. Under the commune, all peasants ate at a common table which I saw two years ago, all received the same income, all worked for the common weal. Apparently, that system did not function well. A kolhoz or *artel* or collective has now been substituted for the commune. In a kolhoz, the working animals, the horses and oxen, and the mechanical equipment, belong to the whole group. All the land of the village is cultivated as a unit. But each peasant is paid in accordance with the quantity and quality of his labor. The labor-day of a tractor mechanic is better rewarded than that of an unskilled or "black" worker. A peasant receives more for 100 labor-days than for ninety-nine labor-days. This was not true in the commune. Everybody there got equal pay irrespective of effort.

"What made the change necessary," I inquired.

We were standing in the open field surrounded by a large group of peasants. The Communist party organizer undertook to reply. "Because we discovered disguised kulaks in the kolhoz," he replied. This organizer's duty was to conduct Communist propaganda and keep the kolhoz management on the party line. He had come to the place only a few months ago, from distant Tambov. He knew nothing about local conditions. He spoke a stereotyped, official language. This was the last question I allowed him to answer. I turned to the chairman of the kolhoz and repeated the original question. He said: "Our nucleus was really Communistic. We had some former Red Army men and a few convinced Communists who understood what a commune implied. But the mass was not ready. Many of our members loafed on the job. We were feeding and paying them for very little work. In the end we had to give it up. The commune descended to the kolhoz."

The kolhoz is today the typical form of the Soviet collective. There are tens of thousands of them. Approximately seventy-five per cent of the peasants and ninety per cent of all arable land in the U.S.S.R. are collectivized. The remaining peasants still operate as individual farmers, but they are at a disadvantage. They are taxed more heavily. They get no loans from the state. They will ultimately drift into the kolhozi. Today, however, nobody is forcing them to do so—except indirectly by the pressure of discrimination.

I had stopped the car at the threshing field. A motor was attached to the thresher. A few tractors in the distance. Two old women were stirring a thick soup in two big cauldrons under which fires had been built. The peasants got their mid-day meal out in the open. I asked the old women whether any of their members had died of starvation in the 1932–33 winter. They said: "Yes, quite a number."

I had spent the month of October, 1932, traveling through the Ukraine. All over the countryside I saw grain which the peasants had left on the fields. It had rotted. It was their winter's food. Then those same peasants starved. They had been practising passive resistance against the government. The violently anti-Bolshevik "Slavonic Review" of London published a rabidly anti-Bolshevik article in January, 1934, which adduced the same facts. ". . . In the Ukrainia," it stated, "the resistance has assumed the character of a national struggle. . . . Whole tracts were left unsown. In addition, when the crops were being gathered (in 1932), it happened that in many areas, especially in the south, twenty, forty and even fifty per cent was left in the fields and was either not collected at all or was ruined in the threshing."

The peasants brought the calamity upon themselves. Yet one can understand what prompted this suicidal action. The Bolsheviks had launched the ambitious Five Year Plan. It had to be financed. It was to cost something like forty-two billion rubles. That colossal sum had to come from within the country, for foreign nations refused loans and gave limited credits at usurious rates. The workers and the peasants had to pay. The worker paid in the form of reduced consumption goods. The peasant paid in the form of huge taxes. In many cases, the government took thirty, even fifty, indeed even sixty per cent of his crop. Without such high-handed measures, the city could not have been industrialized quickly and foreign obligations could not have been met. But the result was that the peasants said: What is the use of plowing, planting and harvesting when the authorities seize a large part of my crop? The peasants accordingly sabotaged—and had nothing to eat.

It was a terrible lesson at a terrific cost. History can be cruel. The Bolsheviks were carrying out a major policy on which the strength and character of their regime depended. The peasants were reacting as normal human beings would. Let no one minimize the sadness of the phenomenon. But from the larger point of view the effect was the final entrenchment of collectivization. The peasantry will never again undertake passive resistance. And the Bolsheviks—one hopes—have learned that they must not compel the peasantry to attempt such resistance.

In the final analysis, the 1932 famine was a concomitant of the last battle between private capitalism and socialism in Russia. The peasants wanted to destroy collectivization. The government wanted to retain collectivization. The peasants used the best means at their disposal. The government used the best means at its disposal. The government won.

Slowly the peasants are beginning to see the advantages of collective effort. 1934, for instance, was a drought year. This region of the Ukraine had no rain throughout the months of May and June. "Then, in July, when we didn't want rain, it came in torrents." The harvest, accordingly, was only half as big as in the bumper year of 1933, but much better than it would have been under the former system of private cultivation. In the first place, the peasants told me, the tractors enabled them to plant earlier and to plow more deeply. In the second place, they had an agronomist who had insisted that they clean their seed. In the third place, they did this year what they had never done before: they cultivated. Large brigades were sent out by the kolkhoz to pull out the weeds so as to conserve moisture. These are simple but very effective measures.

Being a collective, the state, moreover, insures their crops. Most of their winter crop has been destroyed by the prolonged drought. They had also received premiums from the official insurance fund for the death of two horses and four cows.

Nevertheless, Stalin has not yet fulfilled his promise to the peasants of this village: they are not "well-to-do." To be sure, one man told me that his family of six, which includes four workers, had received 5,180 pounds of grain for its year's work. This was good. But it was exceptional. For the "Twelfth Anniversary of October" collective counted 120 households with 600 souls, but only 200 working hands. In other words: one and two-thirds worker to a family of five. There are too few workers because so many have been attracted by the growing cities. And the families are too big for a very obvious reason. In these respects, this kolkhoz was typical of thousands.

Generally speaking, the village lives much more poorly and has advanced much more slowly than the small, not to speak of the large towns in the region. Collectivization has struck roots but has not yet yielded rich fruit. The famine of 1932, furthermore, set back the Ukrainian peasant considerably.

I visited the nursery of the kolkhoz. Now the fact that a backward Ukrainian village has a crèche is in itself an innovation. What Russian cannot tell stories of pre-revolutionary days when babies, left alone at home while mother worked on the fields, had their hands gnawed off by pigs? Who does not know that the playground of the mujhik child used to be the manure pile? Now they are cared for all day in a special building. But the crèche is very bad. It is full of flies which stick to the children's bodies and faces. The peasants who followed me around either thought that flies were not to be taken seriously or that there had to be flies when stables were not far off. What about screens and netting? That was beyond their dreams. The children looked pale, though there had been plenty of sun and though the older boys and girls were tanned and healthy.

Most of the younger ones—those one and two years old—had rickets. But no wonder! Pregnancy in many cases had coincided with the period of general undernourishment. Nevertheless, the nursery was receiving the best that the village had to give it. Each child sleeps in its own bed. This is creating a revolution in the Soviet peasant's home life. No more family beds. As the children grow up they refuse to sleep with papa and mama and the rest of the brood. Each child has its own towel. A doctor sees them regularly. The skeleton of the future, accordingly, already exists. But the task of clothing it with much flesh, firm bones and rosy skin still remains.

The state farms which I visited in the Kharkov district are much better situated. These are large stretches of land, "grain factories" the Russians call them, where the labor is hired and where all the produce goes to the state. Most of them are almost completely mechanized. A few years ago, the Bolsheviks aimed to make them bigger and bigger. One in the North Caucasus was called "Gigant" and was as large as a British county. But since then, the tendency has been towards more moderate acreage. The employees in the Kharkov state farms or "sovkhozi" were comfortably situated. Their standard of living represented a mean between that of the collective and that of the city. They were all dressed in city clothes. Peasant garb was completely absent. They talked an urban language. Most of them, indeed, had had city training. In these sovkhozi, despite their inefficiency, rural life is being cured of the "idiocy" which Marx and Engels detested so cordially.

Soviet newspapers regularly publish photographs showing the penetration of phonographs and bicycles into village life. A little civilization is coming to the peasant, no doubt. Yet comfortable life is a long way off. One of the reasons is that the price of city goods is so high. And prices are high because those goods are scarce. One of the goals of Socialism is a regulated, equitable exchange of commodities between city and village. That exchange is not yet. Until it comes all talk of Socialism in the U.S.S.R. is idle. For Socialism without plenty is a caricature.

Plenty under capitalism produces depressions and economic difficulties. After the fat years come lean years. The Bolsheviks claim, however, that the Soviet Union's future will be marked by a steadily mounting economic curve. When they get plenty they will get more plenty and more and more plenty. There will be no interruption in the progress towards a richer life. The Communists really believe that Russia will reach levels of prosperity unheard of even in America and England.

Scene One

En Route from Kharkov to Rostov

Soviet locomotives are always thirsty: they stop often for water. At several stations I have been noticing one and the same *bezprizorni* or homeless waif. His face and neck are black. His eyes and ears are full of coal dust. His cap shines with dirt. It is cocked at a merry and defiant angle. While he begs he smiles. He is traveling by the de-luxe International car. As soon as the train begins to move, he inserts himself into the six-inch space between the bottom of the car and a large steel box hanging between the car and the rails. This electrical equipment box is his berth. He must be about eleven years old.

At the next station: "I come from Lozovaya. My mother killed my father recently. He had been drinking. They arrested my mother. They took me to a home. What did we do there? We had to work at machines, make our own beds; the teachers were very strict. We could never go into town. I ran away. Three months ago. Now it is beginning to get cold and I want to visit my brother in Baku." Bezprizornis lie like members of the oldest profession. His tale may be true or untrue. I give him a ruble. He runs away. I see him hand the bill to a boy about twelve. He comes back. "That's my comrade. We are traveling together." Suppose he is left behind at some station? "I will wait for him." These young hoboes are the real Communists.

Scene Two

The Hall of the Columns in Moscow

"A few years ago I was sitting in prison in Orenburg." Three thousand people, authors from all over the Soviet Union, prominent political leaders, foreign visitors, fill the Hall of Columns on Hunter's Row in Moscow. Maxim Gorki is on the platform; so also Alexei Tolstoi, Ehrenburg, André Malraux, Sholokhov and others. The first Congress of Soviet Authors is in session. A speaker stands at a rostrum; eight Kleig lights play on him. A bevy of newspaper photographers snap their Leikas right under his face. A. Avdeenko is speaking. He had been greeted with a violent burst of applause. "A few years ago I was sitting in prison in Orenburg," he begins. "A fellow my age occupied the cell with me. He was a native of Orenburg. Once he had had relatives and friends somewhere in the city, and now he had been clapped into jail, like me, for stealing. He was melancholic. He missed his town, his childhood, his family, and he asked me to write a letter for him. It was a letter without an address. We were simply sad and we wrote. Then when I read the letter to him he cried. That was my first literary production." It was Avdeenko who spoke, the author of a very popular first novel, "I Love" which has been translated into English and German, Avdeenko who was once a bezprizorni. Then he worked at Magnitogorsk. Then a year ago, he wrote his first novel.

And so to Rostov with a bezprizorni under my car.

Between Kharkov and Rostov-on-Don, the train cuts through the heart of the Donetz coal basin. The names: Gorlovka, Constantinovka, Lozovaya, Nikitovka are famous in the annals of the Soviet Civil War and of pre-revolutionary revolutionary activity. They were scenes of battle. Now each has head-turning ambitions of becoming a Pittsburgh, a Cleveland, a Birmingham. A powerful metal, chemical and cement industry is growing up in this region. Everywhere—new plants and new homes. At Matveyev-Kurgan Station, peasant wives and wives of railway workers have laid out their wares on rude wooden stands. They sell fried chickens, fried fish, lobsters, Antonovka apples, rings of onions, watermelons, garlic, pickled cucumbers, tomatoes, hot milk in clay jars, sour cream, butter, cheese and brooms. Passengers tired of the monotonous fare in the diner buy eagerly. At Kramatorsk—on one side of the track, a new Soviet metallurgical giant which produces heavy factory equipment formerly purchased abroad. It commenced operations in the Autumn of 1934. On the other side of the track, mud-thatched huts, mud streets, mujhiks.

Chapter XIV

WOMEN AND POLITICS AND CULTURE

The Soviet Union adopted the metric system several years ago. Distances are no longer measured in versts but in kilometers. Russians, however, really measure distances in hours. For it matters less how far away one is from a place than how long it takes to get there. From Kharkov to Rostov-on-Don, accordingly, is seventeen hours by what is called an express train.

Rostov is the center of an important agricultural district in the North Caucasus. But before visiting villages I visited ZAGS. This is the divorce and marriage bureau. These two cognate though different processes are registered at one and the same table by one and the same blond young woman lawyer. Incidentally, the influential Moscow "Izvestia" suggested the other day that there be two tables or preferably two rooms, for marriage ought to be protocoled in a special chamber whose festive atmosphere will not be marred by a grim reminder of marital discord.

Meanwhile, in Rostov, there is one table. A woman walks in. She wants a divorce. She works as a cashier in a drug store; is thirty-two, Russian. Her husband is forty-three, an Armenian. He knew she was going for a divorce, but refused to accompany her. Since there are no children, divorce is automatic. Tomorrow, her husband will receive a postcard from the authorities informing him that he is no longer married. The woman pays 3 rubles for the divorce and 30 kopeks for the postcard.

I ask her a few questions. The couple occupies two

rooms. Now each will take one. She admits that this will complicate life. When I try to ascertain why she wanted the divorce or whether they might not have mended their relations, she became very emotional and was on the verge of tears. She could only say that he "had a difficult character." They had been married eight years and most of it had been hell. I desist. Neither the lawyer-registrar, nor anyone else in authority inquires into the reasons for a Soviet divorce. If a man and woman in the Soviet Union do not want to live together nobody can make them do so for a single day. The reasons are not the government's business. Only where there are children does the law insist that provision be made for them before the separation is legalized.

A couple enters. Both dressed immaculately in white. No one needs to be told that this is a marriage. The lawyer registers the facts about them. She is eighteen and a half (the age minimum is eighteen); he twenty-five. Both Jewish. He is a mathematician and is associated with the Academy of Science in Leningrad. The registrar asks her whether she has a husband. "No." Whether he has a wife. "No." They are told that these declarations are tantamount to statements before a court, and if they are perverting the facts or if they conceal the existence of venereal diseases, the penalty is three years' imprisonment. Both smile. Both beam. She is exquisitely beautiful and he is endlessly happy. The man pays—3 rubles, and receives a receipt which is their marriage license.

Enter a man, woman and child. They have been married slightly over two years. He is a student in the Moscow musical conservatory from which he receives a monthly stipend of 100 rubles. In addition, he earns 500 rubles a month playing in an orchestra during the vacation period. I ask who took the initiative in getting the divorce. Both reply that the desire was mutual. Both are light-hearted. As some information is being entered into the ledger, he unconcernedly reads a newspaper, while Svetlana, their eighteen month old baby, keeps dropping a tremendous house key which papa obligingly returns to her. They have agreed that the mother is to keep the child and that he will pay her 130 rubles a month in alimony until Svetlana reaches the age of eighteen. This is required by law.

Svetlana will carry her father's name. Her mother will resume her maiden name. I ask him whether it will pain him not to see the child. He replies that she and her mother will visit him in Moscow. Mother says softly: "I will not."

Then mother turns to Svetlana. "Svetlana," she asks, "will you live with your papa in Moscow?"

Svetlana cannot talk yet. "She says 'No,'" the mother declares. Father and mother laugh. It is obvious that within a week the young mother will be back at the same table with another man.

The two divorces and one marriage have consumed exactly twenty-eight minutes time, part of which is accounted for by my questions. I go from here to the Rostov Institute for the Care of Mother and Child. In the office where citizens receive free legal advice, a young woman has come for the final documents which record her right to receive alimony.

"How much will her ex-husband pay?" I inquire.

"It is not her husband who will pay," the lawyer replies. "She is still with her husband."

I knit my brow and try to understand. "Then who will pay the alimony?"

"The father of the child," says the lawyer. I am puzzled.

"You see," the woman explains, "I have a husband but

I was living with another man and gave birth to a child from him. Since I am not married to him, he must support the baby; hence the alimony."

"And where is the child?" I want to know.

"The child lives with us. My husband likes it very much."

Soon the whole case develops. It is unusual and unusually interesting. Maria Feodorovna, the woman, is young and quite handsome. She has been married to Pioter, her husband, for eight years. Five years ago, she gave birth to a child which died. Since then they have had no sexual intercourse with one another. But they are good friends and are very fond of one another. Both have affairs, and both know about them.

"Sometimes," Maria Feodorovna continues, "Pioter 'phones from work and says: 'Dear, I have a rendezvous this evening.' Then I know what suit and which shirt he wants to have pressed. When he comes home, he tells me what happened."

"Once not so long ago, he returned late. I was tired and in bed, and when he commenced reporting how he had spent the evening, I sent him away. 'What,' he exclaimed, 'you aren't getting jealous!' And we both laughed heartily."

"Then why do you live together at all?" I interpose.

"We really enjoy it. Believe me. I want to move now to Kislovodsk, and my husband is thinking of going with me. This is rather inconvenient and difficult for him. But I think he will manage it."

Pioter and his wife are under thirty. Maria Feodorovna's lover refused to admit that he was the father of the child. He did not want to pay alimony for eighteen years. This presented a delicate problem to the law courts. The Soviet legal code requires that no matter what the circumstances, fatherhood must be established so that the burden of caring for the child does not fall on the woman. But here was a knotty situation. The lover agreed that he had lived with Maria Feodorovna but denied being the father. The child could not be Pioter's. Yet how were the authorities to know that Maria and Pioter really had no intimate relations. Such a thing cannot be proved. Perhaps husband and wife were lying so as to defraud the lover of money to support the baby.

There were no witnesses and there could be none, although neighbors did testify that they knew the nature of the platonic ties between Maria and Pioter. The court had nothing to guide it except its intuition. But "Soviet law," the woman lawyer said to me, "does not stop at formalities. The judges knew that Maria was telling the truth just as a parent knows whether a child is telling the truth or lying. Moreover, the lover could not know very well that he was not the father. In any event, the verdict was awarded to Maria Feodorovna." That was before the birth of the baby.

The lover appealed the case, but a higher court recently confirmed the decision of the people's court, and now Maria Feodorovna had come for the papers on the basis of which she would call at her lover's place of employment every fortnight and collect one-third of his salary. Where the man willingly pays alimony, however, this procedure is not resorted to. Then he sends the prescribed sum by messenger or, often, he brings it himself.

Maria Feodorovna had no deep regrets. "He is a scoundrel," she said to me. "But not all men are alike." She was young and she would live.

Maria Feodorovna was quickly followed by other women who sought advice or help. Most of them came to learn what specific rights the law gave them. At the end of a long afternoon in which a rich stripe of Soviet life passed before my eyes, I engaged the young lawyer in conversation.

"Men never come here, do they?"

"Only when we summon them. We protect women and children."

"And why?"

"Because they are weaker."

She caught herself right away, for her statement conflicted with the Soviet principle of sex equality. She would have gone into a lengthy historical and sociological dissertation, but I stopped her. "In other words," I said, "women are actually inferior and therefore you make them superior before the law."

In fact, the Soviet legal code and Soviet courts are prejudiced in favor of women, and it has been suggested facetiously that Soviet men should launch a movement for equality. Women are paid the same wages as men on the same jobs but one has merely to watch them work to see that their productivity at certain tasks, in the digging of the Moscow subway, for instance, is far below that of men.

The principle of Soviet law is to prevent women's physical handicap from becoming an economic handicap. Thus, they receive their pregnancy and nursing leave so that child-bearing may not make it impossible for them to be gainfully employed. In like manner, a pregnant woman may not be discharged for any reason whatsoever. The law establishes the maximum weight which women may be asked to lift at work. Factory managers usually assign older women to tasks which require a minimum of standing.

In other fields, the Bolsheviks always urge women into the front ranks. Women are elected as chairmen of soviets and of collectives. Six thousand women preside over 6,000 collectives. Women are appointed to important administrative positions. There are women in the Red Army, women policemen, many women judges, etc. Sometimes such advancement is on merit. Often it is artificial and reflects the Bolshevik desire to place women on a par with men.

Elsewhere in the world, when people argue on the equality of men and women, the protagonists of the latter regularly submit that although women do enjoy equality on paper, there is still a prejudice against them in actual life which prevents them from rising to the top. In the Soviet Union, no such prejudice exists. True, an old Russian proverb declared that "a chicken is not a bird, and a woman is not a human being." Perhaps some peasants and uncultured workingmen have such obsolete notions. But certainly not the authorities, not the Communists, not anybody who has the least influence on Soviet policy.

Why is it, nevertheless, that less than a handful of women have occupied important Soviet posts since the revolution? There are no women in the Soviet federal cabinet. The most powerful body in the Soviet Union is the Central Committee of the Communist Party. Two of its seventy-one members are women—one of them is Krupskaya, Lenin's widow. Madame Kollontai is the Soviet minister to Sweden, but she clothed a much more important office immediately after the revolution.

The revolution, it is submitted, is too young to warrant a conclusion on the relative abilities of men and women. Women, it is submitted, still suffer from their disabilities throughout the centuries. Perhaps so. Soviet experience is certainly too short to justify a dogmatic statement on this vexed sex question. But I think that the actual favoritism shown to women in the Soviet Union and their inequality—that is, their more-than-equality—before the law coupled with their failure to forge unaided to political, economical or even cultural prominence, establishes a presumption of the inferiority of women.

The Bolsheviks like to boast of their progress in the fields of culture and hygiene. And they have accomplished wonders. In Rostov, for instance, they showed me a tremendous hospital city which they had built. There was a fine building for tuberculosis patients, another equally good for internal diseases, etc., etc., all furnished with excellent foreign and Soviet equipment and disposing of an able corps of physicians. But before the inspection, I waited in the chamber where new patients were received. On a table stood a nickel container filled with boiled water, and attached to the container by a chain was an enameled cup. Hundreds of people with God knows what maladies used that cup every day. I addressed myself to a woman in white apron, probably a maid.

"That cup is not very hygienic," I said.

"Why?"

"Well, it transfers germs."

"But each drinker rinses it with some water."

"But cold boiled water does not kill germs."

She was obviously not germ-conscious. She was probably more class-conscious than germ-conscious. "What would you have instead of the container?" she inquired.

"There could be a fountain over which visitors could bend and drink water without a cup," I suggested.

"But then the water would not be boiled," she countered. It did not occur to her that a small tank of boiled water with a fountain attachment would meet every possible objection. Perhaps there is no realistic solution until the water supply of Rostov is made potable without boiling. Meanwhile, the outrage exists in the very midst of an excellent hospital. During the last year or two, factories have introduced water fountains into their shops. But I have seen workers step over to a fountain, swallow the stream which rises from it, and drink with their lips touching the nozzle. To prevent such practices, fountains are being manufactured now with two pieces of metal shaped like inverted V's attached to the bottom of the bowl near the nozzle so that lips cannot reach the mouthpiece.

All this suggests how vast is the task which the Soviet government has assumed. Culture in the U.S.S.R. means not only literature, schools, and symphony orchestras. It includes training in the use of a fork, in drinking methods, in polishing shoes. The acquisition of culture by a nation is not only a prolonged, it is also a costly process. I have several times visited the new coöperative settlement at the Kharkov tractor plant. Once, purely by accident, I came first upon a three room apartment with bath inhabited by an American specialist. It was as clean and well-kept as anything in Western Europe or America. In the same corridor and in the same type of apartment lived a Czecho-slovak couple. The apartment was not nearly as perfect. And then, I entered a third three-room apartment, this time of a Soviet workingman. Kerosene cans and bags of potatoes stood in the bathtub. Several heavy winter coats hung on nails in the living rooms and as a result the plaster had been damaged. Flies abounded everywhere. I need go no further. The point is this: it is not enough to put people into cultural surroundings. They must learn to appreciate and take care of those surroundings. In the process of learning—at the Kharkov tractor homes, for instance—many apartments will be spoiled. When the workingman occupied that Kharkov apartment it was a palace for him. Even in the miserable condition to which he and his family had quickly

reduced it, it was a great improvement on any accommodations he had previously enjoyed. But this apartment ac-
customs him to a higher standard. He sees that his neighbors
have good apartments because they kept theirs good, while
he spoiled his. He will know better how to take care of his
next apartment.

The Soviet press has been paying a great deal of attention
recently to superficial refinements. One paper elaborates on
the benefits of manicure. A member of the Soviet Cabinet
recently threw an important official out of his office because
he was unshaved. One journalist reminds his readers that
civilization has long ago invented tooth picks and that they
are an improvement on forks. Creased trousers are presented
as a cultural desideratum. "Give your seats to old women
and men in street cars. Don't worry; it is not bourgeois."
"Don't stick meat into your mouth with a knife." The list
of politeness commandments grows longer and longer.

I stood outside a food store today, watching people
come out with big bundles of food. A workingman, already
slightly under the influence of liquor, came out carrying a
pint bottle of vodka.

I said to him: "Why do you spend so much money on
vodka?"

"You see," he replied, "I get home from work, there is
not enough to eat. So I drink to forget myself."

"But if you bought food instead of alcohol you would
have enough to eat."

"Yet," he replied, "but then I wouldn't have any vodka."

I went to see Rostov's model milk and ice cream factory.
One must don a white apron and cook's hat before entering
the workshops. The equipment is modern. All employees

must regularly submit to free manicures and haircuts in the plant's tonsorial parlor. In the immaculate restaurant, over a tremendous bowl of delicious vanilla ice cream, I argue with the secretary of the Factory Committee or trade union.

Lenin and Trotzky engaged in an interesting public controversy in 1920. Trotzky declared that Soviet Russia was a workers' state and that the workers therefore required no special protection from trade unions. He would have state-ified the unions. Lenin replied that Soviet Russia was not only a workers' state. It is a workers' and peasants' state. Besides, he added, there is a bureaucracy or official class. The proletariat would have to safeguard its prerogatives against the assaults of these two groups. Time has proved that Lenin was right a thousandfold. But the trade unions have nevertheless allowed themselves to be state-ified, and their first concern, accordingly, is not always the laborer's interests.

"What do you mean by laborer's interests?" the factory committee secretary countered. "The trade union strives to raise production. It wants an efficient plant. Everything which benefits the country as a whole benefits the laborer in particular."

That is the stock Bolshevik argument. "At present, although conditions have improved," he continued, "we are still called upon to make sacrifices. If the workingmen insisted on maximum earnings the state would not have the wherewithal for construction, for building a healthy national industrial foundation, and in the end the proletariat's standard of living would suffer. As it is, we are moving rapidly forward, and each worker too. In the end, the trade union's policy will produce a prosperous individual. The

Soviet Union will reach a level of comfort and luxury higher by far than that attained in the richest bourgeois nations."

There is cogency in this presentation; it is indeed difficult to distinguish between the workingman and his factory. Yet wherever there are wages there is exploitation. And where there are privileges each class fights to obtain a major portion of them. The supineness of the trade unions makes life much easier for the Soviet industrialist. It also enables government officials, engineers, and other strategically situated groups to take the best apartments, to take a more than proportional share of sanatorium accommodations, etc. The Bolsheviks proclaim that the proletariat is the salt of the earth, and the workers do actually enjoy many unique rights and pleasures. But fighting trade unions could win more for them.

Rostov-on-Don (the Don really flows quietly) has several of those very interesting Soviet institutions called "One Day Rest Homes." On the eve of the free day, which is every sixth day, the chosen laborers do not go to their apartments. They go to the One Day Rest Home. They bathe. Get into sanatorium clothes. Receive a thorough doctor's examination. Eat special food. Sleep under excellent conditions. Play and rest and enjoy the whole of the free day, and then return to their families. The relaxation was doing them a lot of good; I found them indulging in children's games. Some had brought along balalaikas. Others accordions. The home possessed a gramophone and miserable Soviet records which everybody enjoyed.

The One Day Rest Home is situated in a park in the new Socialist City. Girl and boy "Pioneers" were dancing with a teacher (but the boys soon left the group); boys and girls were swinging around the maypole (but the teacher, who had no desire to summon an ambulance, soon called the girls away). . . .

Chapter XV

LIBERTY

This afternoon I was invited to lunch at the home of the editor of a Rostov daily. Only the two of us were at the table; his wife was at work. The maid served the inevitable: caviar, white bread which is gray, black rye bread, Narzan mineral water, white wine, red wine, borscht with meat in it, vegetable salad, fried chicken, and compote of dried fruits. We had plenty of time therefore to discuss politics.

Here was an intelligent editor. He had been abroad, spoke German, read foreign dailies. I wanted to talk to him about liberty. We entered into a compact: he was not to spare my feelings and I would not spare his.

"You remember Paul Scheffer," he said. "For years, as Moscow correspondent of the 'Berliner Tageblatt,' he criticized us for our alleged suppression of freedom. Now he edits a Fascist daily in Germany. The liberty argument," he continued, "is a convenient club with which to strike at an enemy whose other policies you detest. Our enemies say we suppress liberty. Actually they mean that we suppress capitalists."

"Some time ago," he said through a spoonful of borscht, "ex-President Hoover attacked President Roosevelt for undermining American liberty. His real thought was: I want to be President again. All your talk about liberty is demagogy."

"But do you write what you want in your newspaper?"

"I write only what I want to write. I am a Communist and my daily is Communist."

"But could an anti-Communist express his views in your publication?"

"No, of course not. I would not let him. And he would know better than to try. We criticize the government and the government's departments severely. We do that, however, because we want to improve the government, not to destroy it."

"Then there is no freedom of the press in the Soviet Union," I summarize.

"We have plenty of freedom. Our enemies have none. There is something you must understand. The crude Marxists say that the British government is a slave of the City or that the White House in Washington takes orders from capitalists. We know, naturally, that no official sits in his office waiting for a 'phone call from General Motors. He knows how to do the right thing by capitalism without the 'phone call. The same applies here. Nobody has to instruct us to defend collectivization or to urge the opening of more schools. Nobody has to tell us what to say about Fascism."

"And does not the suppression of all unorthodox thoughts militate against thinking in general?" I asked. "I know there is no regimentation of material life. That is a silly foreign prejudice. But you have plenty of regimentation in philosophy and political thought. Your youth does not think deeply. It accepts dogma unquestioningly."

"I will make a statement," the editor replied, "which will at first sight seem foolish. But I really believe that an intelligent Soviet workingman, even if he has not read Kant and even if he seldom thinks, has a more correct understanding of the world than your greatest bourgeois philosophers."

"You will have to prove that."

"The basis of the Soviet regime," he began, "is science.

Capitalism has ceased to further the sciences. In its decay, it is mingling religion and mysticism with science. Take your astronomers like Jeans and Eddington, your physicists, your chemists. Their knowledge is at odds with their faith. A brilliant scientist who believes in God is more backward intellectually than a young Komsomol whose principles can stand the test of scientific analysis. Europe is beginning to suppress real science as it is hampering inventions—except for armament purposes. Science will see a new flower in the U.S.S.R. because its realm is unlimited. I do not talk about the concrete stimulus which the Soviet regime has given to scientific research by placing almost unlimited funds at the disposal of individual scientists and of numerous institutions. That is axiomatic. But the other, the philosophic, contribution we have made is no less important. Talk of mental suppression! The bourgeoisie dare not go to the end of scientific analysis because that would kill God, and capitalism needs the strengthening influence of the church. Thorough scientific analysis, the kind that Karl Marx undertook, would reveal the chaotic, illogical, wasteful quintessence of capitalism. Because capitalism fears the ex-ray penetration of science it clothes itself first in patriotism and nationalism. When these clothes grow threadbare, it puts on mysticism, it decks itself in the "Blood and Soil" principle of the German Fascists, it semi-deifies its "Fuehrer." On the day capitalism looked the scientific truth in the eye it would commit suicide. Marxism is not a dogma; it is a science. The Communist is right. One little thought of a man on the right ideological path is worth all the tomes of the mystics."

The editor was waxing oratorical. I got in a word edge-wise while he chewed a morsel of the chicken. "But what makes you suppose," I suggested, "that atheism is scientific?

Does not the really scientific attitude imply agnosticism—doubt?"

"That is an exploded piece of sophistry," the editor cried. "Agnosticism means: I cannot prove the positive, but you cannot prove the negative. This is nonsense. In India, many millions of people believe in incarnation and re-incarnation. You may once have been an ox or a panther. You will become a snake after death. Can you disprove that? Of course not. But do you believe it? No. Imagine a conversation in a totem-pole society. The 'atheist' says: 'I do not believe that a totem-pole can protect us from harm or give us wealth.' The believer replies: 'You cannot prove that.' Yet do you worship a totem-pole? Agnosticism is the refuge of cowards. They dare not say they disbelieve. And religion is that remnant of the cloud which science has not yet dispersed. Once we used to believe that the thunder clap was the angry voice of heaven, that hail was a punishment from God, that illness reflected the displeasure of the unseen ruler. We therefore prayed for fine weather and for recovery. Now science has explained away all those superstitions. There remains an area, however, in which religion still has free play: we do not yet understand the movement of the spheres, the order in nature, and the creation of life. In the same manner, the primitive people did not understand meteorological phenomena. But we are pushing religion back. We can already weigh the planets and measure their temperature. The chemical laboratory is militantly atheistic. So is the astronomical observatory. They will banish your gods from the heavens. It is not God who created man in His image, but man who creates God in *his* image. Today the Nazis are creating a pagan god."

"Now listen," I interrupted. "You are employing the typical Bolshevik tactics in an argument. When I declare that there is no freedom under Bolshevism, you reply that there is none under capitalism. When I affirm that your young citizens don't think deeply, you counter that bourgeois philosophers cannot think. You do not answer the question."

The editor smiled. "That is much the easier way," he admitted. "But something else. You ask me about freedom in the U.S.S.R. because you believe that it exists in bourgeois countries. That is why I first talk about its non-existence in bourgeois countries. You deplore the alleged absence of thinking with us because you are convinced that capitalist thinkers think. They used to once upon a time in the hey-day of capitalism. Now, however, capitalism is declining economically. Today you are living on reserves. And since capitalist economics declines, so also does capitalist science, capitalist philosophy. Western civilization is relapsing into mediævalism from which we will one day save it. Incidentally, how is it I haven't heard the argument of late that Bolshevism can only destroy. Since the capitalists have started sinking coffee into the sea, plowing under cotton and killing off livestock while people starve they have forgotten that once-popular fallacy. We are building faster than ever America did."

"Now come, come," I interjected. "We can discuss these matters if you wish. But then tell me that you refuse to talk about liberty."

"No, nothing of the kind," he said. "To be sure, it is less important than you seem to suppose. Modern capitalism needs the liberty of earning profits, keeping those profits, exploiting labor, safeguarding private property and preventing excessive government interference. The workers and peasants are not interested in such liberty. Freedom has always meant much less to the have-nots than to the haves.

Give a man a permanent job and he will gladly relinquish his vote. The masses would joyfully exchange the so-called privilege of electing and having a parliament for the promise that they would never be called into the trenches again.

"What is the situation in the Soviet Union?" he proceeded. "We do not object to wealth. Soviet citizens own personal property. They have furniture, clothing, libraries, bicycles, etc. In the future, they will own automobiles, houses and country homes. Our government is assigning workers little plots of ground near their homes for truck gardening. Many proletarians own cows, pigs and chickens. There will soon be more individuals in the Soviet Union holding property than before the revolution. But they cannot employ that property to exploit others. They do not obtain that property by exploiting others. It is the fruit of their personal efforts; it is solely for their personal enjoyment and not for the amassing of further wealth. In other words—and I do not wish to elaborate this point—the Soviet citizen is free to live in comfort and luxury, free to study, free to advance professionally, and free to raise healthy, educated children. Such freedoms are real and important."

The editor paused for breath, cut some more slices of lemon and ordered his third glass of tea. I was afraid to interrupt him. "Now," he continued. "Our women have found a new freedom greater than any under capitalism. The capitalist wife is chattel. Here our divorce law, our provisions for the care of mothers, and the certainty of finding employment, make wives and all women free and independent. You will admit that that is important."

I admitted it. "Our children are free in a very profound sense of the term," he affirmed. "Capitalistic individualism cripples your children with father complexes, mother complexes, inferiority and superiority complexes and what not. Your psychoanalysts are sure of steady employment. But our collective training releases the youth from these fatal maladies. We are developing a normal, healthy generation. It will yet startle the world with its achievements.

"Then of course there is the freedom which the Soviet regime granted to national minorities," he added. "The ethnic groups in Czarist Russia suffered under discriminations. The Tartars, Jews and other nationalities could not hold land. The Jews, Armenians and other nationalities were subjected to periodic massacres. No nationality could develop its own culture. National languages were suppressed. Now each racial minority in the U.S.S.R.—and I think the paper said the other day that there were 186 of them—speaks its tongue, has its own literature, its own officials, and schools and courts in which the national language is the official language. They are free. Yet at the same time, their membership in the powerful Soviet federation relieves them from the eternal concern of foreign attack.

"We even allow religious freedom," he smiled. "There is no point in denying the fact that we are combatting religion. But we do not stop anyone, unless he is a party member, from attending religious services.

"I am talking about liberty as it concerns the millions and tens of millions. The masses were always the first object of the Bolsheviks' interest. I will come to the intellectuals in a moment. There is another brand of freedom here which is valuable above all things: the freedom from worry. In many respects the state provides for the citizen's future. Sick and accident insurance, more and more old age pensions, free burial. There are few rainy days in the U.S.S.R. You cannot worry, either, about your children's education. Education is free and does not depend on parents' financial condition. And what is the liberation from the threat of unemployment worth?" the editor concluded.

"I grant that most of these things are true," I said. "But you declare that the Soviets' first concern is the masses. Do the masses, then, govern themselves? Or is this really a government for the people and of the people but not *by* the people? Do the soviets actually rule? We know that your system gives the decisive voice in all cases to Communists. As the Soviet government takes orders from the Communist Central Committee, so village soviets are dominated by village Communists, and city, county and regional soviets are likewise run by party members. More and more, the soviets are becoming educational and executive-administrative organs while the party is the foundation of political power. I will be surprised if you agree with me, but it is true nevertheless."

"We are avowedly a dictatorship of the proletariat," he replied. "The vanguard of the proletariat is the Communist party. The Communist party made the revolution. The Communist party with Stalin as its chief is responsible for Soviet policy. The party is of course supreme. Yet the soviets have a majority of non-party members. In them, peasants and workers are trained to rule the country. For many peasants and workers, election to the soviets is the first step towards admission into the party. Like the trade unions, the soviets are schools of Communism, as Lenin said. You know that we could have many millions in the party if we only opened the door. We Bolsheviks must be highly-disciplined, well-equipped ideologically, and ready for any sacrifice. The Communist party is a shock troop and not every applicant can be accepted. We have about two million adult Communists and five million Komsomols who, since young people past eighteen are permitted to hold important posts here, play an important rôle in the state. Altogether therefore the country has some seven million registered Communists. But there are many more millions who are Communistically-minded. We have their mandate to rule. This is much larger than the ruling party in capitalist countries. The proletariat is bigger than any capitalist ruling class."

"Well, let us drop this subject now," I suggested. "Let us drop the question of political freedom and discuss intellectual freedom. You have considerable intellectual sameness in the Soviet Union. You criticize the misdeeds of this official or that official, but does your criticism ever touch fundamentals? I do not mean fundamentals of principle. But weaknesses of the system. The absence of an opposition leads you into many errors. The moment a person lifts his voice against a holy decision of the party, against one of its time-honored practices, he is branded as a counter-revolutionary and removed from the scene. This code of infallibility is disastrous. Don't I know that many devoted Communists say in private what they would never dare to say in public. Such dishonesty is self-destructive.

"Moreover," I went on, "there is so little intellectual searching in the Soviet Union. Your explorers are doing wonders in the Arctic. But who goes on voyages of discovery through the ice of theory, who investigates the stratosphere of philosophy? It is all acceptance, blind acceptance. Philosophy and theory are handed down from on high like the Ten Commandments."

My editor did not like this. "Oh," he yawned, "you are the typical intellectual. Our Russian intelligentsia told us all these things long before the revolution. Then when the revolution came they were on the side of reaction. We act. We believe in deeds. Maybe one or two of your contentions are correct. Well, what of it? Look at it against the larger background of all our achievements and cultural accomplishments. This is a backward country. As we grow more enlightened many things change. You have seen many things change in your twelve years in the country. You talk as if we were dead and congealed like the bourgeoisie. What is true today may not be true tomorrow. Bolshevism is dynamic. History teaching used to be regarded as reactionary. Now we have introduced it and we are telling our pupils to memorize dates and to study the rôles of big individuals. Nu, and what about dancing? Old Bolsheviks are learning the two-step and fox trot. Army men must learn how to dance. There will be a gradual evolution in other fields as well. Don't worry about us."

I saw that he was tired. News telegrams from Moscow were probably waiting for him in his office. There had been a 'phone call from his assistant editor. We began making our farewells. I promised to come back to Rostov in a year and look him up. "Meanwhile," he said, "watch the progress of intellectual sameness in capitalist lands, and see how liberties are being suppressed and circumscribed in the West."

Chapter XVI

MAILED FIST IN KID GLOVE

Nowhere did the collectivization of agriculture arouse so much active and armed opposition as in the Rostov region. Lazar Kaganovitch, who can rebuild Moscow, has killed kulaks aplenty in the North Caucasus. But since 1932 there is peace.

The Bolsheviks' tactics is to smash opposition with quick blows of the mailed fist and then draw kid over the steel.

The North Caucasus was once the habitat of the Cossacks. They fought under Denikin against Bolshevism in 1918 and 1919. They fought it again with the same and other weapons in 1931 and 1932. They lost both times. They lost much of their wealth too.

The Cossacks used to be the gendarmerie of Czarism. They were Russians colonized in strategic areas or in districts inhabited by politically unreliable non-Russian peoples. The monarchy paid them with land and special privileges. The Cossacks were rich, therefore, and reactionary. They lived in large villages called *stanitsas*. They had many horses and huge herds of live stock.

The defeat of the White counter-revolutionaries in the Civil War of 1917–20 broke up the Cossacks as an organization. Soviet measures against private capitalism weakened them economically during the 1921–28 period of the New Economic Policy. Collectivization was the final purge. Those Cossacks, many thousands of them, who resisted their own death as capitalistic farmers are now digging canals and building roads and railways within the industrial-

educational prison and convict camp system of the Internal
Affairs Commissariat.

"Cossacks" was a term which embodied all that was ab-
horrent in Czarism. The Cossacks were the Czar's praetorian
guard. The common people hated these mounted despoilers
who rode down strikers and recalcitrant peasants and engaged in punitive expeditions against subject races. They
were pictured with their fur caps tipped at a drunken angle
perpetrating pogroms on Jews. Their sabers dripped with
blood. They were once the symbols of autocracy. Now
they are no more.

But having "liquidated" the Cossacks as an organization,
having crushed the Cossacks as a well-to-do and privileged
caste, Moscow gave the Northern Caucasus, and other districts too, the best it had in the way of organizers, scientific aid, financial assistance, and agricultural machinery.
Considerate treatment succeeded ruthless suppression.
Blood and iron yielded their place to balm.

The government realized how very important was the
rôle which its representatives in the villages would be called
upon to play in this difficult healing process. Much would
depend on how the men on the spot interpreted and effected
Moscow's new policies.

Local administration had become a task for experts. Determination would have to mix with a sincere sympathy for
the population and an understanding of its needs. Peasants
only recently "persuaded" by displays or threats of force
would now have to be won over and convinced by proofs
of the state's deep concern for their well-being. Resentment
against the mailed fist would have to be reduced to a minimum. Coöperation had to be courted. Further sabotage had
to be scotched. The past had to be buried under a brighter
and lighter present.

Wisdom, culture, will, strength, knowledge and human kindness were the demands which the situation made upon every government official. In addition, he would have to have at his disposal material resources with which to prosecute the peaceful entrenchment of collective methods of cultivation.

Some day the revealing, exciting story of that period will be written by the patient and, one hopes, dispassionate historian. Meanwhile, the observer can only stop to pay tribute to the speed and deftness wherewith the Bolsheviks executed this radical change from steel to soft leather.

The Communists created a special institution for this complicated purpose: the Political Department or, in abbreviated Russian, Politotdel. The idea in itself was a stroke of genius (they say it originated with Kaganovitch or Stalin), for it entailed the arrival on the scene of new men who had had no part in the resolute repressive measures of 1931–32. And what men!

Since agrarian collectivization had brought with it considerable chaos, much loss of cattle and many knotty political problems in numerous parts of the country, the Politotdels were introduced not only in the areas of major resistance—North Caucasus and the Ukraine, but throughout the entire Soviet Union. Several thousand Politotdels were established. Kaganovitch, who was chairman of the Communist Party's Committee on Agriculture in 1933, chose hundreds of them personally. In any event, he gathered them in Moscow, instructed them, warned them, and prepared them. The success of the second Five Year Plan depended first of all on them.

A peasant's son, pressed forward into the limelight by the revolution, was graduated from a Soviet university and after special study, became a "Red" professor. His major interest was economics. The government sent him abroad where he worked for three years in the capacity of economic observer for a gigantic Soviet commercial organization. He learned a foreign language and met the finest brains of the bourgeois country in which he was stationed. He is now the chairman of a Politotdel in the North Caucasus; I know him well. He has written a book about his experiences down there. This is the type of person which guides the fortunes of the collectives.

Jonescu. A Roumanian. A revolutionist who fled from Roumania and joined the Bolshevik fighting forces in 1917. Between 1918 and 1930, he was an officer in the Red Army. Then he became assistant director of a factory in Leningrad. Subsequently, he was in charge of party organizational work in a large agricultural district in the Ukraine. Since September, 1933, he has been the chairman of the Politotdel of the Aksai county near Rostov. There I visited him.

One has only to take a good look at Jonescu's face and figure to know that he possesses temperament and energy. He knows his mind; he is accustomed to handle peasants (in the army) and workers. He has had a good general education. His words reveal a clear, analytical brain. He brooks no interruption while speaking; he must pursue his thought to the end; then he invites, he begs for objections. Having heard the objections, he lays out a new plan of attack, and his eloquence pours forth again. His wish to convince convinces. The peasants respect and like him.

Jonescu is a big man in a small district covering only 12,000 hectares and including only four village collectives. Those farmers have an unusual opportunity. Mere contact with him broadens their horizon and enriches their outlook on life, for he brings the big outside world into their two-by-four existence. Occasionally he delivers lectures to them about foreign politics, general economic trends and larger Bolshevik policies. He is a cultural leaven.

But that is incidental. His job consists in raising the agricultural yield, organizing agriculture on modern, collectivistic lines, and establishing a new, higher standard of living. The task is too great for one man. But the Politotdel is a department. It includes two assistants—one for work among the Communists, the second who is a direct agent of the Commissariat of Internal Affairs; two other members —one who organizes the Young Communists, the second who organizes the women; and a sixth member—the editor of Politotdel's weekly newspaper which is printed in an edition of 800 copies. Four of the six are natives of the district. I entered their wooden office hut during a meeting of the Politotdel.

Threshing was the chief point on the agenda. I visited the North Caucasus in 1930 and again in 1931. I remember walking through village after village and noticing men sitting on the steps in front of their homes at the height of the threshing season. Then I went out to the threshing fields. Young girls and boys of sixteen and eighteen were doing all the work. The elders were sulking—practising passive resistance. Collectivization had alienated them and they refused to work. Now the village of Aksai in which the Politotdel's headquarters were located was empty. Every man and woman was in the fields.

The Politotdel had done that. But the more basic cause of the change in these people's attitude was the change in Soviet policy from force to assistance—and that policy had changed when the opposition had been crushed. As a result, threshing was proceeding at a fast pace. Indeed, harvesting, and, before it, harrowing, planting and plowing had been carried out in unprecedentedly short periods. The old Russian village used to go about its work with Slav sluggishness and in blind slavery to ancient weather superstitions. Collectivization has brought the agronomist and science and Bolshevik "tempo" to the Soviet countryside. Jonescu was proud of the district's achievements: "We finished our sowing in two and a half days," he boasted, "and exceeded our plan by 165 per cent. Sowing was completed by April 10th—twenty days earlier than last year. Last year this district reaped in September and was still threshing in December. We are already two months ahead of last year's threshing schedule." It was chiefly a matter of organization, planning and winning the peasants over to non-traditional methods.

"During the entire growing season," Jonescu continued, "we had only one heavy rain. Yet our crop is good. The dispatch with which we worked was a telling factor in the result. Also, we conserved moisture, and cultivated."

Jonescu and his Politotdel had won success. Yet other districts in similar circumstances had suffered. The Communists understand now that much depends on the individual official. And the peasant understands it, too.

The Russian peasant was formerly dependent on the weather, the landlord and the usurer. Now he depends on the official whom he has not elected. There are many ways in which the peasant can redress his grievances, but what percentage tries? The Politotdel and the Communists of the village are the masters of the situation. The arm of Moscow is very long, and the misdeeds of officials are rigorously punished. But Russia is big, communications are bad, and much remains unrecorded.

Poor official! Moscow or Rostov issues strict orders. He tries to obey them. The results are disastrous. Then suddenly, Moscow scraps its former policy and blames the official for the disaster. Exactly that happened twice during the early collectivization period. If only policy remained stable! The peasant wants fewer gyrations. And if only the officials were more permanent! They would perhaps learn to love and spare their wards. Yet the official is nothing more than a helpless manikin. There is a big field in which his ability and character play a rôle. But in most things, he, the "master of the situation" is really the pitiful tool of a higher and distant master.

Planning is one of the virtues of Sovietism. But the necessity of fulfilling the Plan is one of its worst curses. The official has one God: Plan Fulfilment. Costs do not matter. Suffering is not counted. The Plan's the thing. The official must be able to report to Moscow or Rostov or Kiev that he has carried out the Plan. How he carried it out, whether national economy will benefit, whether quality has not been sacrificed to quantity, whether part of the grain delivered to the state will not have to be returned to the peasants for next year's seed—all this does not matter. He needs paper results—because headquarters demand a telegram in which he announces those paper results. Officials frequently act against their better judgment. But what can they do when the Plan seizes them by the shoulder and points a cold, implacable finger towards the eternal goal —Fulfilment. If the Soviet official, especially the Communist, knows anything, it is discipline and obedience. Discipline is excellent—when it is not too rigid. Moscow, for the best reasons, is insisting on Fall fallow planting. This measure increases the yield per hectare. There are regions, however, where soil and climatic conditions make Fall fallow planting injurious. Yet some officials are afraid not to obey universal instructions.

This stiffness of officialism in the U.S.S.R., the disinclination to accept responsibility, "passing the buck," the race for percentages of Plan fulfilment, the worship of the letter of an order lest punishment overtake one who ventures to deviate from written instructions—this is what Russians call "bureaucracy." The press criticizes it, ridicules it; the party persecutes it. Yet it remains. For bureaucracy is an inevitable concomitant of the centralization of authority, and of the lack of culture and material goods. If it had not been for Moscow's stubborn insistence, the Soviet village would not have deepened its plowing, cleaned its seed, introduced Fall and Spring fallow, cultivated, irrigated, planted new cultures, built schools, piggeries, cow stables and bathhouses, etc., etc. The Bolsheviks had to take the burly mujhik and shake him out of his century-old hibernation. They had to rid him of his pessimism and disbelief in progress and in better conditions. They had to destroy that terrible, most-Russian of all Russian words: "Nichevo," or "never mind, it doesn't matter anyway." For these purposes, the bureaucracy had to be sent into the villages. The peasantry, on its own, would never have turned to collectivization and the new life.

The peasantry, however, did not like the new, and the bureaucrats did not know how to make it palatable. Peasants and officials lacked culture. Bureaucratic officials often found it easier to achieve by force what they could just as well achieve by persuasion. These are vestiges of the days of Military Communism (1918–21) when the bayonet ruled the village.

The Politotdel has introduced officials with culture and understanding—though exceptions, of course, are numerous. Now the lack of goods still hampers the smooth relationship between peasant and government. The collective farmer has been shown the road towards modern, productive farming. He has been dragged and pushed forward on that road. He would now move ahead without much prodding if sufficient incentive existed in the form of consumption goods. But the city, with all its factory-building and increased output, is not yet in a position to pay the peasant in full for his crop.

That is today the Soviet Union's major problem. The country needs a fair commercial exchange of commodities between city and village. In the kingdom of Jonescu I saw bicycles, gramophones, tractors, city furniture, city clothes, factory shoes, iron beds. These are newcomers. But the factories are not yet manufacturing a sufficient quantity of these and other articles. The peasant, accordingly, has no incentive to sell his crop, especially since the scarcity of commodities raises their price. The collective farmer must pay an excessive quantity of grain for shoes or under-wear or kerosene. He therefore has little stimulus to market his produce. Since the government, however, must feed the cities it must extract the peasants' grain by other than commercial methods. The method of extraction consists in levying high taxes and putting pressure on the village to sell at low prices. This evil will remain until Russia has more consumers goods. This evil makes the official unpopular. The official would like to be popular, and he would prefer to disregard or forget the central government's orders. Hence the rigid discipline; hence the need of blind obedience.

When the supply of goods equals the rising demand for goods, the Bolsheviks will be able to discard the mailed fist. Then the Politotdel will disappear. Meanwhile, the Moscow Commissariat of Agriculture, shrewdly, pays the salaries and expenses of Jonescu's department.

Jonescu sends one of his assistants, the Communist organizer who is also an agronomist, to take me about the countryside. The land lies flat—broad steppe or prairie, much like the American Midwest. I visit several villages. I enter a few homes in one village. The houses are made of clay mixed with chopped straw. They are regularly white-washed inside and out. I stop along "Main Street" and visit a family. The hut is an oblong divided into three rooms. In the first, the man and wife sleep and eat; in the second, the children sleep and grain is stored; the third room, during Winter time, is used as a pigsty. The floor is the natural ground. In the "parlor," high up and touching the ceiling, across a corner formed by two walls, hangs a gilded ikon.

"Do you believe in God?" I ask the lady of the house.

"I almost don't believe in God," she says literally. She never goes to church. Her husband wants her to remove the ikon, but she thinks it might as well remain there. "It doesn't bother anyone."

This family, like all others, receives compensation from the collective for the husband's and wife's labor days on the fields. But in addition, it owns private property from which it receives all the benefits: one cow, two pigs, twelve chickens and a sheep. It also has the use of one hectare of land around the house for vegetable gardening. The Soviet kolkhoz or collective, accordingly, is now a bastard form of economy: it is chiefly socialistic, but partly capitalistic. The Bolsheviks countenance the private section for a simple realistic reason: it raises production and helps to solve the problem of food. But its years are numbered.

The mechanization of agriculture proceeds apace. The village enjoyed the help of 21 tractors during the plowing season; that was seven more than last year. The Politotdel lent it a combine for one day during the ingathering period. It threshes with electricity; huge electric search-lights have been set up near the threshing board so that threshing can be continued through the night. The Politotdel has promised this village two motor trucks for next year—if it fulfils the Plan for next year's sowing. This suggests the methods that will be applied by Soviet village officials in the future: kid glove and gold in place of steel. Machines to replace men. Voluntary exertion in lieu of superimposed organization.

The extent to which the needs of the Soviet peasantry are satisfied is an economic matter. But the peasant mood which results from non-satisfaction or partial satisfaction is a political matter of tremendous importance in view of the war menace. The Bolsheviks have exaggerated this menace ever since 1927. Undoubtedly, however, it exists, and the Bolsheviks would be fools not to prepare for an emergency. They have a powerful army with mechanized equipment produced in factories built during the Five Year Plan, and they have a large, efficient air force. Military defense, nevertheless, is not only a question of for-tresses, cannons, tanks, and aeroplanes. In a modern war, the rear is almost as important as the front. Without a con-tented civilian population it is impossible to conduct suc-cessful military operations. And the Soviet government, in preparing for a war which may not come soon, must ask itself: Shall we strengthen the front or shall we strengthen the rear? By strengthening the rear one strengthens the front. But the strengthening of the front does not always strengthen the rear. At times, on the contrary, it weakens the rear, for the money and materials and men that are devoted to military purposes could produce shoes, houses, suits, furniture, etc., to raise the spirits of the population. Just now, I believe, too much energy and wealth is being consumed by activities for the front. The inadequate Soviet transportation system too is overburdened by these activities, and therefore goods which are available for peasant consumption occasionally cannot reach their destination.

If a war were imminent, if it threatened within three or four months, preparations for the front would, of course, take precedence. But the Soviet foreign political position has improved in recent years, and the capitalist Powers are too divided among themselves to form a constellation which might effectively attack the U.S.S.R. Moscow must be ready for any eventuality; that is the first law of every state. But for the moment, at least, no national interest would suffer if a larger proportion of the limited resources of the state were placed at the disposal of the peasants and workers. Indeed, national interests would be served.

I go back to talk to Jonescu.

"Of course, the costs have been very heavy," he replies. "But do you realize what the socialization of agriculture means? The world is too near collectivization to see its significance. This is the first change in agriculture since the serf became a peasant. Now we are transforming the peasant into a collectivist. The nearest parallel is the industrial revolution of the West which converted the artisan into a factory laborer. We are staging the agricultural revolution which the rest of the world will have to imitate. For the peasant or farmer to own his own land or his own plow is as anachronistic as would be the private ownership by each worker of the lathe or motor which he operates. Agriculture everywhere else is still in the Middle Ages. The Bolsheviks have made the first long step towards the modern, scientific organization of farming."

From Rostov, the main line to the Lower Caucasus runs south and east through prairies bounded by hills and mountains. And so from Rostov-on-the-Don to the Mineralni Vodi junction point: "mineralni" means mineral, "vodi" means waters.

Chapter XVII

THE CRADLE OF THE WHITE RACE

From Mineral Waters a broad-gauge railway twists slowly up the mountain stopping to unload stomach and liver invalids at Essentuki, women with female disorders at Zheleznovodsk, rheumatics at Pyatigorsk, and heart sufferers at Kislovodsk or Sour Waters. This is Russia's natural hospital, once the playground of the wealthy. Hot curative liquids bubble under the hills and mountains.

I am en route to Kislovodsk. A young man sits opposite in the train. He has green piercing eyes and "Arrow Collar" features: curled lashes, eyebrows as if painted on, a long head, delicate long nose, sharp angles in his lips, angular chin, a marked angle where jaw meets cheek bone. Red-tinted cheek contrasts with bluish jaw. On his head is a flat karakul cap with sides sloping outward. He rises to alight. He wears a thin, pressed-woolen tunic from neck to knee. Broad shoulders, and very narrow waist held firm by a narrow leather belt from which hangs a silver-tipped dagger scabbard. The dimensions of the chest are exaggerated by two breast-pockets with cigar-like partitions containing wooden silver-headed pegs which now substitute for the real ammunition of Czarist days. These Caucasians walk on their toes, lightly, like ballet dancers. But the real delight comes in seeing them ride. They were born in saddles. Many have certainly died in saddles. In cool seasons, they wear huge black fleece capes which hang from the square, pointed shoulders down to the animal's hind quarters. When the rider races over the fields the cape flies in the air, his white neckscarf flaps in the wind, and horse and man together look like a creature from another world.

This and the territory to the south is said to be the cradle of the white race. Hence the name Caucasus. Pyatigorsk is the capital of the North Caucasian region. The North Caucasus united Russians, Kabardinians, Balkarians, North Ossetians, Dagestanians, Chechenchi, Ingushi, Karachi, and many still smaller races. Where the cradle stood is now Babel. The mountainous character of the terrain has conduced to the evolution of distinguishing ethnic traits. Sometimes a race is limited to one single village. The next village is inhabited by a different national unit. Several years ago, not far from here, scientists discovered a pass in the mountains inhabited by a people which was ruled by its women—a matriarchate. Among the Cherkessi—a warlike, horse-riding race of this region—women are not allowed to milk cows or wait on tables. Their touch, apparently, contaminates food. The men monopolize the light chores while their wives reap and thresh. The collectives have been trying to break this ancient tradition, with only scant success.

It is no simple task to rule almost two hundred races with varying pasts, varying cultures and varying notions of a good future. The Soviets have undertaken not merely to rule them but to remake them. The task would be impossible without a large measure of freedom and self-determination. But it would be equally impossible without considerable centralized dictation.

Kislovodsk, its chief physician told me, "is the biggest health resort in the world"—another proof of the Soviet obsession with bigness. On the hills around the bowl which is Kislovodsk one can see sixteen sanatoria in the process of construction. They will contain 2,455 beds. One of them, with accommodations for 200 patients, is being erected by Intourist for foreigners. In all the preceding years of the revolution only five new sanatoria were built for 930 patients. But other, pre-war sanatoria have been enlarged, and the private villas of millionaires which formerly accommodated one family have been transformed into *pensions* so that Kislovodsk, which prior to the revolution treated only five or six thousand heart-sufferers a year, took care of 89,198 in 1933 and 103,000 in 1934. This result was achieved, in part, by intense crowding and, moreover, by extending the cure season over the entire year. Before the revolution, Kislovodsk was chiefly a pleasure resort and "Nachkur" during the four summer months.

Soviet citizens on vacation. The fact that the men here do not have to attend meetings, answer telephone calls, weave and cut red tape, bear responsibilities and take care of their daily needs is alone enough to heal weak hearts and sick nerves. Alone the fact that the women have no queues to stand in and no material concerns should make them strong and healthy. Some people pay a small sum, many pay nothing—and the sanatoria supply them with their food, physicians' care, clothing (if they want it), entertainment, everything.

The atmosphere is restful. No air of sickness hangs over the town. It is just a place for happiness and relaxation, and, naturally, of health repair.

The curative elixir is Narzan which, in an ancient tongue, means "Giant Water." We have drunk it from bottles these many years. Here the sick bathe in it. In the sanatoria, however, all maladies are treated. The patient regularly immerses himself in heated Narzan for the sake of his heart, but at the same time these busy Soviet citizens eagerly seize the opportunity to go through intensive cures for everything else that ails them.

About half of the Kislovodsk patients are ordinary workingmen. The others are government clerks, scientists, army commanders, high state officials, writers, engineers, etc. The workers and the majority of the remainder could never have dreamed before the revolution of spending at least four, and sometimes six, weeks restoring their health in an expensive spa. But I believe the ruling proletariat is yielding ground at Kislovodsk to a competitor: of the sixteen new sanatoria going up at the resort, almost all are being built by government offices like the State Bank, the Commissariat of Heavy Industry, the Commissariat of Posts and Telegraphs, the "Pravda," the Commissariat of War, the Commissariat of Agriculture, etc. All these employ workers too, but my guess is that officials will find easier access to the beds and Narzan baths than the workingmen. The pen-pusher and engineer are pushing out the lathe tender. In their defense, the officials might submit that it is harder on the heart to work in a Soviet office than to work in a coal mine. A Russian journalist was once given the assignment of describing an insane asylum. He got the address wrong and walked into a commissariat. Neither he nor his editor noted the mistake, and psychiatrists were very much interested in his data. . . .

Karmashov, a gold mining engineer from Siberia who is taking the cure at Kislovodsk, tells me that South Africa's gold output is falling, the Soviet Union's rising, and in five years Russia will be the world's first producer of the yellow metal. Every year new deposits are being uncovered. The engineer sojourned two years in the United States studying American methods. . . . The Commissariat of Heavy Industry has a construction department which supervises the building of new plants. In 1934, one of the department's chiefs tells me, it spent one billion two hundred million rubles. It could not invest the remaining three hundred million of its budget because of transportation difficulties. . . . An Armenian directs a new synthetic rubber factory at Kazan on the Volga. It yields 25,000 tons of rubber a year. It has planted thousands of acres of potatoes for the purpose; potatoes make good rubber tires. The Volga is becoming an automobile republic. Yaroslav on the Volga produces five-tone trucks and rubber; Nizhni Novgorod, passenger cars and small trucks: Kazan, rubber; Saratov is constructing an automobile factory; Stalingrad manufactures tractors and steel. The Volga is deep in the heart of Russia and cannot easily be reached by an invader. It is on a direct line to Siberia where a war may have to be fought against Japanese aggression. And it is being connected with Moscow: three sufficient explanations for the choice of the Volga district. But why cannot the entire automotive industry be concentrated in one city?

An Armenian escaped from the Turkish city of Van in 1915 at the age of eleven. He walked to Tiflis; was the only member of his family left alive after the Turkish massacres. He walked two weeks. Part of the territory was in the war zone. He could not speak a word of Russian. He arrived footsore, sick and hungry. Now he edits a Soviet agricultural magazine and the Soviet agricultural year book—in Russian. . . . A prominent engineer—I met many of them in my six days at Kislovodsk—who drafted the plans for the new freight car plant at Tagil, in the Urals. It has an annual capacity of 64,000 cars, and has already started to produce. The engineer states that the Tagil enterprise is one of the largest of its kind in the world. . . . A woman,

chief judge of a Moscow district. Thirty-four years old. At
ten she became an orphan. Served as a nurse maid. Then
became a seamstress's apprentice. Never slept in a bed.
Spoke only Yiddish. When the revolution broke out, she
went to the Civil War front. Learned Russian in the
trenches; became interested in law. Became a clerk to a
field tribunal. With the advent of peace, she was sent to a
high school and, later, to the law school. Served as judge
in Kharkov. Promoted to Moscow last year. Very handsome young woman. Long-standing member of the Communist party. . . . Sergo Ordjonikidze is also taking a cure
at Kislovodsk. Architects showed him the plans for his commissariat's sanatorium here. He asked what sort of accommodations were being provided. "Every patient will have
his own room," was the proud answer. Sergo objected. A
man on vacation should have his wife with him. And his
children. He immediately ordered all the plans changed
accordingly. Two and three room apartments will now be
built. In that case, some one suggested, there should be a
kindergarten. No, Sergo again objected. Parents on vacation, parents who are so busy all year around, will not want
to give up their children for a whole day.

The best sanatorium in Kislovodsk belongs to the G.P.U.,
now converted, with narrowed prerogatives, into the Commissariat of Internal Affairs. The former G.P.U. also has
the best office building in Moscow, and in Leningrad, and
in Kharkov, and in other cities. Its employees buy in the
best coöperatives. It tries to supply them with comfortable
apartments. It is an efficient organization, probably the most
efficient Soviet organization. The majority of its staff are
devoted, self-sacrificing comrades who never spare themselves when on duty. The G.P.U. and its predecessor, the
Cheka, have invaluable services to their credit: but for

them the revolution might have been crushed. They destroyed the hidden enemy while the Red Army mowed down the foe in the field. Subsequently, however, the G.P.U. committed many errors and subjected the Soviet government to no end of embarrassment with foreign countries. It exceeded its authority on numerous occasions, and its zeal was often greater than its discrimination—especially in relation to engineers and other intellectuals during 1929, 1930 and 1931. There were then so many arrests on little or no ground that the population ceased to regard incarceration by the G.P.U. as a disgrace. It was more often a mistake than a disgrace. Beginning with 1931, Stalin gradually and delicately clipped centimeter after centimeter from the wings of the G.P.U. until today it is shorn of the absolute power it once possessed. Nevertheless, its privileged position, as incorporated in its buildings, is still an eye-sore.

Apropos the Red terror of the Cheka and G.P.U., Lincoln Steffens tells this story. In 1919, President Woodrow Wilson sent William C. Bullitt, later U.S. ambassador to the Soviet Union, and Lincoln Steffens, the talented American author, to discuss peace terms with Lenin. The delegates met Lenin in the Kremlin. Having talked about many subjects, one of them said: "And the world would like to know when the Red Terror will end." Lenin wheeled around in his chair, screwed up his narrow Tartar eyes, and pointing a finger, exclaimed: "Who wants to know? The men who sent millions to death in the trenches, the statesmen who bartered populations and territories as though they were fish and cabbages, the diplomats and generals who sowed havoc and destruction throughout the world?"

"Beregis," "Look Out," "Look Out" yell the drivers as their three-horse "Troikas" rush through the narrow streets. The Moscow merchant almost fills the carriage completely. In the morning he took the regulation Narzan bath. Tonight he is feasting on borscht and roast beef. Wine and champagne flow. Friends have arrived from Pyatigorsk. There is a cabaret program in the rich restaurant. Half-dressed girls sing and dance. Later they come and sit at his table. The Moscow merchant orders the entire menu. A Moscow merchant was never known to economize. Finally, heavy with food and drink, he is helped into his broadcloth coat, he is helped into the cab. The bells jingle in the misty night. At three a.m. he reaches his bed. In the morning he will take another Narzan bath to cure his heart. That was the Kislovodsk of merchant, officer, and land owner.

The carriages have disappeared entirely. No horse-back riding. Walking into the hills along carefully graded and charted pathways is part of the cure prescribed by the physicians. Each sanatorium has its curfew. Gymnastics at 6.30 a.m. Strict diet. Sensible living. Self-staged entertainment in the form of little acts, cinema, dancing, an occasional lecture. Much reading on park benches. But no knitting.

From Kislovodsk to Pyatigorsk is an hour by train, and then, in an open Soviet "Ford" or Gaz, through a dark night, through the mist and cold that blew down from Elbrus, Europe's highest mountain peak, over a flat plateau 90 kilometers wide dotted by completely unilluminated villages, with an occasional wild goat and owl as the only signs of life, southward, to Nalchik. The three-and-a-half-hour ride froze our ears and stiffened our toes.

Karmashov, the gold mining engineer, and a colleague who works for the Ural platinum and gold mining trust had come along. Gold is now being mined in the Kabardino-Balkarian autonomous territory of which Nalchik is the proud little capital. The doctor at Kislovodsk had warned Karmashov and Noskov not to interrupt their cures. They had gone despite his orders. It was not work, nor was it pleasure that drew them to Nalchik. The local director of gold mining operations would take them up into the hills. They were experienced and could give him valuable advice. The service would of course be unpaid. They, in fact, paid their own expenses.

Two gold miners arrive to meet a third—in the Klondike, let us say. The third is afraid. What are they up to? Do they wish to dispute his claim? Or get rid of him by foul trickery. His mouth is closed. Perhaps his finger is on his trigger. But in Nalchik that night three comrades sat down over roast goose and vodka to discuss freely how to carry out the gold production plan sent from Moscow to Kabardino-Balkaria. Yet it was interesting that though the gold would not be their own they had the "gold fever" nevertheless.

Nalchik is inadequately supplied with electric light. I had no impression, therefore, of the city or its setting. When I awoke in the morning and looked through the window, I might have been in the stalls of a theater. For the view seemed almost unreal. A semi-circular paved square —the stage—and behind it, the backdrop: an immense park, filled with bright flower beds, short firs and young elms, stretching far off and curling up gradually into wooded hills on the wings; directly in front but furthest away— high, snow-covered mountains sparkling in the early sun. Soon the skies became overcast and the distant range faded out of the picture. The air was soft and warm. I strolled through the spacious park. A stadium is hidden in it. Boys of thirteen and fourteen wearing the regulation red

"Pioneer" or scout tie were playing soccer. Most of them had removed their shoes. Some had on one shoe for kicking. They were tall and lithe, and full of mischief. They talked Russian as well as tongues that were unintelligible to me. When the game broke up, I accosted a small group of boys with text books under their arms. The books were in Russian. Were the boys Kabardinians? No. Then Balkarians? No, they were Kumiks from near Mozdok in the direction of the Caspian and Dagestan. Kumiks constitute only one half per cent of the population of Kabardino-Balkaria. These youngsters were from the distant mountains. They attended a secondary school in Nalchik because their own villages had none, and they lived in the school's dormitory. I had never before heard of the Kumik race.

They spoke Kumik among themselves. But they needed Russian for contact with the Kabardinians and Balkarians. The Kabardinians needed Russian for contact with the Balkarians. And so on. The Kumik boys told me they were glad to study in Russian because that opened wider horizons to them. They could work anywhere in the Soviet Union. Russian literature would be accessible to them.

A pleasant column of smiling, singing, round-faced nursery children passed. The young woman teacher could scarcely keep up with them. They babbled in Russian. "Are they Russian kids?" I asked. "No," she replied, and ran on.

In the big restaurant of the brand-new, stone hotel. A graceful Kabardinian girl in pink silk dress down to her high heels, holding her long, fur-collared coat tightly around her with one arm and a vanity case under the other. No headdress. She looks to all the world as if she would step into a limousine the next moment and ride to the opera. But she was only standing in a queue trying to pay for her breakfast steak.

Kabardino-Balkaria has a population of 250,000. There are 150,000 Kabardinians in it—and in the world; 37,000 Balkarians, 39,000 Russians, some Germans, some Ossetians, some mountain Jews, some Kumiks. Ethnographers declare that the Kabardinians are related to the Basques of Spain, that the Basques originally came from the Caucasus, and that the Kabardinians stood near the cradle of the white race. Some of the races in this region are partly Tartar; most are Moslem in faith. They speak with the Arabic guttural intonation, and until the Bolsheviks Latinized it, their script too was Arabic.

I met the director of the Lenin Study Town of Nalchik, a Kabardinian educated in Moscow. The 1,140 pupils of the "Town" range from the ages of sixteen to fifty. Some have had only three or four years of preparatory schooling. The courses last three years. The "Town" might be called a high school for adults. But it must serve the purposes of a university and normal school. It consists of several institutes: a Pedagogical Institute with 450 students, of whom forty-five per cent are women, which trains teachers; a Medical Technicum with 160 pupils, of whom eighty-seven per cent are women, which graduates nurses and physicians' assistants; a Soviet and Party Political School which turns out party propagandists, secretaries of village soviets, etc. (120 students); and an Agricultural Institute with 220 pupils which prepares agricultural experts. Fifty per cent of the enrollment is Kabardinian, and twenty-five per cent Balkarian. All the seventy-four instructors are university graduates. Seventy of them are Russians. Russian is the language of instruction.

The "Town" is overcrowded and operates in two shifts. I went from room to room. A biology laboratory with

A Kabardinian Peasant

mounted specimens of the birds of the region including one
large eagle. A class of twelve, with two women, studying
soil structure; the teacher was explaining some elementary
questions in chemistry; the large glass cases all around the
room contained test tubes, microscopes and physics equipment. A class in practical agriculture: the German-Russian
instructor was explaining plowing methods; nineteen students, three of them women; several pupils were gray-
haired; the cases are full of regional plants; all the pupils
have had long experience in farming. An empty zoological
laboratory with lantern slide fixture. A geography class:
many big maps on the walls; several old men; all the pupils
have geography text books on their desks; they speak Russian poorly; their lesson covers conditions in the Antarctic
—seventh grade material. A class in Russian grammar; excellent woman teacher.

Then I entered an economic class. This is what I had
been waiting for. There were eighteen persons in the class
of whom three were women. All the men were dressed in
blouses, breeches and boots; the women in waists and skirts.
They had all obviously had a difficult time in life; all had
worked hard at crude outdoor tasks. The lesson was in the
theory of surplus value. After listening for a while, I whis-
pered into the teacher's ear; he sat down with the director
of the "Town" at the rear of the room and I stepped in
front of the class. I told them I had come from the capitalist
world which they wished to destroy and wanted to ask
them some questions. All sat up eagerly.

"Tell me," I demanded, "what is capitalism?"

Several raised their hands. I called on a man of about
twenty-five.

"Under capitalism," he replied, "the working class has

no freedom. The workers have only their hands. They sell their labor. But the capitalist owns the machines, the machinery of production, and exploits labor."

"Do you think any workers live well under capitalism?" I now asked.

Many were ready with answers. I pointed to one young man with a heavy-featured face. Later I asked him some personal questions. Until 1927, he had not known anything about the Soviet system. He had worked in a village for a kulak. Then a Komsomol propagandist talked to him and made him understand a few things. He went into the Red Army for two years and learned to read and write. Except for that he had never had any schooling. Now he was going through a two year course.

"No," he said with conviction, "capitalists and kulaks never allow workers to live well."

I pointed to another young man. "The aristocracy of labor," he said, "lives well in capitalist countries. But the masses suffer."

A young woman demanded the floor. "The capitalists," she felt, "divide the working class against itself by giving good conditions to one part and bad conditions to the other part. Capitalist thus seeks to prevent proletarian solidarity."

"Does it make any difference to those who work," I asked, "that some workers are unemployed?"

The best pupil in the class, a Russian, answered: "Unemployment enables the capitalists to reduce wages. The unemployed press on the labor market and depress the incomes of the employed. The capitalists see to it that there is always some unemployment. They build their factories where labor is cheap."

"And don't you think that the capitalists want the workers to live well?"

A loud chorus of "No's."

I went to the blackboard. A group of factory owners produce 100 automobiles, 100 suits, 100 pairs of shoes, etc. "The workers constitute part of their market," I stated. "If those commodities cannot be sold the capitalist suffers. He is left with goods on his hands. The capitalist class, therefore, is interested in raising the standard of living of the workers."

The class eyed my diagram suspiciously. Soon the objections came thick and fast. "In other words, the capitalist always thinks first of himself. The workers' conditions are a by-product. In the Soviet Union, our interests are first." "In reality, each capitalist wants the other capitalist to raise the standard of living. A wants his competitor B to pay higher wages so that he, A, can earn bigger profits." "Profits always mount more quickly than wages." "In times of crisis, there are no wages but the exploiters still receive their dividends." The teacher took a hand. He quoted Lenin to the effect that though the absolute status of the proletariat might improve, its relative participation in the national income continues to fall as capitalism develops. In judging the affairs of the working class, he added, one must not look at those who work. What are the wages of the entire working class, employed and unemployed? What are the wages of the working class not in any given year but over a period of years covering a cycle of prosperity and depression?

The bell had rung ten minutes ago. I was detaining the class. I nevertheless asked some questions about themselves. They were all from villages. Each received a scholarship of 250 rubles a month from the government. They lived in the "Town's" dormitory. Lodging cost them 22 rubles a month, food 50 rubles a month. Text and copy books free.

All sent money home to their families. They regretted that the course lasted only two years. This was their first opportunity, since earliest childhood, to study and broaden their horizons.

One point stood out after this experience: those pupils were sure that capitalism was rotten, cruel and bad. They were equally sure that their life was an improvement on capitalism.

Kabardino-Balkaria is 10,000 square kilometers in extent —a small state made still smaller by its untillable mountains. South, Kabardino-Balkaria is cut off by very high ranges behind which live the Swanns, until recently inaccessible. The people of Swannetia would, when driven by hunger, brave the perilous passes to buy bread from the Balkarians. Swannetia was a country without roads, and it had no roads because it had no wheels. It had not reached the wheel-stage of civilization. The Swanns saw aeroplanes fly over them before they saw wheels. Now Tiflis, from which Swannetia is governed, has hewn highways into that wild territory and sent vehicles into it. Nalchik proposes to follow the lead of Tiflis. . . . North, the country of the Kabardinians and Balkarians abuts on the Mineral Water region. Afraid lest these races, embittered by poverty, raid the spas or cut the main railway line to the Caucasus, the Czarist regime resorted to its time-honored policy: it planted armed Cossack farmers across the hypothetic path of the discontented. That was shortly after the liberation of the Russian serfs in the sixties of the preceding century. Gradually, the Cossacks pushed the Kabardinians and Balkarians towards the mountains and even into the inhospitable mountains. In 1912, the Kabardinians and Balkarians revolted against this pressure. Betal Kalmikov, now the Communist leader of Kabardino-Balkaria, then a boy of eighteen, received his first revolutionary baptism in that explosion of popular resentment. The revolt succeeded in relieving the pressure somewhat, but the land hunger remained. The Bolshevik regime took 250,000 acres of arable soil from the landlords and princes of Kabardino-Balkaria, and subdivided them among the peasants. It took, further, some 350,000 acres of pasture land and placed them at the disposal of the villages. The estate owners and the nobles were expelled. The bulk of the Cossacks was not molested, and only the kulaks among them—five per cent was the estimate given me—were exiled to colder climes when they resisted collectivization.

Kabardino-Balkaria is 98.8 per cent collectivized. This is a record; for all practical purposes its agriculture has been completely socialized. I went to see the socialist village of Kendje, not far from Nalchik.

Kendje used to be called Koshorokov. Koshorokov was one of the three big landlords of the present Kendje. On a bluff overlooking the village, a school building is nearing completion. Two stories high, pure white, fashioned firmly of stone, with many windows, it is a prominent feature on the horizon. It has eleven big class rooms, an assembly hall, work shops, restaurant, kitchen and office. On the front wall of each class room, workingmen were plastering a small area with a mixture of cement and soot. This will serve instead of a slate blackboard. Slate is unavailable. The school will give a ten-year course. It will combine, in other words, primary, secondary and junior high schools. Nalchik is paying seventy per cent of the cost of construction; the village pays the remainder in the form of labor and means of transportation.

The school building is a pleasant introduction to a good

collective. I cross the almost-dry, pebble-covered bed of the Kendje, and climb up a bank into the village. Kabardinians dressed in woolen suits and wearing broad, round-rimmed, brown hats of pressed felt are standing on ox-drawn basket carts made of plaited twigs an inch thick, and pouring baskets of corn ears into enclosures. These enclosures are likewise made of twisted twigs. They are about a meter deep, two and a half meters high, ten meters long and stand on foundations of stone. When these primitive harvest bins are filled, they are covered with straw. Next spring they will be opened and their contents used for seed and food. But the collective had built several such enclosures of boards, and roofed them with removable red clay tiles. These new structures afford better protection against the weather.

The harvest bins represent two sides of a square. On a third side are new, well-ordered barns. In one I saw tanks of honey—from the collective's 250 beehives; in another, large compartments filled with wheat, oats, barley, buckwheat and sunflower. (After three days' assiduous cracking and spitting, my overcoat pocket still yields some sunflower seeds.) I had never seen such accumulated plenty in a Soviet village. A whole cellar filled with barrels of evil-smelling fermenting cheese. Piles of wool. All for the collectivized peasants.

The kolhoz office is situated in the same square. In the office all placards and signs are in Russian. The bookkeeper, a Russian, gives me figures—striking figures: Kendje includes 312 families counting 1,558 individuals (five in a family) of whom 723 work on the fields. This is a good proportion and one expects better conditions. Only six members of the kolhoz are employed in industry outside of it. Three hundred and forty of the field hands are women. Since there are 312 families and 723 laborers, each family has almost two and a half workers to two and a half non-workers—a favorable ratio in the Soviet village.

Kendje owns 1,812 hectares of land. It is increasing its holdings by reclaiming uplands overgrown with brush. In 1934, 134 hectares of such virgin soil yielded their first crop. The kolhoz grows berries, hay, apples and pears (tremendous ones; they gave me a load-full to take home), wheat, oats, buckwheat, barley, beans, corn for eating, corn for silos, sunflower, potatoes, tomatoes, cabbage, carrots, onions, beets, cucumbers, watermelon, pumpkin and gourds. This is a rich, many-sided economy, much more so than one encounters in most Ukrainian collectives.

The Kendje collective has 3,907 animals: 576 horses of which 402 work, 57 oxen, 183 cows, many calfs, 1,139 sheep, goats, rams, etc. No tractors. It scarcely needs them.

Kendje has already paid its taxes to the state; is now laying in its seed supply for next spring; has planted its winter crops; has created a special reserve for communal feeding out on the fields in the coming planting and harvesting seasons—and has commenced to compensate its members for their work during the past year. On the average, each laborer worked 135 days during 1934. This means that the average family has 330 labor-days to its credit. Having divided the balance of the harvest among the total number of labor-days of the kolhoz, the management knows what it must pay for each labor-day. An average family receives for its efforts during the year:

6,660 kilograms of corn (about six and a half long tons),
   1 metric ton of wheat,
264 kilograms of buckwheat,
 36 kilograms of beans,
474 kilograms of sunflower seeds,
 14 kilograms of honey,

  725 kilograms of hay,
  330 kilograms of straw,
and cheese, and wool, and vegetables, and fruit, and berries.

"When will you distribute all this?" I asked the chairman of the kolhoz who had meanwhile come in from the fields.

"We have already distributed most of it."

"You mean that the peasants have already come and taken these commodities away?" I persisted.

He smiled. "We delivered it to their homes," he declared.

I went to the homes to confirm this information.

On my way, I meet a teacher of the village school. He is a Russian. The school has eleven teachers of whom three are Russian. Except in the class on the history of Kabardino-Balkaria, the language of instruction is Russian. The parents and pupils demanded Russian, and the teachers must attempt, vainly, to restrain this desire. They are now beginning to teach Russian in the first grade. "In schools where Russian is used," the teacher tells me, "the children behave better." Later I encountered a young woman who taught in a school at the stone quarry nearby. She was married to a Kabardinian Komsomol. "If you have a child," I asked, after ascertaining that they had none, "what will it be?"

"Russian, of course."

Two fierce mountain dogs bar the way. An old woman quiets them, and I enter her stone, one-story house. She is Chaba Bekulova, age sixty-one. Her husband, she recalls, stole her from her father's house when she was eighteen, and married her. The poor, who could not buy wives, simply stole them. Such abductions were common in Russia in Moslem regions and elsewhere too. "For two years thereafter," she continues, "I was never allowed to leave my room, for my relatives lay in wait for me. Food was brought to me. I was practically a prisoner and a slave. Twelve years later, my husband was stabbed in the woods up there in the mountains. Probably my brothers did that."

I wondered how a person bred in such a primitive society reacted to the collective. "When they started talking about the new life," she said, "I was afraid and did not permit my children to join. We old ones thought that the new life was only for the young, that our children would desert us and we would starve."

"And how has it been in fact?"

"We all work together, young and old. Betal (Kalmikov) honors us, and our children have come to respect us more for that reason. The old men are 'inspectors of quality.' They give advice on how to care for the horses and live-stock. I always awake early," she said. "In the beginning when the kolhoz was organized, my two sons refused to rise when I woke them. Now I rouse them at the break of the day and they jump up immediately. We all work to-gether because we are living better."

I looked around. "What have you bought this year?" I inquired.

She pointed to the flannel dress she wore. Then she showed me some large tin pots and pans in the kitchen. There was a loudspeaker in the living room. She lifted the bed covers; they had recently acquired two mattresses. "We could buy much more," she added, "but the coöperative is not well supplied." The family owned a cow and a calf which I saw, three pigs, several turkeys, and some poultry. In the barnyard stood a twisted-twig enclosure bursting with corn.

"Did you get any honey?"

"Yes."

"How much?"

"Oh," she remarked, "they brought us a canful. I don't know how much was in it."

I next visited the Kazanshev family. The woman at home did not speak Russian. She had a child of four, a child of two, and a child six months old which already sat up, and was sitting, half naked, on the stone floor. "Why do you have so many babies?" I asked through the agronomist who accompanied me.

He translated, and she blushed beet-red and hid her face in her hands. Her old toothless mother had meanwhile come in from the neighboring house. "Why," the mother said, "that is what she exists for."

I had seen the usual corn enclosure in the yard of this family too. "Yes," the young woman said, "we have received three carts already." A chest in the living room was filled with wheat. The agronomist estimated that it contained 18 poods,—about 650 pounds. They had also received honey, fruit, sunflower seeds, etc. I saw three large sacks of sunflower seed. There was buckwheat in a bin. The family owned two cows, sixteen chickens. It had milk and butter for its own purposes and some surplus which was sold in Nalchik.

The mother did not know how old she was, but she had been living in Kendje for fifty years, she declared.

How did the new compare with the old?

"Formerly we served the princes and landlords. They took away the land which my father once owned. We had practically no pasture land. Now that the landlords are gone we are freer." She believed in God, had a radio, and thought there must be some connection between the two. But the fact that the radio sometimes told her not to believe in God puzzled her. Before the revolution, the family had owned two desyatins (approximately five and a half acres) of land; it had received an additional desyatin and a half when the landlord was dispossessed. But they could not work it. They had no equipment and few animals. "If collectivization had been postponed," she stated, "we should have perished." She was illiterate. "Tell Betal we would like to have electricity," was her parting request.

No inspection of a Soviet village is complete without a visit to the coöperative store. Prices were very high, and goods therefore lay on the shelves. This is a strange and new phenomenon in the Soviet Union. The Bolsheviks had raised prices because goods were scarce. But the prices were so high that the scarce goods were not being bought. The high prices were calculated to force the peasant to deliver larger quantities of his grain in exchange for the manufactured commodities. But the Bolsheviks had overreached themselves and defeated their purpose; the peasant was keeping his grain.

A new system of coöperative selling had been introduced: articles were sold only to the buyer who paid part of the price in kind. Thus, five liters of kerosene cost 3 rubles 30 kopeks. The collectivist paid half of this in cash (and he could get the cash by disposing of his dairy products on the free, open market); the other half, or 1 ruble 65 kopeks he paid in corn at the rate of 55 kopeks a pood (36 pounds). In other words, 5 litres of kerosene for his lamps cost him 1 ruble 65 kopeks and three poods of corn, which was exorbitant. Kerosene was typical for other commodities: sugar, for instance, sold at 4 rubles a kilogram, of which 3 rubles 20 kopeks was in money and the rest in grain—about a pood and a half of corn.

I would talk about these matters to Betal Kalmikov, the Communist chief of Kabardino-Balkaria, one of the most striking personalities in the Soviet Union.

Nalchik is the bud of a socialist city. Before the revolution it was a small town or a large village with a population of 8,000. Now, 40,000. It is still scarcely a city. But Kalmikov had laid out parks everywhere; some streets have been paved; three or four policemen are practising, on ox carts and about a dozen autos, methods of directing the traffic of the metropolis to be; and many new two-story and three-story buildings made of a white pumice stone have been erected. Between the small residential district and the small factory district lies a vast open field perhaps a mile wide. Nalchik is expected to grow. It has a plan, and if it has a plan it will have to fulfil it. The scaffold is already there. Everywhere in Nalchik, and, for that matter, everywhere in Kabardino-Balkaria, one feels the hand of a master who plans, builds, judges, rules—the hand of Betal Kalmikov.

Chapter XVIII

BETAL KALMIKOV

I sat for a long time in Betal Kalmikov's waiting room. He is the Communist party leader of Kabardino-Balkaria, and Kabardino-Balkaria is merely a small district in the North Caucasus with a population of 250,000. Yet the entire Soviet Union has heard of him. In his own area, he is No. 1. Everybody is subordinate to him, including the president of the autonomous territory. Everybody willingly submits to him, for he is a unique personality, a Socialist Timur, a constructive Genjhis Khan.

I sat and listened to his voice as it issued from the adjoining office. It was a rich, melodious baritone. It was the voice of a man who knew he had so much authority that he did not have to impress anyone with it. He neither argued nor commanded. He simply talked in a soft, mellifluous flow. But that was law for Kabardino-Balkaria.

An old Balkarian peasant woman with deep folds in her face and wearing the garb of two generations ago comes into the office and bows deeply with a gesture of her hand towards the floor. "I want to see Betal," she announces to a secretary. She will not tell the secretary her business. "I will tell Betal." Everybody in Kabardino-Balkaria knows Kalmikov and he must know half the population at least. He certainly knows every village, every road, every mountain pass. He was born here; he was a shepherd in his youth.

His father was very strong physically. He taught Betal to tame wild horses. At the age of eight the boy rode untamed mares without saddle or bridle. His father wrestled with him regularly. One day, when the father could not longer throw the youth, he sent him forth from the house, and said: "Go, now, be your own master." His father gave him these commandments: "If you see a cart in a rut, lend the peasant your shoulder. If you find a stray animal, find its owner too. Help the poor. Kill the rich."

In 1912, when Kalmikov was eighteen, the Kabardinians and Balkarians rose up in revolt against their princes and against the Russian Cossacks who were stealing their land and pastures. Betal led an armed band. The insurrection was unsuccessful and the rebels fled into the barren, snow-covered uplands. Kalmikov would not tell me his experiences in that episode. Kalmikov is a modest person who talks little about himself. "Ah," he said, "that is a long story." But comrades relate how he remained a long time in hiding high up in the mountains. He was always a lover of nature. He lay and observed an eagle's nest. The eagle attacked him and he fought with it on a pointed crag. He lived on moss and wild berries. The young man's will grew as hard as his muscles. He would live, and fight and conquer the enemies of the people. It was his first revolutionary baptism.

Came the Bolshevik revolution in November, 1917. By 1918, all the Russias were plowed up by civil war, and the North Caucasus was especially affected. The Bolshevik party sent a representative to Kalmikov to win him over to the Communist cause. Kalmikov sympathized with the poor and oppressed, and he joined the Reds against the Whites. In 1919, the Whites killed his father whom he had deeply loved. Betal Kalmikov organized Communist guerrilla bands, and with Sergo Ordjonikidze, helped to conquer the mountainous Caucasus for the Soviet regime.

When peace was reëstablished, Betal naturally became the leader of his native Kabardino-Balkaria.

Kalmikov neither drinks nor smokes. He hates smoking. No smoking is allowed at meetings which he attends in Nalchik. He believes in the influence of physical labor on morals. He is interested in the personal lives of his officials, visits their homes and criticizes their mode of life, the condition of their lavatories, etc. He has a patriarchal relationship to his entire territory. Recently he assembled the mothers of Nalchik and made them a speech. Why are your children's faces dirty? Why don't you mend their clothes, he demanded. The Kabardinians and Balkarians are a slow-minded race, partly, no doubt, as a result of isolation and inbreeding. Kalmikov proposes now to "import" one thousand Ukrainian women.

He himself, though he claims to be pure Kabardinian, probably has much Kalmick or Mongol blood in his veins. His surname and his facial features support the hypothesis. Kabardinia once felt the iron heel of Timur the Lame. Earlier, it had fought the Tartar khans. Mongol blood and Moslem influence abound in this territory. In many families, the blood has grown cold. In Kalmikov's it enriched an extraordinary man.

Kabardino-Balkaria suffered less from the revolution than most other parts of the country, and the chief reason is Betal Kalmikov. Throughout the Soviet Union, for instance, agrarian collectivization was accompanied by the wholesale slaughter of cattle. Women were never nationalized by the Bolsheviks but cows were. The wily peasant, however, instead of entering the collective with his cow and thus surrendering her to the community, ate or sold her just before he entered the collective. Kalmikov, on the other hand, allowed the peasants to join the collectives and keep their cattle. The rest of the country woke up to the advisability of this method only after millions of animals had been killed unnecessarily.

Similarly, relatively few kulaks of Kabardino-Balkaria were exiled or economically destroyed. When Kalmikov commenced to collectivize agriculture he did not send strangers into the villages to guide this painful process of adjustment to socialism. Everywhere, local people carried out the distasteful tasks, and they usually had an understanding and a tact that made for smooth sailing and peace. This explains why Kalmikov had little or no trouble with the Cossacks in his territory whereas the Cossacks of the Kuban and Don were driven to violent opposition.

For the entire country, collectivization began with a highly destructive phase which did not end until 1933, and in some sections until 1934. But the destructive phase in Kabardino-Balkaria was short and mild. The result is that the territory has plenty of meat and plenty of working animals. It is making rapid progress. Its harvest in 1934 was sufficient to feed it for three years, and its taxes to the state, which elsewhere may amount to twenty per cent of total yield, amounted to only six per cent. Their own sustenance, therefore, is no longer a sufficient incentive to the peasants. They have enough to live on without working. They need an additional stimulus. There are collectivized farmers in Kabardino-Balkaria who could buy automobiles. But no automobiles are on sale. Peasants told me they want bicycles, gramophones, the best city clothes, brass beds. But they cannot get them because the U.S.S.R. is not yet manufacturing enough of these commodities. The general economic condition of the country, accordingly, is retarding the growth of Kabardino-Balkaria. This is a unique situation and the first time it has been observed in revolutionary Rus-

Betal Kalmikov, Communist Leader of Kabardinia-Balkaria

sia. I talked to Kalmikov about it and he admitted that I
was right. "But we will get out of it," he said. His territory's
forward motion exceeded even his expectations and he was
unprepared for it. He would try to make contracts with
several cities or factories or trusts for an exchange of food
for manufactured goods.

Nevertheless, it will be several years before the goods
shortage in the Soviet Union disappears, and meantime the
Bolsheviks must evolve supplementary means of improving
living standards and stimulating agrarian production. Kalmikov has found one very effective means.

"You see those villages," he said as we drove through the
countryside in his Lincoln car. "That is not the way for
human beings to live. We will wipe them from the face of
the earth like this" and he turned his hand over with a
powerful twist. The work has commenced. The conception
is Kalmikov's. This son of a shepherd, who has never been
abroad and who might well be so accustomed to the backwardness of his distant district as to regard it as normal, hates
the heritage of poverty and ugliness bequeathed by Czarism.
Last year, in the little city of Nalchik, his capital, he con-
vened a congress of architects of the entire Soviet Union.
He talked to them, he placed his ideas before these experts
and artists, and then he said: Put these ideas into blueprint.

The plans are ready. "The word 'village' smacks of the
dismal past," Kalmikov maintains. The new settlements
will be called "Agro-Cities." The village of New Ivanovka
is already transforming itself into an agro-city, and Kendje
is taking the first small steps in that direction. Each collective farmer will, according to the draftsman's plans, have
a house with four large rooms. Fronting it will be a flower
garden. Behind the house will stand a corn barn, a pigsty,
a chicken house, a small storehouse and an individual garage.

A private fruit orchard will be planted in the rear of each home and the entire oblong area will be surrounded by a row of trees.

New Ivanovka will have 580 such households with large open spaces between them. The streets will be wide and lined with trees. In the center of the agro-city will stand the office building of the collective, the office of the soviet, stores, a school, a home for aged farmers, a hotel, and a dormitory for technical specialists. Beyond the confines of the agro-city, large barns, a cheese factory and a brick kiln are to be erected. "This is what Stalin has called 'well-to-do-life,' " Kalmikov said.

Kalmikov can commence home and city construction because building materials lie all about him in the hills and mountains. The peasants will contribute their labor. Yet work is proceeding slowly because the architects have gone back to Moscow and Rostov, and Kabardino-Balkaria has very few of its own architects and engineers. "We cannot depend on the outside. People are too busy. We have sent our own young men and women to be trained. We must begin from the ground up."

The prospect of the construction of agro-cities has stirred all of Kabardino-Balkaria and the people worship Kalmikov for his initiative in this matter. They detest the rude dark hut which has housed the Russian peasant for ages. The passing of the "Village" will be the beginning of a new stage of Russian civilization. Kalmikov points the way which the Soviet Union will follow. He talked of the peasants' low standards and of the necessity of teaching him to want and demand more from life. "So much depends on this," he declared as he knocked the knuckles of his perfectly manicured fingers against his forehead.

But housing is not everything. Better breeds of cattle

must be developed. "Why should human beings go to rest homes and sanatoria and not horses?" Kalmikov asks. In all villages, he compels the collective managers to send their working cattle to the hills for vacation. He wants to introduce new stock. He heard somewhere that a bee whose sting is lengthened will produce more honey. He has written for all the literature on the subject. Kalmikov is a man with many thoughts and ideas, but little education. One sees him think as he converses. He weighs my replies as we talk. Throughout the Soviet Union, policies or suggestions from Moscow are often blindly and mechanically applied. If flowers are the vogue, every restaurant table and factory shop is decorated with them. They may be dusty and withered and contribute towards ugliness rather than beauty. But they remain because somebody in the "Pravda" perhaps, or Kaganovitch in a speech said that flowers must be part of the good life of the proletariat. Kalmikov thinks for himself, and if he had arrived at flowers before Kaganovitch he would have popularized their use. There is therefore something very refreshing about Kabardino-Balkaria. Kalmikov takes the initiative not only in doing but also in thinking. That explains why a little far-off district sets the pace in some matters for a whole Continent.

His body is solidified energy. But calm and under perfect control. No flamboyance. He is modest, and suppresses public praise of himself. He knows his own shortcomings. He realizes that he is handicapped by his poor education. He had only three years of schooling in his early youth, he tells me. But though he said his Russian was not as good as mine, it is in fact better, and excellent. That is his own achievement, for as a boy he spoke only Kabardinian. When he has time he reads, but he has little time. I doubt whether he has studied Karl Marx, and he has probably never read even

Lenin thoroughly. He lacks a good grounding in theory, and theory, conscious or unconscious, is the gasoline of action. No big policy can be consistent and wise unless rooted in social theory.

"How old are you?" I inquire.

"Oh, quite old," he replied. "Forty."

"No, he is quite young," his wife says with a look filled with affection. She is Russian-Polish. They have three children; one of them, a girl of three, is a little female Betal full of fire, mischief and will power.

Can Kalmikov become a big Soviet leader? That is the question that went through my mind constantly as I talked with him. I brought up the subject of foreign affairs in order to judge how well he understood it. He had a firm grasp of the interplay of factors and of many facts. His information was not detailed and could not be, but his penetration was impressive. The absence of formal schooling is no handicap to prominence and power in the U.S.S.R. And yet I felt that he could only be a great leader in a relatively small area.

Kalmikov's methods are unique. Several months ago, for instance, a congress of the Communist and agricultural officials of Kabardino-Balkaria took place in Nalchik. Usually, such a meeting in the Soviet Union begins with a long report by the highest official, Kalmikov in this case. The delegates discuss the report at great length and through thick clouds of cigarette smoke. Then resolutions are adopted and everybody goes home perfectly satisfied with the holiday. But Kalmikov did not want any such assembly. He dispensed with his own introductory address. The conference met in the open. Kalmikov stood at the chairman's table. Immediately in front of the table stood a horse. "Comrade Kambiev," Kalmikov exclaimed, "please step up here.

Do you know how to improve this breed? Must it be crossed
with another?" Then, after an exchange of questions and
answers, Kalmikov said: "You have shown here, before our
entire territory, that you yourself do not yet understand
how to take care of horses. How in those circumstances can
you lead others?"

Two pigs are led up to the chairman's table, and with
them one Communist leader, head of the political department of a collective. They discuss the enrichment of the
stock, the food, and the treatment that hogs should receive. Kalmikov studies these matters first; then he demands
that others know at least as much.

The spring of 1934 brought no rain at all. The fields of
Kabardino-Balkaria lay parched and cracked under a merci-
less, baking sun. "There will be no harvest," the peasants
sighed. Kalmikov summoned the old men and women of
the villages to Nalchik. "What can save us from disaster?"
There was only one solution: the streams must be damned,
and the land flooded. No time to be lost. The crops were
being burned on the stalk. The participants in the conference, Kalmikov included, promised not to go home, not to
rest, until the task was finished. Every adult and child of
Kabardino-Balkaria was mobilized for the big adventure.
They built dams of boulders; they dug canals. Night and
day the hasty temporary reconstruction of nature continued without interruption. Farther and farther the refreshing waters swept. More and more yellow and gray
fields changed to deep brown as they drank in the large
draughts of moisture. The harvest was rescued. More,
Kabardino-Balkaria that year grew a tremendous food surplus. Its yield per hectare was among the highest in the
Union. Kalmikov was its savior.

Before the revolution, Kabardino-Balkaria was not only

economically backward; with its princes and landlords, with its harems and bride thefts, it was also socially backward. It passed from this semi-feudal status directly into socialism. Some of the old psychology, therefore, has of course remained. Betal Kalmikov is the patriarch of Kabardino-Balkaria. Old and young look to him as a sort of big father and protector. He is the head of a family of 250,000, and he must concern himself with their bed linen, their children's ears, the depth of their plowing, the health of their horses and the morals of their new generation. There is, to be sure, a trace of the patriarchal in the relation of all Soviet leaders to their followers, but in Kabardino-Balkaria the entire relationship, for practical purposes, is patriarchal. This may be very effective in a little district but the habit of maintaining such a relationship would be a handicap for a national figure. For given the patriarchal tie, too much depends on actual personal contact and example, and much less on organization and general leadership.

Kabardino-Balkaria has no industries and no proletariat. Yet socialist Russia is based on the proletariat, and the U.S.S.R. is becoming more and more industrialized. In fact, rapid industrialization is one of the chief functions which Russian history has assigned to Bolshevism. Kalmikov has no experience in handling workers or in directing industrial developments. He is young and talented, however. He might learn to govern industrialized regions too. But it would be a pity to remove him from his Kabardino-Balkaria. For Kabardino-Balkaria is a stimulus to all of Soviet Asia. Its example makes them envious. Social competition is an important factor in Bolshevik politics, and the success of Kabardino-Balkaria impels other districts forward. In this sense, Kalmikov is a blessing not only to his native state but also to his neighbors, and he is perhaps accomplishing as much indirectly as he could directly. Bolshevism split the social atom in all the national minorities of Russia, but the process was not a wasted explosion. The Communist party, acting through Kalmikov and others, captured the energy and applied it without much loss to the gigantic task of the economic upbuilding and social reformation of eastern races once oppressed by Czarism.

Just a little south and east of Kabardino-Balkaria lies North Ossetia. It is an instance of the healthy jealousy which has replaced the ancient wars and armed feuds that tortured the Caucasus before the revolution. The North Ossetians are a cultured people. Long-headed, finely built, with their dancing gait and broad-rimmed hats of white felt, with their piercing black eyes and clear-cut facial features, they are the embodiment of grace and beauty. They are milder than the Georgians and livelier and lighter than the Kabardinians. They resent the fact that Kabardino-Balkaria has earned itself a reputation throughout the Union whereas Northern Ossetia, whose civilization is more advanced, is only another of the many Soviet minor nationalities. The Communist leaders of the Ossetians cultivate the rivalry between Kabardinia and Ossetia. Socialist competition is raging between them. As a result both move ahead.

It was from Vladikavkas, the pleasant capital of North Ossetia, that Sergo Ordjonikidze set out in 1919 to wrest his native Georgia from the rule of the Mensheviks. He could not march down the picturesque Georgian Military Highway to Tiflis, for it was guarded by the enemy. So his ragged army of volunteers and guerrillas pulled their cannon and carried their supplies over snow-clad mountains, over Mt. Kazbek, higher than Mont Blanc, to which, the myth has it, Prometheus was bound, through lofty passes and thick forests, beyond the reach of the sleepy foe, until, after suffering untold hardships and losses, they joined with the local Communist insurrectionists, and were able to surprise the Georgian nationalist socialist regime and drive it in panic to Batum whence, with Allied assistance, its chief made their way to Constantinople and later to Paris into the embraces of Sir Henri Deterding and French intriguers. Now, with every warrant, Vladikavkaz proudly bears the name of Ordjonikidze. In its parks, the surging Terek is white with foam. The city smiles. From here, one has only to ride a day on horseback to be in regions as wild and exotic as any in the Western world. Ordjonikidze is the cork of a long-necked bottle. The long neck is the Georgian Military Highway. The bottle is Georgia. Both the neck and the bottle are full of wine. The cork too is saturated with it.

Chapter XIX

GEORGIA

A road creeps around the waist line of a high mountain. Tall cedars and firs hide the sun and darken the path of the two automobiles. In the first sit the guards—six fierce looking Georgians with inverted sheepskin bucket-hats, two bandoliers of cartridges across their chests, Mausers on their hips and rifles in their laps. Their scraggy black beards seem like a continuation of the goat fleece which they wear on their heads. Their sharp eyes are strained upwards; they try to penetrate the forest. They are ready for an attack. A moment behind, a second car, a German journalist, a German professor, I, and more guards. The sound of the motor and the wheels drowns all other noises and then it swallows itself. Only the dread silence of the woods remains. Suddenly, a shot rings out. The first car was invisible around a bend. In a fraction of a second we were upon it. It had stopped. The six guards had jumped out of the car and were lying flat on the road, their rifles pointed, their heads searching in all directions. The chauffeur sat stiff at his wheel with drawn revolver. Our machine halted too. A loud laugh is heard. The chief Chekist in our front seat had fired the shot to test the guards. What they said to him in Georgian I did not understand. But I could imagine. Sparks flew from their black eyes.

There had been a Menshevik uprising against the Bolshevik regime in Soviet Georgia. I was moving on the heels of the rebellion. The mountains were said to be infested with political bandits. We were in Kahetia, famous for its vineyards. Oxen and barefooted women press the juice from luscious grapes. Those clay jars, taller than a man and bigger than a man's embrace, will soon hold the new harvest's precious Kahetian wine. In Telav, the capital of Kahetia, cobblers making heelless mountain boots and shoes sit sullen in their narrow shops. A boy aged fourteen cannot speak a word of Russian; or does he refuse on principle? We ride on heavy cavalry bays to the wine cellar of the Grand Duke Nicholai Nicholaievitch, uncle of the last Czar. The director entertains at dinner. The toastmaster fills a ram's horn with wine, pronounces a toast, and drains the liquid. He toasts to "The Guests" and names them: the German journalist, the German professor, me, and Chaikovsky, the commander of the cavalry regiment at Telav.

"But I am not a guest," Chaikovsky good-humoredly interrupts.

"Russians are always guests here," replies the Georgian Bolshevik master of ceremonies.

That night I slept in the broad bed of the grand duke, and the next morning we drove to the Allaverdi of Georgia, at the foothills of the Dagestan Mountains. Tribesmen had come down from mountain villages. Girls dressed in velvet and embroidery. Bards sang ballads in unwritten tongues while they strummed on two-string musical instruments shaped like truncated gourds and richly decorated with mother of pearl. Around the Allaverdi church, young couples danced the Lesginka. And if two danced together several times it was the beginning of a courtship. The festival was the annual Allaverdi marriage mart.

From Kahetia back to Tiflis and then to the manganese center at Chiaturi which the Mensheviks had occupied for several hours. Thence to Novo Senaki, Samtredi, Poti, and other tiny hearths of revolt. At Samtredi a young man said:

"Why did America not send tanks to help us?" He did not
know how far America was, or that most Americans know
only the one Georgia which produces peaches. But his leaders had promised that if they raised the standard of revolt
all the capitalist nations would rally to it and overthrow
Bolshevism. The foreign press, as usual, lied about the extent of the insurrection.

All this was in 1924. Since then more than a decade has
passed. . . .

The Bolsheviks faced a difficult task in Georgia. In other
parts of the Soviet Union, the bourgeoisie was weakened and
its morale undermined during three years of Civil War and
Military Communism. But Georgia went Bolshevik in 1921,
when the more moderate New Economic Policy had been
inaugurated by Lenin. Georgian capitalism was scarcely
interfered with. And when Tiflis, under Ordjonikidze's
leadership, did begin to put pressure on the property-
owners, did start to close private stores, did begin to persecute the church, did commence to squeeze out the "princes"
(I visited Georgian "princes" like the Mdivanis who owned
nothing more than three acres of land and a wooden house
that rested on wooden stilts), did, in other words, remind
the population of the advent of Bolshevism, there came the
1924 flare-up. Georgia had few workers. In the insurrection,
the workers sided with the Bolsheviks. In fact, these day
laborers had suppressed the Mensheviks even before the
regular army could arrive on the scene. Yet the proletarian
support on which the Soviets could count was very weak.
All that was long ago, but it is the background of the present picture. . . .

In Tiflis, capital of Georgia and of the Trans-Caucasian
Federation, less building has been done than in any other
Soviet city I know. I saw Tiflis in 1924, 1927, 1932, and

now, but the eye which has become accustomed to urban reconstruction that makes recognition difficult registers few fundamental differences in Tiflis. The spirit too is strangely un-Soviet. There is much more private trade in Tiflis than in most Soviet cities; foreigners are accosted and invited to engage in currency speculation. The town seems lazy and stagnant. The top of a hill in the center of town affords a marvelous view of the surrounding scene and relief from the torrid heat of the summer day. But the flat summit is as neglected now as it was a decade ago; at most one can buy Borzhom mineral water at a stand and some sunflower seeds from an old woman. A place which could be a very delightful and pleasant amusement spot is dark and inhospitable.

This is one instance of many. The Georgians are a beautiful, wine-drinking, pleasure-loving race—a race of tenors —and so proud of their ancient origin and culture that they think they can rest on their oars while the rest of the Union pulls away from them. The Georgians are kind and hospitable and I am being unkind to some most friendly hosts who have entertained me in Tiflis, Tchiaturi, Batum, Poti, Telav, Sukhum, and other Georgian towns. But I have crossed them before and they have forgiven me. Once, when a big company was regaling itself with young red wine or "Most," I asked for tea. Children drink wine in Georgia. Men start the day with cognac or vodka. And I was asking for tea. They were too polite to display their contempt. They simply said they would send to the drug store for it, whereat I revoked the request.

Banquets are set on any and every excuse in Georgia. Banquets are, at least, as enjoyable as work. Meat in the highly spiced hors d'oeuvres, meat in the soup, a chief meat dish, and meat in the form of the famed Caucasian "shashlik" which, washed down with copious ram horns or goblets of Georgian wine makes one valiant, joyous and eloquent. The "Tamada" or toast-master is endlessly resourceful. A toast is pronounced to the guest's parents. He cannot refuse to drink. Another toast to his wife and children. Obviously he cannot refuse that. A toast to the host. A toast to the victorious proletariat. A toast to the greatest of all Georgians, Joseph Stalin. A toast to the host's beautiful wife. They are all toasts that vanquish the most temperate. If the Georgians were as determined in prosecuting socialist construction as they are in pressing more wine on the helpless visitor they would accomplish marvels.

Stalin is one of the greatest organizers of men that civilization has seen. Sergo Ordjonikidze, likewise a Georgian, has achieved wonders in developing Soviet industry; he was a daring and able warlord as well. My old acquaintance, Budo Mdivani, of the family made famous in America by American heiresses and film stars, is capable of a fire, a strength of conviction, and a readiness to suffer for ideals which would do credit to a race with more iron in its veins. Yet taken together, the Georgians lack the capacity for work, the stick-to-itiveness, and the stamina of many other Soviet nationalities with less glorious histories.

Perhaps there was too much inbreeding among Georgians; they hated the Russians of Czarist days and regarded themselves superior to the Moslem peoples and the Armenians who were their neighbors. Never having had much industry, being essentially a land of barren rocks, small fields, and mountain pastures where one can drowsily watch sheep and goats graze on perpendicular slopes, having sulked as a nation for generations because the monarchy suppressed their language and culture, oppressed them, and obstructed their material growth, perhaps Georgia's past weaned her from the habit and traditions of labor. Perhaps the crazy-quilt of Caucasian nationalities and the incessant tribal warfare among them taught the Georgians that it was more advantageous to be a good fighter and horseman than a good worker. The Georgian did not even take to trade. Armenians were the merchants of Georgia. In Tiflis sat the Czar's Viceroy for the Caucasus. Tiflis was therefore an official's town. It has remained the administrative center for the Caucasus; that is bad.

Elsewhere in the Soviet Union, even in backward Turkestan, the Bolshevik revolution represented a violent wrench with the past. But if Georgia had any wrench it was not very violent and it came only recently.

When I told Germann Mgaloblishvili, the prime minister of Soviet Georgia, that I did not notice much progress in Tiflis since 1932, he partially concurred, but he explained that whereas the rest of the U.S.S.R. actually built during the first Five Year Plan, Georgia had to use that period for preparations, for geological explorations, for surveys, etc. If I came back two years hence I would see a huge difference, the premier promised. Georgia had already struck its stride. It too was moving forward at "Soviet tempo."

Mgaloblishvili was educated in Germany, graduated from a university in Dresden. He has a warm, mild manner. This was my third meeting with him. At the first, he lent an air of intimacy to the conversation which made our second encounter seem like a reunion of old acquaintances. And this third time, there were no formalities; only friendly interest and cordial spirit. Most Georgians are like that. Most Russians are not; certainly not Moscovite Russians. In the provinces they are less frigid than in the capital. To do them no injustice, one must add that officials in Moscow are overworked and terrifically busy, more busy than is good for their work and their health. Few big Bolsheviks know how to delegate tasks to subordinates.

Germann Mgaloblishvili regretted my unfavorable impression of Tiflis. To correct it he would have had me travel at least three months in his little autonomous republic visiting all the scenes of boiling economic activity. I was sorry I did not have six weeks at my disposal as in 1924. Then Ordjonikidze, the party leader of the Caucasus at the time, gave us his machine for trips in town and for long excursions into the interior. When we traveled by train his word got us the best accommodations. Horses were always at our disposal. And for a hurried visit to Baku and return he lent my colleague of the "Berliner Tageblatt" and me an aeroplane in which we were almost wrecked when three gales, one from the Caspian, the other blowing up from the Muggan steppes and the third tearing down from the mountains caught us at a dangerous corner and held us immovable—like a huge bird checked by the wind—while the frail plane creaked and shivered. Finally, after some terrible minutes, Spiel, the able German pilot, managed to escape unscathed only to be burnt alive in the same machine with three prominent commissars just a fortnight later.

As a substitute for a thorough, first-hand survey, Mgaloblishvili would tell me what Soviet Georgia was doing. I took out notebook and fountain pen. "This week we are opening the Rion River Hydro-Electric Power Station with a capacity of 48,000 kilowatts. You will see it on your way to Batum. (I did.) We have dammed the Suram River, and the railroad which runs over the Suram Divide has been electrified. It uses giant Diesel motors. This year the railway from Tiflis to Segsaphon was electrified, and next year we will complete the electrification of the line from there to the Black Sea. By the end of 1935, Tkvarchelges with

38,000 kilowatts, Sukhumges with 10,000 kilowatts, and Kanakirges with 60,000 kilowatts will commence operations. Today, the Caucasus produces 310,000 kilowatts of electrical energy; in 1937 this will have been brought up to 800,000. You see we are working."

"But electrification," the Georgian Prime Minister continued, "is only one phase of the task of changing the face of the country. You saw in today's newspapers a call for settlers to occupy newly reclaimed land in the Kolhida marshes near the Black Sea. By 1936, the entire Kolhida swamp, 500,000 acres in extent, will have been opened to agricultural cultivation. We are not only draining, we are also irrigating. In East Georgia and in Azerbaijhan there are 2,500,000 acres of arid soil. Together with the Baku government, we are now constructing a wall one kilometer long and sixty-three meters high to dam the Kura River at Midandukhaura and create a huge water reservoir. We expect that this enterprise will enable the Caucasus to multiply its cotton crop by five. That will give the Armenian textile mills more raw material. We want the Caucasus to be self-sufficient in cotton and independent of the Central Asian cotton fields."

"All this will be ready only in several years," I interrupted.

"Yes," he replied, "but we had to begin from the bottom. We had nothing. The Czarist regime prevented our industrial expansion because it did not want to see the rise of a working class here which might organize revolutionary protests. The capitalists of Russia preferred to transport our raw materials up north and there transform them into finished articles instead of developing an industry at the peripheral source of supply. We were a colony, and we were treated like step-children. Now only we have commenced to study the resources of Georgia. In the mountains near Kutais we have discovered molybdenum. There appears to be a 10,000 ton deposit of that precious mineral. We also found arsenic and gold recently. Coal lies at Kutais. It is of a poor quality but it contains slate from which we can make aluminum. In Eastern Georgia, furthermore, in Shirak, we are developing a new oilfield. We plan to mine 1,000,000 tons in 1935. A whole forest of derricks has already been erected. Baku and Grozni are not enough. We want to exploit every particle of natural wealth we possess. And why not?"

"But why is Tiflis so stagnant?" I demand.

"We have been doing many things in Tiflis," he replied, "which do not strike the eye. For instance,—Tiflis used to be famous for stomach diseases because the population drank the waters of the dirty Kura. Now we have brought water from a distant mountain spring, and stomach troubles have disappeared. In two months, a mill to fill all of Tiflis's flour requirements is scheduled to be opened. This summer we introduced an automatic dial telephone system. Before starting to build houses and offices we had to erect a number of auxiliary enterprises like saw mills, brick kilns, etc. These are now ready. Moreover, we feel the lack of industrial workers. We never had many. Only in Western Georgia did the landless peasant seek work in the town. Today our peasants are too busy expanding their farm work and introducing new cultures to have time for industrial activities. We must import workingmen from Russia and the Ukraine."

"Isn't that just what Czarism did?" I asked. "Didn't it colonize Russians in Georgia? Will not the arrival of non-

Georgian laborers arouse jealousy and competition, and fan the flames of nationalism which are not dead in Georgia?"

"No, how could it?" he responded. "There can be no jealousy when there is no unemployment and even a scarcity of labor. No worker from the North will take the job of a Georgian. He will only help the Georgians carry out their plans. As it is, we sometimes cannot begin operations on a building project because of the lack of hands. The newcomer actually helps the local population to find work."

"Yes," I argued, "but some day you will have unemployed. Some day the rapid expansion of the Soviet Union will stop."

"Never," Premier Mgaloblishvili affirmed. "Our progress will never be interrupted. You must not measure a socialist economy with a capitalist yardstick. It is capitalism which must have the ups and downs of boom and slump. In the first place, it will be several decades before we shall have exploited to the full all the known resources and all the unknown resources which certainly exist in the uncharted and unexplored regions of the vast Soviet Continent. And after that there can be no limit to the prosperity and well-being of the Soviet individual. Every person can have a house and a country house, an automobile, or two automobiles, a fine library, excellent home furnishings, and all the benefits of all the best inventions which science will give us in the future. Why should not every workingman own his aeroplane? And then as we grow richer we will reduce the working day. We have already reduced it from eight to seven hours. Why not a three hour day? That would enable us to give employment to everybody. But such a short day would mean that there would be more leisure and we would need more employees to provide that leisure. Leisure will some day be our greatest industry; it will give employment to millions of men and women."

"And the forward advance, you think, will never be interrupted?" I question.

"No," he said. "You see, we have abolished the profit system. You have it in capitalist countries. In modern capitalist nations there is always a surplus of production which cannot be consumed because profits take too big a slice from wages. Therefore, production exceeds consumption. Therefore you must export goods and capital. And when your debtors default and you cannot safely export goods and capital you are in a blind alley. Karl Marx explained this decades ago, and it is just as true today. Every capitalist crisis digs deeper under the capitalist system. This is not the final crisis but it has lasted longer than the previous ones and its victims have been more numerous. We, on the contrary, look forward to a bright future."

We sat for a long time and discussed foreign conditions and foreign politics. "We need machines," he said, "automobiles, drills, automatic lathes, everything. No capitalist country became industrialized without outside assistance. Only we have had to do everything alone, and the limited credits we got were extraordinarily expensive. We still need millions of machines. If the capitalists had sense they would give us credits. But I suppose they have no sense," he concluded.

I outlined my program to the prime minister and told him I proposed to go in a few days to Batum and then up the coast to the Black Sea. He was pleased. "You must see our tea plantations," he suggested. "They have political significance."

"How political?" I wondered.

"Western Georgia," he explained, "was always the

stronghold of our enemies, the Mensheviks. Tea has now killed Menshevism. The peasants were poor because the land was overgrown with weeds and regarded as unfit for cultivation. Poverty made the peasants an easy prey to anti-Bolshevik propaganda. Beginning in 1926 when we decided to free the U.S.S.R. from dependence on foreign tea, we sent agronomists and machines into Western Georgia, cleared the fields, gave the peasants credits for seed and food, and started them on the road to prosperity. That was the end of their Menshevism."

I promised to see the tea plantations.

"And the tea factories," he added. "We have sixteen. In 1937, we will have forty. By 1937, the Soviet Union will grow all the tea it needs, and you know it needs a great deal." The Soviet government imported 53,000,000 pounds of tea in 1930, 35,000,000 pounds in 1932, and continues to buy large quantities in China, India and Ceylon. Tea and vodka are Russia's national beverages, and how could one live through the long, northern winter without either or both? The state has a monopoly of vodka-making and vodka-selling. The government also has a monopoly of tea-selling, but tea-making, in samovar or kettle, is still the monopoly of the housewife. It is the irony of geography, however, that the tea-loving Russians should have to look to the tea-hating Georgians for their tea. The Russians probably learned the use of tea or "Chai" from China.

The factory plays such a tremendous rôle in the social and cultural life of the Soviet Union, that even when one is interested only in men and not in machines, one tries to visit a factory in each urban center. In Tiflis, I went to a cigarette manufacturing plant. From the point of view of machines there was nothing to see; it was an old, pre-revolutionary enterprise in which little of the equipment had been changed. It has a good nursery. But I carried away only one big impression: every adult employed, 454 in all, went to school in the factory for an hour before work. This was compulsory. They devoted the first hour of each day to education because the workers were fresher in the morning.

At the exit of the tobacco factory a group of boys gathered around my car. I noticed two who were just as black-haired, just as swarthy, just as brown-eyed as all the others. But they seemed different nevertheless. They told me they were Georgian Jews.

"How do you know you are Jews?" I asked.

"Our father told us," the brothers replied.

But for that, they would not have known. Ask an English Jew what he is and he answers: "An Englishman." Ask a Soviet Jew and he answers: "A Jew." Nationality is a prominent factor in Soviet life. Every Soviet questionnaire —and there are unfortunately hundreds of them—contains an item called Nationality, and the reply is "Russian" or the name of one of the numerous ethnic minorities in the U.S.S.R. Many Soviet citizens, however, do not feel their nationality. It is a reminder of something which does not exist in their hearts or minds. The multiplicity of races and the weakening of nationalistic antagonism makes for considerable intermarriage in the Union. Now the offspring of a mixed marriage will probably speak Russian rather than the language of, let us say, his Lett father or Jewish mother. There is nothing in his daily life or education, moreover, which suggests that he is Lettish or Jewish. Yet he is certainly not Russian, and he cannot assert that he is "a Sovieter." No such category exists. He must write "Lett" or "Jew" in his application, and that is unnatural and, in a deep sense, untrue.

This is an unsolved Soviet problem. In lieu of the Czarist policy of forcibly russifying ethnic minorities, the Bolsheviks have stressed the cultural autonomy and separateness of national groups. The Soviet Union, consequently, is witnessing a high flower of racial culture which emphasizes the divergent character of different groups. On the other hand, there is coöperation between races, there is intermarriage, there is no economic rivalry, no fighting. National enmity persists here and there but its roots have been deprived of their food. The Bolsheviks persecute it relentlessly. This, instead of stressing the separateness of national groups, strengthens the ties and lessens the difference between them. Nevertheless, the official Bolshevik ideal is not a melting pot.

What of the future? Intermarriage, the eclipse of religion, and the nature of socialist economy undoubtedly conduce to racial assimilation. This process of assimiliation has proceeded faster among such groups as Poles, Finns, Letts, and Jews which, not being concentrated on their own compact territories, are more likely to lose their individuality. Among the other ethnic groups, and they are the majority, the revolution has accentuated national characteristics.

The sharp Soviet emphasis on the distinguishing features of nationalities is perhaps the first step towards the merging of those features into a homogeneous whole. That day, however, is far far away. Will the Kazak who is more Chinese than anything else, the Tadjik who is more Hindu than anything else, the Laplander, the Ukrainian, the Armenian, the Tiurk, the White Russian, etc., etc., etc. ever amalgamate into one nation?

Stalin has said that the Bolshevik system is nationalistic

in form and socialistic in content. Each national unit has administrative and cultural autonomy—that is the form, and it is a disrupting factor—but all those units are building socialism—that binds them together. Under the planned economy of the Soviets, no national republic can compete with another. The various sections and republics complement one another. Friction is thus eliminated.

Bourgeois nationalism implies that blood is stronger than economic interests. Tartar workingmen, accordingly, should feel a bond with Tartar capitalists. The Bolsheviks say: "No. The Tartar workers must destroy their capitalists." The Tartar proletariat will then become the ruling class. In such a worker's state, the form will be nationalistic, it will be a *Tartar* republic. But economically and socially it would be socialistic. It would be a Tartar *Soviet Socialist* Republic. The content would be socialistic.

Ergo, even if Tadjik never merges with Ukrainian, if Russian never assimilates with Buryat-Mongolian, a Soviet nation can arise on the common denominator of socialism. Since the Spring of 1934, and with increasing intensity, the Bolsheviks have propagated the idea of "Fatherland." "Fatherland" glares brightly in Soviet declarations. A unifying Soviet patriotism is being inculcated. The Kremlin, apparently, believes that a new national cohesion is already in the making. Without erasing the boundaries between national minorities, the new nationalism will weld them together into a Soviet nationality.

But a Soviet nationality will be more than a nationality. It will be a kind of hitherto unknown super-nationality. It would be as if a nationality emerged in India. The various blood strains in the United States, in the British Isles, in Germany, are all very similar. But the Georgian has little in common with the Kamchatkan Eskimo. Nor is the Uzbek akin to the Volga Germans. A Soviet nation, if it develops, will be a federation of easily distinguished races bound together by a philosophy, economy interests and a political system.

In Tiflis, as in other Soviet cities, the janitors sprinkle the streets in front of their houses several times a day during the warm months. Last summer, the Tiflis Soviet staged a "socialist competition" among the janitors, and announced that it would award a prize to the janitor who used the smallest volume of water for this purpose. The janitors competed and competed, and they competed so vigorously and so enthusiastically that soon they were using no water at all, and the streets were dusty and hot. Nothing could induce the janitors to resume the sprinkling of the streets. They all wanted to win the prize. It required the intervention of Beriya, the Communist leader of the entire Caucasus, to persuade the Tiflis janitors to bring out their rubber hoses once more.

Beriya is the secretary of the Communist Party Committee of the Caucasus. Like so many Bolshevik leaders of the post-revolutionary vintage, he is in his thirties. When I met him in 1924, he was the president of the Georgian Cheka. He sat in on an interview I then had with Mogilevsky, the president of the Caucasian Cheka. It was immediately after the Menshevik insurrection, and with my German colleague, I was trying to ascertain how many rebels had been executed. Of course, I did not ascertain. Beriya sat there and never said a word.

At that time, Beriya was one of Ordjonikidze's rising men. Now he is the big leader. He is an excellent organizer. He is the little Stalin of the Caucasus. To him goes the credit for the region's achievements. To him all pay homage. His words are quoted. His picture appears in many offices.

Every section of the Soviet Union has its little Stalin who is leader. In Leningrad until his assassination it was Kirov. In Moscow it is Kaganovitch, in the Ukraine Postishev, in Rostov Sheboldayev, in the Caucasus, Beriya. The Bolsheviks spend much energy in the attempt to awaken feelings of personal loyalty to local chiefs. And especially, of course, to the big chief in the Kremlin. He is "the great Stalin," "our much-beloved Stalin," "Stalin, Lenin's best disciple," "Stalin, Bolshevism's first theoretician," etc. The engineers, factory directors and Communist leaders of Soviet heavy industry recently met in congress in Moscow. Like practically every other Soviet gathering, it sent greetings to Stalin. "To the inspirer and organizer of the victories of Socialist industrialization, to the beloved leader of the toilers, to the great Stalin (it read), the conference of heavy industry leaders sends its flaming greetings. In the years when our industries made their first steps on the road towards reconstruction, thou, loyal pupil of the immortal Lenin, with the perspicacity of genius and leadership, penetrated into the depths of coming years and gave us and the party the great program of socialist industrialization."

"With this program as our battle flag," this oriental document proceeds, "under thy personal guidance and with thy close daily attention, the working class, caught in the sweeping pathos of construction, created in the years of the first Five Year Plan a mighty socialist industry furnished with excellent equipment."

Further: "Under thy wise leadership, there were established new cadres of industrial workers, there was founded a new productional-technical intelligentsia of the proletariat. In the years of the stormy growth of socialist industry it was thou who proclaimed the slogan: 'The Bolsheviks Must Master Technique'; thou didst give us the six conditions of victory; thou didst summon us to supplement the pathos of construction with a pathos for efficiency. Thy instructions became the indestructible foundation of the next triumphs of socialist construction.

"We," this saccharinal hymn of praise concludes, "in closing our conference, promise thee, dear Comrade Stalin, our friend, leader and teacher, that we can again and again prove it—there are no fortresses which the Bolsheviks cannot take. . . . Long Live Our Stalin, the great organizer of great victories."

Stalin has a mountain-high collection of such published pronunciamentos. Apparently he likes them else he could easily stop their flow. Having attained the dizzy heights, he wants to be reminded of it every moment. This thirst of Stalin for public adoration is not exactly in the best Communist spirit. Lenin certainly never allowed it. But let no one now parrot the old shibboleth that the Bolsheviks deny the rôle of the individual in history: those declarations addressed to Stalin stress that rôle every day. And so do the daily resolutions, couched in similar styles to the Beriyas and other lesser Stalins of the provinces.

Stalin towers above all other Soviet leaders in ability, wisdom and will power. Agrarian collectivization is his outstanding contribution to history. While many of his colleagues thought the burden too heavy, feared the pace was too fast, wanted to turn off the gas and stop for breath, his hand held firm to the wheel and steered a straight though perilous and expensive course towards the present incline up in the direction of prosperity and a new social form.

Stalin is undoubtedly a great statesman. He can dictate, but he can also listen. G. B. Shaw has described him as "the great listener." I know an instance in which a very minor official in one of the many government commissariats telephoned Stalin at home late at night and urged that a decision of the supreme Politburo which concerned that official's department be canceled. The next day the decision was canceled. I recall the Gorki celebration in the Moscow Grand Opera in 1932. While Gorki spoke, while Nizhni Novgorod was being renamed Gorki, while orators lauded Stalin, while orators lauded Gorki, Stalin sat on the platform talking, talking for more than an hour to a young, unknown man from the provinces whom he was obviously trying to convince on a certain point. Stalin is the patient, plodding, brick-by-brick upbuilder of his own power and of the new, industrialized Soviet Union. The Bolsheviks think he has done a good job. The Soviet Union and particularly Soviet Georgia are proud. If one considers Soviet history for the eighteen years since November, 1917, I am not sure who has influenced it more, Stalin or Lenin. In any event, the U.S.S.R. today moves completely within the orbit of Stalin and Stalinism.

Tiflis always had a large Armenian population. Many Armenians regarded it as an Armenian *irredenta*. I have heard Armenian Dashnaks say that it should have been included in the Armenian republic. Between the Georgians and Armenians very little love was lost. In fact, in 1919, when nationalist socialists called Mensheviks ruled Georgia and nationalist socialists called Dashnaks ruled Armenia, the two countries went to war, actual bloody war, over some terrritorial crumbs.

Now Soviet citizens look back upon that ridiculous episode with incredulity. Was it really possible? Georgia and Armenia are today two friendly neighbors in a federation, two brothers in a family.

Chapter XX

LAND OF CONTRASTS

On entering a new country, it is well, before investigating the present, to visit its ethnographical, historical and even art museums for a glimpse of the past. Erivan, the capital of Soviet Armenia, has a very poor museum. But the ethnographical section is not bad. Here one finds, among other interesting exhibits, two agricultural instruments: a plow which is simply a bough of a tree with a crooked, sharpened point, and a neolithic threshing board consisting of a flat plank about two inches thick in which rows of stone flints have been imbedded.

A few days later, I went by automobile to the mountain Lake Sevan. At a distance I saw a man standing practically motionless yet moving round and round a cleared space. On approaching I discovered that he was standing on a board pulled by a donkey. Flints were stuck into the board. The peasant was threshing his wheat. The threshing board was not only a museum piece.

Near Erivan, I visited a village collective. The peasants were busy threshing. The village had been electrified, and at the threshing field, a mechanical thresher using the current from an overhead wire to which a pole had been hooked was quickly separating the seed from the straw.

Soviet Armenia is a land of a million contrasts. Peasant women sit by their houses on their haunches and spin balls of dirty cotton into thread. But in Leninakan, the former Alexandropol, a textile mill with 100,000 modern spindles is being erected. Forty thousand of these are already operating. Leninakan is "Armenia's Manchester." . . . Black, lumbering water buffalos and stupid oxen hauling heavy carts retard the progress of high-powered foreign machines and of Soviet "Fords" on perfect asphalt roads. . . . In Echmiadzin, in the "Armenian Vatican," sits the Pope of the World Armenian Church whom the Bolsheviks helped to elect. In the same town, and throughout Soviet Armenia, anti-religious education continues in normal fashion, yet without the vigor, and without the success, which attends it in other parts of the country. . . . Tractors draw plows and, in the same field of vision, a donkey harnessed to a camel. . . . A village half collectivized, half inhabited by private capitalistic cultivators. The one half argues for collectivization. The other half is not convinced. Most of the peasants here live in stone box houses built deep into the soil and rising only four feet above the ground. These semi-subterranean hovels look exactly as Xenophon described them centuries ago. Their winter fuel is animal dung which the women fashion into rude brickets and pile in front of their homes. A hole in the roof of the houses allows some of the smoke to escape; the rest is on active duty choking the household and irritating mucous membranes. Nearby are modern two-story dwellings with chimneys, stoves and electric light. These have been one of the most cogent argument for collectivization in a region where the government allowed the peasants a free choice. . . . The Bolsheviks are rapidly industrializing Armenia and introducing Western production methods and new conceptions of quality and speed. But an Armenian proverb says: "What you gain in time you lose in dignity," and one sees many citizens who apparently make this adage the principle of their lives. Yet generally speaking the

Armenians are an industrious, patient, painstaking people. They merely conduct Western activities orientally. . . . An ancient Shiitic mosque in Erivan. In the center of its court, around a water pond, is a café where Armenians, fatigued by the heat of the day, sip hot tea or Turkish coffee. All around the court, under heavy dome-arches, are deep alcoves which formerly served as "hotel" accommodations for pilgrims and now serve as permanent dwellings. In one lives a young fireman with his wife. I ask him whether he is a member of the Young Communist League. He says: "You would not expect anything else, would you?" His neighbor is the Moslem bishop of Erivan, likewise occupying an alcove room. A "descendant of the Prophet" lies immured in one of the walls. A bronze plate marks the spot. One foot away, on a bed of precious rugs, sit the bishop and his beadle. He answers my questions but I wonder what he thinks. His gnarled, olive-colored face tells me nothing. "Yes, religion is doomed, and no youth come to the mosque." "No, no mosques were closed in Erivan." "No, there are no harems now. Before the revolution, Moslems had three, sometimes four wives,—those were the rich. Two wives were more normal. But the Koran teaches that a man may have only one wife. The revolution brought this about." Ergo, Bolshevism is realizing the word of Mohammed, and the bishop, by implication therefore, is a friend of Bolshevism. He is rather the Last of the Armenian Mohicans, and he is too wise not to know it. When he goes, another member of the Young Communist League will move into his room. . . .

Nowhere does the old clash so sharply with the new as in Erivan. Broad, well-graded avenues lined with thousands of new seedlings are diligently watered several times a day.

In the ancient quarters—ruts that are called streets but have no names. The dust is as thick as the stench. Low stone houses with practically no furniture; the ground is the floor; cooking is done on a clay hearth just outside the door; the flies buzz in a powerful, persistent monotone. But in the modern sections rise modern apartment houses with walls of the beautiful rose-colored tuff stone in which Armenia abounds. They are high, with large windows. The architecture is German. Gardens surround the houses. Here baths, electricity, and parquet floors are axiomatic. Nearby, the Armenian National Theater is being finished—a structure that would do honor to any city in the world. Elsewhere, numerous public buildings and government offices are in construction. Many have already been completed. Wherever one looks—tearing down, digging up, building, hauling for building purposes, painting, planting of trees and parks, etc. If ever a city had a "boom" it is Erivan. Even persons accustomed to the usual mad Soviet construction "tempo" are astounded. The old city, which was one big slum, is quickly disappearing. Soviet Erivan is out-Sovieting the Soviets. Erivan had a population of 13,000 a hundred years ago. It counted 13,000 inhabitants in 1913. It has 110,000 inhabitants today. A high official said to me: "Berlin has 12,000 university students; we have 11,000." Even if he errs by several thousand both ways, the attempt at comparison is in itself significant.

And—another contrast. I stand in a street of Erivan, hot, perspiring, praying for the cool breeze of the evening. I look up. There is the snow cap of Mt. Ararat on which, if the geography of the Bible is correct, Noah rested his Ark. There are two Ararats, one with the eternal snow peak, and the other with a rounded gray knob top. Ararat Major is connected with Ararat Minor by a curve which goes

The "Covered Wagon" in Soviet Armenia

down, then straight over, then up, and the whole therefore resembles a Caucasian saddle. . . .

But the greatest of all Armenian contrasts is the difference between Armenia's political status before the revolution and now. The word "Armenia" immediately calls up the word "Turkey," and the two conceptions unite to form "massacres." Armenian history is one long conveyor of blood baths which culminated in the horrible slaughter of the World War. Hundreds of thousands of Armenians lost their lives either by Turkish scimitars or from the ravages of disease and starvation. Comrade Erzinkian, the acting Prime Minister, or, in Soviet terminology, the acting chairman of the Council of People's Commissars, of Soviet Armenia, told me that the Armenian population of Turkey was reduced to one-quarter its size by the war. Now, for the first time in 500 years, the Armenian nation has a separate existence with complete cultural autonomy—Armenian schools, officials, newspapers, courts; Armenian national heroes; old Armenian art and literature being studied; an Armenian theater—some political autonomy and considerable economic independence. Above all, it has peace, and not only peace today, but a guarantee of peace tomorrow; security against the throatcutting which emptied the nation's arteries for century after century. Peace and security are always good things, but in a people that had forgotten what they were, in a nation that had been bled white, they awaken a deep sense of gratitude. Not only the Armenians in Soviet Armenia are grateful to the Bolsheviks. Many foreign Armenians have concretely expressed their appreciation of the new page which the Soviet has added to the sanguine record of their race. One Armenian millionaire, of course not a Soviet citizen, donated the money for the building and equipment of a modern eye hospital in Erivan.

A group of foreign Armenians presented Erivan with its car tracks. A number of rich American Armenians have built themselves homes in Erivan.

How simple are the annals of England, France, and especially the United States compared with the checkered past of a country like Armenia which lies on the high road that ancient Europe took to Asia. The Khaldians, the Medes and Persians, the Romans, the Arabs, the Turks, the Mongols, the hordes of Tamerlaine, and finally the Russians all marched and re-marched across this isthmus between two continents. All took their booty, all left their wake of destruction, all stamped their mark on the culture of the province, all contributed their blood to the originally Aryan veins of the Armenian race. And all built roads. Armenia seems to have the best net of highways in the Soviet Union.

In the seventh century of the present era, the Arabs invaded Armenia. In 885 A. D., the Caliph of Bagdad appointed a member of the Armenian Bagratid family as king of Armenia. And the Moslem bishop of Erivan told me that until the revolution, he paid allegiance to a superior in Bagdad. Old ties last long. During the reign of Nero, Armenia became a vassal of Rome. The Romans introduced some Hellenic influences. Soviet scientists are now excavating ancient Roman ruins. Going still further back to the dawn of history, the cuneiform script was brought to Armenia from Assyria, probably. Cuneiform tablets have been found near Lake Sevan.

Erivan's construction fever has unearthed many buried treasure hoards of ancient days. One consists of Byzantine coins of the seventeenth century. The second discovery consists of coins of the Arab caliphs dating back to the ninth century. Another hoard contains 550 silver money pieces of the Mongol period. Here are concrete reminders of Armenia's troubled history.

And now Soviet ideology is being grafted on this complicated Armenian past. The Bolsheviks are clever enough to do it gradually and to let their works be their propaganda.

Acting Premier Erzinkian says: We are an ancient people. There are now only 3,000,000 Armenians in the world. Once we had 20,000,000. Armenia formerly occupied the Eastern Villayet down to distant Cilicia and including the fruitful valley of the Ararat. The Armenian kingdom was crushed in the 14th century in the struggle between Byzantium and Persia.

"The Czars gradually conquered Armenia 120 years ago," Erzinkian continues. "Erivan became Russian in 1827. Russia gave us nothing, built us nothing, and only took away what we grew. We were politically, culturally and economically backward. Industry constituted no more than four per cent of the income of the province. Eighty per cent of the population was illiterate."

The World War was the climax of Armenian woes. Some Armenian towns in Azerbaijhan and Armenia were converted into Pompeiis and Herculaneums. Agricultural yield dropped almost to zero. The whole land was plowed up by advancing and retreating armies. Then, in 1918, came the régime of the Dashnaks, the Armenian Nationalists. For over two years they ruled. But the country lay in ruin around them, and they could not relieve the distress or present a program for Armenian reconstruction.

In 1920, Erzinkian recalls, the Bolsheviks came to power. What a task they faced! They had to raise the standard of living and renew the province's economy. They had to restore Armenia's tortured spirit.

Soviet Armenia, Erzinkian thinks, can be proud of her achievements. At the moment of sovietization, the population numbered 700,000. Now it is 1,200,000. Fifty thousand Armenians immigrated into the Soviet Union from other countries, especially Turkey and Greece, since 1920. Nine thousand arrived in Erivan last year from Greece. Tens of thousands of Armenians came to Soviet Armenia from other parts of the Soviet Union when Bolshevism was established. Many Russians and members of other nationalities were likewise attracted by the employment opportunities offered by Armenia's vast industrialization program.

Three hundred thousand Armenians, some of them refugees from Turkey and Greece, live in Soviet Georgia. Six hundred thousand are counted in other parts of the Soviet Union. This, according to Erzinkian, makes 2,100,000 Armenians in the U.S.S.R., as against 900,000 in the rest of the world.

The economic retrogression brought on by the rule of the Dashnak nationalists between 1918 and 1920 was in considerable part due to the separation of Armenia from Russia, Erzinkian affirmed. Russia is Armenia's natural market, and the source of innumerable indispensable raw materials and of much engineering, scientific and technical aid. Membership in the big Soviet commonwealth gives Soviet Armenia the additional advantage of a planned economy and of appreciable financial subsidies from Moscow.

Armenia is rich in natural resources. Nevertheless, it was a predominantly agrarian country until 1920. To-day, industry accounts for fifty-eight per cent of Armenia's national income. The Bolsheviks' first task was to explore and map Armenia's subsoil wealth and then to launch its exploitation. Before the revolution, a French concessionaire worked some copper deposits at Allaverdi and produced 1,500 tons a year. In 1934, the same deposits yielded 6,000 tons; and the plan for 1935 is 10,000 tons. Copper is now also mined at Zingazur in the South. Lead and zinc have recently been discovered, but the most important find is precious molybdenum. A deposit of 16,000 tons has been located hard by the Persian frontier and another of 12,000 tons near Zingazur. Theretofore, all the known molybdenum resources of the U.S.S.R. amounted to only 3,000 tons. The country is still obliged to import this expensive metal from abroad, but Erzinkian hopes soon to relieve Moscow of that necessity.

Being a mountainous district with many streams, Soviet Armenia is busy developing its hydro-electric power possibilities. From the engineering point of view, the problem is very simple. The great natural feature of Armenia is Lake Sevan. Situated more than a mile above sea level, its immense expanse of pale blue, translucent waters is a delight to the eye. The lake in some places reaches tremendous depths and even near the shore of the small Island of Sevan which I visited swimmers are warned that the clarity of the water and the bright marble and limestone bed create a dangerous illusion of shallowness at spots which may be twenty to forty feet deep. Residents in the rest homes on the island instruct the newcomer, moreover, that the specific weight of the water is below one. It has no buoyancy, therefore, and it requires a special effort to keep from sinking. This was my second swim of the year. The first had been in Palestine's Dead Sea which is so saline that one can sit in the water, put one's wrists around one's knees, and twiddle one's thumbs.

Lake Sevan is a gigantic natural water reservoir out of

which several rivers flow. The fall of these rivers, particularly the Zanga, is now being harnessed for power purposes. Several big hydro-electric stations are already working. All in all, the Sevan electric grid will, some years from now, yield 500,000 kilowatts. The entire investment required is 300,000,000 rubles. Erzinkian stated that it costs an average of 2 kopeks to produce a kilowatt of electric energy in the entire Soviet Union, but only eight tenths of 1 kopek in Soviet Armenia.

The availability of cheap and plentiful electricity explains the rapid growth of the chemical industry in Armenia. In the city of Karaklis, a carbide factory with an annual capacity of 20,000 tons has been erected. In 1934, it manufactured 16,000 tons. A huge aluminum plant is in construction. The synthetic rubber factory which, Erzinkian said, would be the world's largest, is nearing completion in Erivan. The combination of more power and more cotton has also given the textile industry of Soviet Armenia a mighty fillip. Its production grows by leaps and bounds, and still construction of new mills continues. Armenia, too, is rich in fruits and vegetables. A new canning factory which makes 16,000,000 cans of fruit a year is operating. But a bigger one with an annual capacity of 100,000,000 is being designed. "Yet before our advent," Erzinkian proudly interposed, "Erivan had only one factory, a cognac distillery, and several small carpet and silk and handcraft shops."

One third of Armenia is arable. Part of the remainder is used for grazing purposes. Tobacco culture was introduced by Armenian refugees from Turkey and now 3,000 hectares have been sown with it. Cotton acreage has been extended; also vineyards, silk growing, etc. In general, an interview with any high Soviet official nowadays is an avalanche of figures representing a sharply rising curve. This applies especially to Soviet Armenia, which was a distant, neglected Czarist province and is now experiencing a wildfire "boom."

Erzinkian's "dry" economic figures are the spice of Armenia's life. But the acting prime minister does not limit himself to economic matters. He speaks of the advance of collectivization and of the progress of culture. They have 135,000 children in their schools. Erivan has a ten-year compulsory education system. Erivan has a university, medical, veterinary, architectural institutes, etcetera. Armenia had an old culture. They were not destroying it. They were merging the new with the old. This applied to architecture, fine arts and music. The government had opened many clinics in hospitals, in cities as well as villages. It was draining swamps and fighting malaria in the lowlands. Several spas had been developed. I visited one at Arzni, not far from Erivan. The population was healthier than ever before, Erzinkian declared. And more literate. Ninety per cent of the inhabitants can now read and write.

Soviet Armenia, however, was not only for Armenians. Just as the Soviet Union gave the Armenians autonomy, so the Armenians granted autonomy to the Turco-Tartars who have their own territory within Soviet Armenia and to the Kurds. Armenians, Turco-Tartars and Kurds have their separate schools in which their national language is the language of instruction. Each ethnic group has its own newspapers, courts and officials.

Armenians are intermarrying with Turco-Tartars, or Tiurks, as they are called in Russian. These are the Turks who used to massacre the Armenians. Now they coöperate to build a new Armenia. And as a concrete illustration of the accord between those two traditionally hostile races, Erzinkian pointed to the man who sat at his right hand.

"I am the assistant premier of Armenia," Erzinkian said. "This comrade occupies the same position. I am an Armenian. He is a Tiurk."

In conclusion, Erzinkian speaks with deep emotion of the aid rendered to Armenia between 1919 and 1923 by the Near East Relief and other American and foreign philanthropic organizations. "The children which the Near East Relief saved from a sure death," he declared, "are now among our most valued citizens."

Until 1924, Erzinkian used to visit the home of Archbishop Horen who is now the Catholicus or Pope of the Armenian Church of the world. I went to interview the Catholicus in his "Vatican."

The Armenians were converted from paganism to Christianity in about the third century of the present era. By 400 A. D. a full-fledged Armenian Christian church had been established. But the Armenians never recognized Rome and always rejected the advances of the Greek Catholic (Russian Orthodox) church. The Armenian Christians are monophysite; that is, like the Copts of Egypt, they regard the dogma of two natures in Christ as a heresy. But in fact the Armenian church has borrowed some elements of faith from the Roman Catholic church and some rites from the Greek Catholics.

The road from Erivan to Echmiadzin, where the Armenian Pope resides, leads through the famous Valley of the Ararat, sub-tropical in its summer heat and rich in its vineyards and verdure. But the heavy stone churches of the "Vatican" are an absolute refuge from the rays of the torrid sun.

When I arrived at Echmiadzin to keep the appointment which Catholicus Horen had graciously granted me, he

could not receive me. An archdeacon was being buried in
one of the three churches of the "Vatican." I went to
witness the solemnities. The dead priest lay in an open
coffin. He was garbed in a robe of silver brocade and on
his head was a high, domed, ecclesiastical crown of silver.
A veil of silk gauze covered his face but did not hide his
expressive though waxen features. In the long delicate fingers of his right hand which rested on his body he held a
half sheet of white paper, a message to the other world. On
his breast lay a prayer book bound in green velvet and
decorated with silver filigree.

The church had no benches or pews in it. The hundred
or more people in the church stood grouped in front of
the altar. About a score prayed, kneeling, touching their
foreheads to the stone floor Moslem-fashion or raising their
open hands to their faces. Now and then children ranging
from the ages of five to ten approached the bier and kissed
it in three places. They all kissed the same spots in the same
order. The paintings on the whitewashed walls were peel-
ing, and the whitewash itself, in thick layers, had curled
off the walls and hung ready to collapse.

The singing was exquisite. A choir of young women,
singing from sheet music spread in front of them on stands,
rendered refrains while the chief officiating priest sang the
funeral ritual on the gilded altar. Acolytes diffused incense.

The Catholicus sat on a throne under a canopy of carved
wood. After a while, the open coffin was lifted from its
pedestal by four handsome priests and placed with one end
on the low step of the altar and the other on the floor. The
Catholicus now took a position at the feet of the dead
archdeacon. From a distant door, a powerful priest appeared carrying a graceful gold cup filled with wine. He
sang as he strode through the church to the altar with the

cup in his two extended hands. The officiating priest touched the cup to his lips and set it down. Then another singing priest appeared carrying a gold dove. The officiating priest took the dove, inclined it slightly, and allowed drops of oil to drip ever so slowly on a piece of cotton wherewith he anointed the brow of his deceased colleague. Then, with another bit of cotton similarly treated, he moistened his right palm. Before doing so, he removed the letter to the next world. Then he replaced it.

Now six priests arrayed themselves on either side of the coffin. In pairs they bent low over the deceased, one took the prayer book from his breast, kissed it, handed it to the other who likewise kissed it and returned it to its former position. So six times. Finally the Catholicus, who had stood tall and immovable all the while, went through the same ceremony. At that he turned; twelve priests formed a double file in front of him and accompanied him out of the church and through the court to the gate of his residence near by.

Half a moment later, a bishop holding a long staff mounted with a gold ball came to fetch me. "This is the so-called Throne Chamber," the bishop said as he led me through a long room where stood a carved hardwood chair on a raised dais. I was then ushered into a small study where the Catholicus of all the Armenians sat at a flat desk. He rose to receive me. He was dressed in one all-enveloping garment of heavy, dark blue, Chinese pressed silk which reached from neck to heel. On his head he wore a very high conical hat of the same material which almost touched his eyebrows. A cross of precious stones was fastened to the cap just above the eyes.

The Catholicus speaks an excellent Russian with scarcely any accent. It was not long before a man-servant brought delightful Turkish coffee. But even prior to that the audience had lost all constraint. The Catholicus spoke his mind freely. He was obviously a warm Armenian patriot.

He was struck by a coincidence and he mentioned it twice, at the beginning and towards the end of our conversation. All the previous night he had read "Martin Eden." In fact he had slept only two hours. The story was probably autobiographical, he thought. And this afternoon he had a visit from a "representative of the American people." The Armenian nation had an especially warm feeling towards America, a feeling of gratitude and of sympathy.

He had gone to the United States in 1920. He was still Bishop Horen at that time, and went to the United States as the plenipotentiary of the then Catholicus. He also represented the Armenian government of the day. "I interviewed Secretary of State Colby and President Woodrow Wilson," he said. "I met American bishops and brought them the thanks of Armenia to the honest and excellent American people for their succor in time of distress. We are happy when Americans come here.

"If all President Wilson's plans had materialized," he mused, "things might have been different. But the U.S. Senate was in disagreement with Wilson. I, of course, wanted the United States to accept a mandate for Armenia. I do not know what would have happened in such an event. American laws, however, permit of no interference in the affairs of other states. Who knows what would have developed?

"Armenia is surrounded by hostile nations—Persia, Turkey, Azerbaijhan—which have hostile designs on us. The Armenian people is pleased that it enjoys peace and security. Everybody received something after the war. Only the Armenians lost. At the Lausanne Conference in 1923, we were promised $5,000,000 by Prof. Nansen. I felt that those were like unto thirty pieces of silver. We lost 1,500,000 Armenians during the war. We lost Turkey. . . . Turkey used to be regarded as the real Armenia. Now it has disappeared.

"The Armenian people, in general, is not satisfied," he continued. "To be sure, there are many who understand, but the fate of a nation is decided by its intellectuals, and many of those think that the Dashnak Nationalists should not have handed over power to the Bolsheviks late in 1920. The Armenian people, however, deeply appreciates the fact that it now lives in peace and that efforts are being made to put it on its feet.

"Our orientation, therefore," he stated firmly, "must be on Moscow. More than anything else the Armenians want peace. If we wish to retain our territory and our independence, our orientation must be on Moscow. Azerbaijhan leans towards Turkey and that is a menace to us. Georgia has aggressive plans against us. Our safety, therefore, is in Russia. The Armenian people, in general, is satisfied. It has what it has: a federated Soviet Union. It is as autonomous as any member of a federation can be. There is a central authority in Moscow, and our autonomy, accordingly, is limited."

My stenographer was writing down every word the Catholicus uttered. He had said: "The Armenian people, in general, is dissatisfied," and a moment later, "The Armenian people, in general, is satisfied." But he was not contradicting himself. As a staunch nationalist, he, like many members of the intelligentsia, had hoped, as he told me later, that "a free Armenia would be altogether in the hands of Armenians." They regret that such an Armenia

was not established. But they know that only an American
mandate or some other miracle would have allowed a tiny
unattached Armenia to exist unmolested. Armenia, the
Catholicus declared, would have been continually subjected to the aggression of her hostile neighbors were it
not for membership in the Soviet federation. In other
words, they are dissatisfied that world conditions made it
impossible for them to be totally independent. In view of
those conditions, however, they are satisfied that they
enjoy the security which the Moscow orientation grants
them.

I asked him how the Armenians fared under the Soviets.
"Well," he replied, "they live somewhat poorly. If you
consider Socialism—every working-man understands that
he is creating his own fatherland. If he is deprived of certain things, he knows that he is building; he is planting, and
the fruits will be excellent. We have not the comforts
which you have, and we may never have them. But 'the
millionaire in his palace, the pauper in his hut.' Your workers live well, too. America might have been the first country to enter the kingdom of Socialism. Take Henry Ford's
book. Many laborers feel that they are part-owners of their
factories." The Catholicus was somewhat enigmatic.

We came now to speak of his own position in the Soviet
Union. Early in 1920, the Dashnak authorities had raided
his house and searched for Bolsheviks. He returned to
Erivan in November 1920, a few days before the Soviets
assumed office. They raided his house and searched for
Dashnaks. Subsequently, however, the Bolsheviks did not
disturb him, and until 1924, Comrade Erzinkian had entertained him.

"But how had it happened," I asked, "that the Soviet
government allowed a world religious congress to meet

right here in Echmiadzin, on Bolshevik territory, and elect you Catholicus?"

Catholicus Horen attributed the circumstance to Bolshevik consideration for Armenian public opinion abroad. Moscow welcomed the aid which Soviet Armenia receives from foreign Armenians. The Bolsheviks want the entire Armenian nation to feel that Soviet Armenia is its homeland. "The convocation of the congress," the Catholicus affirmed, "was a very serious matter. The highest authorities deliberated upon it. Stalin himself insisted on the meeting being held."

"Here," he proceeded, "everyone knew that the majority of Armenians wanted me. And yet in the beginning, it looked as if I would not be elected. In 1932, the elections were postponed. Then the Soviet government decided: 'You may elect whomever you wish.' The Armenian foreign press supported me. Here they then decided: 'If you insist, we do not object.' Perhaps the government and some foreign Armenian elements had another candidate," he intimated.

The Bolsheviks are anti-religious. But their public policy has never been one of universal blanket suppression of the church. Their policy *vis-à-vis* the church has always had nuances and variations. They have moderated their attitude in one section of the country and made it harsher in the other. They have intrigued and tried to maneuver one church organization against another. In the beginning, for instance, they refrained from harassing the fanatic Moslems, and only gradually did they penetrate with their atheistic propaganda into the regions inhabited by the followers of Islam. Similarly, Moscow endeavored to undermine the Greek Orthodox Church by supporting schismatic movements like the Church of the Resurrection

and the Living Church. In like manner, the Kremlin nego-
tiated with the Pope of Rome with a view to introducing
the Roman Catholic Church into the Soviet Union as a
counterpoise to the predominant Greek Catholic Church.
Early in those pourparlers, the Vatican was not averse.
Each party thought it would gain by the strategy.

With respect to the Armenian church, too, the Bolsheviks have been realists. The Armenian church enjoys many
privileges which have been withdrawn from religious
communities in other parts of the Union. The national
minorities in the U.S.S.R. are frequently accorded more
liberal treatment than Russians.

I asked the Catholicus about his relations with the Soviet
authorities. "Naturally," he began, "difficulties occur. But
when one is cultured, when one reads everything, when
one knows the tendencies of the state, one must occasionally
make concessions. I realize that at times it is impossible to
reopen a church. If they close ten and reopen two, it is
also good. I understand that they will not be reopened anyway. The government should be friendly towards me, and,
in fact, it is. Is it conceivable that I would oppose any one
who constructs and builds?"

"Has the Armenian church a future?" I now inquired.

His reply was characteristic of his double-track manner
of thinking. "Of course," he said, "the church has no future. If you approach the question from one angle, the
church has no future. But as an optimist I believe that
things will be well. The dictatorship will come to an end,
and decrees which now exist will be carried out—decrees,
for instance, which permit each community to have its
priest. Of late, there has been a let-up. Our situation has
improved. I am not a statesman and I do not understand
international politics (there was a slight curl on his thick

lips), yet perhaps Soviet membership in the League of Nations will make a difference."

Certain developments encouraged the Catholicus. "The Armenian nation," he suggested, "is closer to the church now than fifteen years ago. Last Easter many young people came to church. The Armenians are a peculiar people: when it is persecuted it is less religious, when life is better it believes more. The youth is attending services."

I had stayed over an hour and made a move to go. The Catholicus then asked about a number of foreign countries, and gave me a detailed explanation of the incident in New York where his chief representative, an Armenian high priest, was killed by Dashnaks. He told me he had sent two bulls on this subject to Bishops Manning and Berry. Two bulls lay on his table. I wondered whether he would show them to me. He unrolled one. It was a broad roll of parchment. At the top, delicate miniature paintings of Christ and angels in exquisite coloring. Below, decorative Armenian lettering on fields of gold, and then the hand-written text. Finally, the seal and signature of the Catholicus. This bull was ready to be sent to the Archbishop of Canterbury. It urged the Archbishop to discuss with King George V the right, which the Catholicus claimed was his, of confirming the Armenian patriarchs in Jerusalem and Bagdad. He thought the British were prejudiced against him because he lived on Soviet territory. The second bull, likewise brilliantly executed, was for the eye of Carol, King of Rumania. Both looked like ancient illuminated manuscripts, but the Catholicus complained that the dyes used were not as good as before the revolution.

My stenographer, who was also my photographer (and my wife) now asked the Catholicus to pose for her. He went to another room and soon returned with a long silver

chain around his neck from which dangled an ecclesiastical
ovular emblem in the form of a colored miniature. I stood
beside him in my shirtsleeves. Unfortunately, the photographer was a better stenographer, and the snapshot did not
turn out.

Soviet Armenia is one of the most interesting parts of
an interesting continent. The old with its color and dirt is
retreating before the attack of a new life. The old has no
resistance. The new is only beginning to entrench itself.
The people still feel strange in it—just like a boy of fifteen
in a new suit.

Chapter XXI

JUNGLE AND RIVIERA

Russia, to most people, means snow, frost and sleighs. But Russia extends from the frigid Arctic to semi-tropical Turkestan. And Batum has jungle.

From Erivan one must double in one's track and return to Tiflis in order to reach the seaport of Batum.

From Tiflis to Batum a torrential rain wiped out the scenery and transformed the earth into moving mud. But Batum was bathed in sunlight, and the colors which I had seen only in Mediterranean countries are native here too. Palms grow in the streets of the city, and cactus blooms in stone courts.

On one of my previous visits to Batum, in 1924, there was a lone steamer in port, but the commandant of the port, who took me around in a motor boat, did not know the name of the ship or what flag it carried. Now the harbor was jammed full of large and small craft loading oil brought from Baku in the old and new pipelines and purified and cracked in the new refineries, loading citrus, tea, building stone, and cotton for Central Russia, loading mountain climbers who had just descended from Mt. Kazbek, loading Kurds, Abhazi, Adjari and sons of other tiny races, and loading American, British and French tourists, some of whom are filled with the self-importance which good clothes presumably lend them in this poorly-dressed land, some of them obviously conscious of the superiority which birth in the rich West has supposedly given them.

A small area around Batum is the only corner of the Soviet Union which has heat and moisture enough to grow lemons, tangerines and oranges. Even so, many precious citrus trees need individual kerosene stoves to protect them during cold evenings and nights. The Soviets have also commenced to grow grapefruit in this district, but the Russians will have to cultivate a taste for this breakfast delicacy. They reject it now as being too bitter. The taste, however, will come with the eating. Up to the present, less than a dozen fruits have been plucked, and they have gone into the Kremlin. Joseph Stalin, who annually visits Sochi, just north of Batum, for a two-month vacation, is particularly interested in the development of citrus growing, and he has given this "Soviet Florida" his special patronage, for the Bolsheviks want to become self-sufficient in respect to sub-tropical fruit too. They have even been thinking of planting Turkish coffee in these parts, and then almost the only thing they would lack is bananas. The banana tree actually grows in the Caucasus, but its fruit is diminutive and inedible.

Meanwhile, millions of lemons and tangerines ripen in the Batum region every year, but Moscow and other northern cities suffer from their absence for long seasons. In December, 1932, when I was in Batum last, one could buy any number of tangerines at 10 kopeks apiece. In Tiflis, eighteen hours away, a tangerine cost 40 kopeks. In Baku, another twenty hours away, it cost 100 kopeks or a ruble. And in Moscow tangerines were scarcely obtainable. The reason was inadequate transportation facilities, and the same condition to-day obstructs the proper distribution not merely of citrus products but of all products. The explanation is simple: Russian industries have increased their output several fold since the revolution (and people travel

more since the revolution), but the building of railroads
has not kept pace.

From the base of the road which leads out of Batum,
angry Black Sea waves have been biting large concrete
blocks and rolling them into the water. The road runs
north, up and up, until it winds itself into an impasse at the
botanical gardens. The horticulturist who toiled for years
to create the gardens lies buried within them. He did not
want a gravestone. The gardens would be his monument.
Japan. A little climb and one is in Mexico. A short ascent
to another terrace carries one into Java. This botanical
center is the experimental station for the citrus and tea
regions round about it.

From the gardens to the tea plantations. Along the road,
warm soggy moss drips with water. Tubular creepers,
strange plants and rich ferns cover the rocks and the earth.
Bamboo trees. The tales of their very rapid growth almost
create the illusion that one sees them add to their stature
as the automobile passes by. Bamboo trunks are used as
water pipes in this region.

Kurds sleepily lead their sleepy oxen along the road.
Adjari in primitive homes. Batum is the capital of the small
autonomous territory of Adjaristan. This is part of the
Georgian republic. Abhazia at Sukhum is another autonomous territory included in Georgia, and so is South Ossetia. They enjoy special status because they are not
Georgian. The Adjari, being neighbors and former subjects of Turkey, are Moslem, while the Georgians are, or
were, Christians; their language is Turanian, and their
script was once Arabic. The Bolsheviks take cognizance of
these distinguishing features and allow each race a certain
amount of administrative autonomy (Batum has its own

cabinet of ministers), as well as complete cultural independence.

On hillsides and on flat fields grows the short, deep green tea bush. Tea culture has obviously assumed much larger proportions in recent years. The big tea plantation at Chakwa has likewise made considerable progress since my last visit. And the tea factory where we drank tea from a samovar (which means "self-cooker") while the director explained how tea should be brewed, is operating more efficiently. The director, who is a pre-revolutionary expert, has visited most of the tea-producing countries of the world. Only Java protected itself against a Communist uprising by barring him.

On the table of the director lay a large book in which many visitors had entered their views. A young American lady who has distinguished herself by unbridled lecture attacks on the Soviet Union wrote that she was greatly impressed by the tea factory and wished the Soviet Union success in all its undertakings.

The tea farms of Soviet Georgia, like practically every Soviet economic enterprise, must cope with the problem of labor scarcity. The picking of tea leaves is tedious and slow, and requires many hands. Could there not be a machine for the purpose? The Bolsheviks consulted foreign tea experts, but these were not very helpful: in Ceylon and China labor is plentiful and cheap. The machine has not yet been invented, but already some Soviet tea is harvested with shears which are said to be three times as effective as deft fingers.

The Western world is beginning to object to machines which take the place of men. In Germany, Italy, and other countries, mechanical devices are proscribed on certain public works and in agriculture. For what is the point of eliminating labor by introducing machines when the purpose of so many ventures is to create employment? This attitude must ultimately exert a far-reaching influence on the efficiency, economic status and culture of Western nations. If they will not go backward they will at least not go forward as steadily as they might. Labor-saving inventions and technical improvements will become an embarrassment. But if labor scarcity continues to trouble the Soviet Union—and that is quite likely—its technical progress should be very rapid. There is another consideration. The cheaper the labor the weaker the incentive towards mechanization. If Soviet living standards will continue to rise, the incentive towards mechanical improvements will be very strong. These circumstances inspire the Bolsheviks with confidence in their ability to "overtake and outstrip" capitalist countries. Though we scarcely notice it, the world is witnessing a gigantic competition between its two parts: the socialist and the capitalist parts. Whichever asserts its economic supremacy will also win the political struggle. Granted that the economic situation of the capitalist world improves so appreciably as to flatten the crisis into a depression. If, by the time the next crisis arrives, the Soviet Union will have become a prosperous, happy nation—it is not that now—the moral will be a devastating one for the bourgeoisie. This is Red Russia's real challenge to capitalism. Not Communist parties and the Third International, but this.

Returning to Batum, I saw a private railway coach parked on a sideline, and stopped. On the car was an inscription which informed the reader that the occupants were boy and girl scouts, "Pioneers," who had performed very valuable services for the Commissariat of Posts and

Telegraphs. Soon I received an invitation and climbed in.
More than a score of youngsters between the ages of twelve
and fifteen, advised by two adults, had made the car their
home since they had left their families in Leningrad several weeks ago. They had stayed in all the big cities, and
now they were enjoying themselves in Batum, bathing and
seeing the sights.

"And what is all this for?"

The Leningrad post office had organized a competition
among "Pioneers." It needed their help. Many letters remained undelivered because the addresses were badly written. The work of the postmen was made difficult by the
absence of numbers and names on doors, by obstructions
on stairways, etc. Would not the children help? They must
start with their own apartments, then their houses, then
their streets. They must report. The reward would be a
trip through the Soviet Union in a private car. These are
the winners. And what a joyful time they have been having! In Moscow, the Commissar of Posts and Telegraphs,
Alexei Rykov, entertained them. They visited the Kremlin. In other cities, big receptions were arranged for them.
But it was not all entertainment. The receptions offered an
opportunity for propaganda. They met the "Pioneers" of
Moscow, Rostov, Baku, etc., and explained how they had
worked in Leningrad. They summoned the children of
each new city to imitate their example and to improve on
their achievements. In each city, with the aid of the Posts
Commissariat, the private car published its own newspaper
wherein it recounted its activities in Leningrad and described its meetings with the boys and girls of other places
and the results of those meetings. This was civic training
of children by children.

The boat which travels from Batum north along the Soviet Riviera to Odessa was built by Krupp in Germany. When its lavatories are not out of order it is an extremely pleasant ship. The crew and officers go about their work with business-like precision. Strict discipline prevails. Immediate dismissal is the punishment for any infringement of the rules. When on duty the captain is the unquestioned commander-in-chief. But let him or his subordinates step into the clubrooms of the crew which are located on the best "A" deck. There all are comrades. And the stoker may roundly scold the first mate for not doing enough party work. Every person employed on the steamer took some kind of a course in his off-duty time.

The boat carries many foreign tourists. Some are surprised that Soviet hotels and trains are clean. Some brought food and roach powder which they never used. Some had been reconciled to "conducted tours" and were pleased that they could see so much of the bad along with so much of the good. Russia, in their minds, has been added to the list of civilized countries. Often a town is excellent and the revolution wonderful if the Intourist hotel in the town has a good chef and if the hotel rooms have running hot and cold water. If they are deprived of these benefits the Soviet "experiment" has been a failure.

In years gone by, foreign tourists came, saw, and then decided: "The Soviet Union is bad," or "The Soviet Union is good." But now those who could think, said: "What does all this mean to my own country? How much of it can we apply at home?" Those who could think began to read Marx and to worry.

They had visited this strange red planet. It was interesting in itself. But they also used it as an observatory from which to look back on their native land.

One evening on deck I overheard a conversation between an American girl and a Russian man.

"What is this dialectics I always hear about?" she was saying.

"Ah," he replied in quaintly accented English, "this is not a night for philosophical dialogues."

"But I must know before I get back to Boston," she insisted.

He laughed. "You won't understand anyway," he said.

She coaxed coquettishly, and he consented. "You see," he began, "this dialectics, as you call it, is a fundamental feature of Marxist revolutionary thinking. It teaches that any conception also includes its opposite."

"And what does that mean?" she queried.

"Well, for example, if you say 'Ivan is a man,' you are actually saying that Ivan is a Chinaman, a Congo savage, a Lenin, a Rodin and a bandit. You are uniting a general conception with an individual and giving to him some characteristics which he has and some which he hasn't. Every conception must be examined in this wise. Take 'nation.' A nation is supposed to be a unit with general characteristics. But actually 'a nation' expresses lack of unity, for it combines the bourgeoisie with the proletariat. Similarly, an imperialist war contains the elements of a war against the imperialists—witness the Bolshevik revolution. Do you understand?"—he paused.

"Yes, go ahead, but slow," she said in American. "I'm beginning to get you."

"Now why is this so important? Because the two opposites struggle with one another incessantly, and the struggle makes for movement, dynamic movements, and change. Marxism abhors that which is static. But the bourgeoisie asserts that human nature never changes, that man will always need religion, that capitalism has come to stay. We Bolsheviks reject such silly notions. Capitalist prosperity bears depression within it, and the depression either merges into a boom or explodes into a revolution. Feudalism carried in itself the germs of capitalism, and, as Marx and Engels said in 'The Communist Manifesto,' which you should read, capitalism prepares its own gravediggers in the shape of the working class."

"Then your Soviet system will dialectically disappear too?" she questioned.

"The Soviet system is a class society," he replied. "But it already contains elements of the classless society. Our classes will destroy themselves and establish a classless society."

"That will be Communism, eh?" from her.

"Yes."

"And what will succeed Communism?" she persisted.

"I don't know," he said. "Besides, you and I will be dead by that time," he added playfully, "and meantime there is a moon."

"Is the moon dialectic?" she teased.

"Yes, it changes all the time," he said seriously.

"I suppose Russian men are very dialectic," she suggested.

Therewith silence set in.

Sukhun lengthened into a white line above the dark water. "In Abhazia," a girl said, "there lives a man who is 151 years old. He has a son 100 years of age."

She was leaning against a lifeboat. Her toe nails were lacquered red. Her sandals showed her tanned feet. She showed her tanned legs and arms. "Before you grow old," a professor of chemistry, member of the Soviet Academy of Science, replied, "we will have conquered the problem of growing-old. A colleague of mine in Moscow had the operation made for him in order that he might finish a valuable volume of research. He lives economically only for this task."

"Yes," the beautiful girl persisted, "but Communism cannot solve the greatest of human problems: death. It is not only that we die, but that we are always aware of the ultimate doom. That is what bothers me."

A handsome Komsomol, likewise browned by his month on the Sochi sands, obviously ached to mock her and demolish her. But the group which had gathered near the prow of the boat was too dignified and he was too young. Yet he could not refrain altogether. "Those who live richly," he declared, "rarely think of death. The man who has nothing to live for dies every day. One would think death would become a habit to him. Yet it is he who fears dying most."

"Twaddle," she exploded. "All that is just the Communists' dogmatic glorification of life. You might suppose from listening to a Bolshevik, that he never had any doubts, never had any moments of melancholy, that he was always enthusiastic, excited, automatically happy. You make me sick."

Nobody answered. The group watched the beautiful scenery unroll. Then they returned to the intellectual gymnastics the love for which has withstood the revolution.

The girl was the first to resume the argument. "You Communists," she said, "always talk in the best platform manner. Orations instead of conversations. But what happens when you are alone with yourself? Don't you ever ask yourself what is the purpose of life?"

"When I devote myself to the improvement of life," the Komsomol replied, "I forget to think of death. I love the world, love life, I want to make it better for myself and others. We all know that death is the end, but you want to have a beautiful dress, nevertheless. And I want to build a better world in which, while there is life, there will be less suffering and less injustice."

The girl with the red toe nails scoffed. "We are all ants driven by our instincts, and too busy to think." Later I saw her and the handsome Komsomol promenading arm in arm on the top deck. As the Soviet saying goes: "They sat on a park bench discussing Marx, and nine months later it was a boy."

Chapter XXII

TWO UKRAINIAN CITIES

Last January, on a day that was full of sleet and cold rain, I sailed from Odessa in a 750-ton, rat-infested Soviet freighter for Turkey, Greece and Palestine. Especially when the tiny vessel bobbed like a cork in a violent gale off Crete or fell with a thump into deep troughs opposite Cyprus I vowed I would never make another avoidable boat trip. But here I was back again in Odessa, at the end of a most delightful voyage on the now tranquil Black Sea.

Before October, 1934, not a single Soviet steamer had ever entered a Roumanian port. Roumania and Bessarabia, which are Odessa's hinterland, were until then entirely closed to Russian shipping and Russian trade. Odessa's significance as a port has been further reduced by the competition of Novorossik, which has easy access to the grain-growing North Caucasus, and of Kherson, which has benefited by the locks of Zaporozhie. Odessa, moreover, is too exposed to foreign attack to expect very much industrial development. The revolution, accordingly, has transformed Odessa from a port to a resort. The city has beautiful sand beaches, an equable climate, and curative mud. It possesses the soft, relaxing atmosphere of a Southern city unspoiled by the noise and haste of industry. Odessa before the revolution was famed for its humor—mostly vulgar—and for its gaiety. Neither has disappeared.

Whether it be the sea, or the wide tree-lined avenues or the height of the sky, Odessa is endlessly spacious. It is spaceless. Only the street on which you stand exists. That street seems to be isolated in the very middle of a vast prairie. Odessa is only Sergei Eisenstein's 200 steps above sea level, yet one has the sensation of being on a lofty, undisturbed plateau green with verdure and white with homes. The streets are clean; the people are well-dressed. Odessa was born for vacation-making. The revolution has robbed it of its business and returned it its character. A few houses have been built in recent years, but most of the new structures are universities and technical institutes. Odessa is destined to become a famous center of learning and bathing.

Who would think of visiting a factory in Odessa? Or of inspecting the harbor? Rather one asks the orchestra to forget foreign jazz and strum Ukrainian melodies and gypsy songs. Cafés are just beginning to venture back. More parks with luxurious vegetation. Round-faced, dark young girls arms linked with romantic-looking men. Private stores. Private artisans. Doctors, dentists, midwives galore—all with pre-revolutionary shingles. The past has not been banished. Where there is less of the new there is more of the old.

Kiev has been restored to its ancient dignity; it is again Ukrainia's capital. Once upon a time, indeed, it was the capital of Russia. Kiev is near the Polish frontier. In 1920, Marshal Pilsudski suddenly invaded the Ukraine and captured Kiev. The Bolsheviks, to be sure, almost returned the compliment by marching square up to the outskirts of Warsaw. But Kiev was obviously too exposed to be a safe capital in times of stress. Kharkov was chosen. Kharkov is a big industrial center. It is the gate to the Donetz coal basin. The Soviets could count on strong proletarian support for Kharkov, whereas Kiev was buried in a broad sea

of undependable peasants. Kiev, moreover, was too closely
associated with the patriotic nationalistic emotions of numerous middle class and intellectual Ukrainians. The Soviet
administration, it was feared, might be infected with that
spirit. But when it was found that Kharkov itself was not
impervious to this very spirit, and when the Bolsheviks no
longer dreaded internal opposition or easy sallies from
abroad, Kiev resumed its traditional rôle.

Kiev is also the mother of the Russian church. Here
stood the cradle of Greek Orthodoxy. The child has since
grown to hoary old age. In fact, the Bolsheviks regard him
as a living corpse which drags helplessly through the minds
of the untutored. Soon he will stumble into the deep grave
which the atheists hold prepared for him.

The child was not born on Russian soil. Holy men
brought it from Constantinople. Prince Vladimir, later
Saint Vladimir, fathered it. A more-than-life-size iron
statue of Vladimir holding a huge cross over his shoulder
stands untouched in a park on the shore of the angry
Dnieper. His face is to the water. Has he turned his broad
back on Kiev since the red iconoclasts invested it?

Vladimir has been spared. But what of his handiwork?
St. Sophia is opened only to the privileged few while Soviet artists faithfully restore its precious mosaics and fres-
coes. The holiest of holy Pechora Cathedral and its famed
lavra or catacombs have been converted into an anti-
religious museum. This means that everything in the church
and the subterranean passages has been kept strictly intact;
but a number of atheistic exhibits now invite a critical attitude towards the unmolested relics of the past. Thus:

The catacombs reach deep into the damp earth almost
to the walls of the Dnieper. In them the monks buried their
dead. Bolshevik archeologists have recently opened hith-

erto unknown labyrinths and burial chambers. Some cells are packed tightly with grinning skulls. The catacombs, apparently, served as a place of imprisonment and penance too. Sacred tradition has it that sinful priests buried themselves up to the neck in the floor of the catacombs and lived for months, for years, in prayer. Before the revolution, perfectly-preserved but never-embalmed mummies were taken from the catacombs and displayed to believers as proof of the saintly qualities of these deceased servants of God. These mummies are still on display in the cathedral. Parallel showcases, however, contain undecayed corpses of rats, bats, cats. The soil in this district, according to scientifically-presented explanations, possesses properties which occasionally prevent animal decomposition. The mummies, perhaps, never provoked disgust. But their juxtaposition with rodents and dead kittens has an inevitable suggestion.

Before the war, Kiev counted 25,000 priests and only 14,000 industrial working-men. This speaks volumes to the Soviet mind. Kiev boasted innumerable rich churches. Whence did they derive their income? In the Pechora Cathedral a chart reveals the sums which reached the church from various sources. The figures were taken from the official ecclesiastical records. In the first place, the girl Komsomol guide impresses on the Soviet visitor the immenseness of the funds that poured into this useless institution. The pinched peasant gave his mite that the monks might wax fat, cynical and licentious. She refers to classic Russian novelists to recall the loose living of the clergy. Then the itemization of Pechora's income: so many rubles from the sale of holy books, from box collections, from the sale of icons, from the profitable operation of hotels, from a brick factory, from the sale of candles, from pray-

Socialist Construction (in this case a tower for the Moscow
subway) crowds out the Church

ing for dead souls and sick bodies, from the sale of grain, and so forth. The impression is created of a huge business organization.

The chart shows how church collections dropped steeply after 1906. "Why?" the guide asks. It was after the 1905 revolution. "The masses were resentful because the church had fought at the side of the Czar against the people." "The Greek Catholic church," the Komsomolka adds, "played the same rôle when we took power. Did not priests bless the White armies which marched against us?"

Holy services were discontinued at the Pechora Cathedral on January 5, 1930, and at St. Sophia in the Spring of 1934. "The congregations were too small." Agrarian collectivization closed the one, and the second Five Year Plan the other. Every new wave of revolutionary sentiment and activity submerges another religious stronghold. The strength of religion in the U.S.S.R. is in inverse proportion to the success of Bolshevist economy. What one thinks of the future of religion in Russia depends on one's estimate of Bolshevik economic prospects.

I argued about the church with the Komsomolka. "How is it," she asked, "that whenever the people rise, be it in Mexico or Spain or Russia, they always attack churches, burn monasteries, and expel priests? The workers and peasants are never really religious. But the church awes them by its wealth and by its reputedly good connections with God. It keeps them in darkness. It frightens them with the prospect of death. It promises them reward in heaven that they may not rebel on earth. The church is therefore an active agent for combating revolutions. Capitalists use it for that purpose. Did the churches of the world condemn the World War? No, because it was a capitalist war." She spoke with religious fervor.

"Eat Swift's Ham." Many citizens of Kiev would be happy to follow this injunction painted high on the side wall of a building opposite the excellent Continental Hotel, but they are forced to content themselves with Soviet ham —when they can get it. "Eat Swift's Ham" is a reminder of pre-revolutionary days. It has remained on the wall since the days of Czarism. Russia, that vast agricultural country, land of grain and cattle, ate American-raised meat. It is difficult to explain how far away "Eat Swift's Ham" sounds today. It is the call of another age. In Moscow or Leningrad or Kharkov, moreover, such a remnant of foreign capitalistic commercialism would long ago have been erased by the fire company's hook and ladder brigade. But Kiev, the beautiful princess, hibernated during all the years of revolution while Kharkov and other towns grew new streets and more faubourgs. Her gaze was backward to the times when shops sold imported delicacies to merchants' wives. She was ignored—a step-daughter out in the shadow. Her lights were dim, her thoroughfares silent. Then, in 1934, the revolution came and touched her shoulder with its finger. The princess awoke. Prince Charming did not woo her; he ordered her to manicure her houses, comb her streets, lay out new parks, construct new buildings, open new universities, new clinics, new schools. "We have stood Kiev on its head," local Bolsheviks said to me. "Two years from now we will put it back on its feet." Meanwhile, streets are dug up, houses are dressed in scaffolding, the bank of the Dnieper is being re-shaped—in other words, Kiev is assuming the visage of a normal Soviet city. "We will make Kiev more beautiful than Vienna," residents boasted. But they will not destroy Kiev's individuality. They could not if they would, and they would not. Cities have personalities like human beings. We may grow old, wear different clothes, grow taller or fatter, grow beards and mustaches or become bald-headed, suffer, attain richness or fame, but "the child is father of the man." The revolution was typhoon, fire, earthquake, war, epidemic—all rolled in one. Yet some cities of old Russia, Kiev, Leningrad, Tiflis, have emerged with their essential character intact. Moscow, I think, has changed most both externally and intrinsically. The Moscow of the merchant and "forty times forty churches" is now the Red capital, Bolshevik Moscow, city of big apartment houses, city of rushing tempo. The new in Erivan is larger than the old and the whole is therefore very different from the old. Yet city nature resists change as stubbornly as human nature. In one generation, nevertheless, towns and men have yielded to the revolution's touch, yielded in varying degree, yielded partially without surrendering altogether, but yielded none the less. "The revolution," reads an inscription on a Moscow building, "is a whirlwind which sweeps away everything that stands in its path." Not everything, and not immediately; Russia is still a mixture of what was and the beginnings of that which is to be. The two elements are in conflict. The course of that conflict is the history of the Soviet Union.

What was, was very terrible. The first socialist revolution took place in Russia because the masses had little to lose and much to gain. But the sad heritage of the past does not make the task of the revolution easier. It makes it much more difficult. For people with the past in their bones and blood are building the future. Bolshevism did not begin with a clean slate. It began with Russia.

The backwardness and natural virginity of Russia were not an unmixed disadvantage. The Soviet nation is unspoiled, full of the physical energy needed to bear hardships, and capable of great enthusiasm and faith. The human material with which the revolution has been working is both bad and good. It is bad when culture, technique, skill, and a highminded relationship between individuals are demanded. It is excellent when the situation requires it to live on a shoestring, a promise and partial fulfillment, requires it to lay sacrifices of comfort and freedom on the altar of hope.

History will register this age as the age of collectivism. And as the age of hope. Hope of a return to the better times of old sustains capitalism. Hope of further progress towards new and better times sustains socialism. The Bolsheviks are a race with a mission. In an inspired moment that capable, much-loved and much-lamented leader, Sergei Kirov, who fell at the hands of an assassin, said: "Comrades, many centuries ago the great mathematician dreamed of finding a point of support from which he could move the world. Centuries passed, and that point has not only been found, but we have created it with our own hands. It will not be long before we, supporting ourselves on the achievement of socialism in our Soviet country, will switch both hemispheres to the road of communism." Soviet success would bring about the world revolution; that was the implication.

Chapter XXIII

AND SO?

And so back to Moscow, the Moscow that is Mecca to some, anathema to others and a Chinese puzzle to most, to the Moscow that is more than a city and more than a capital, that is a symbol, a promise and a threat.